COINCIDENCE

The Freedom of the Press in Ireland
The Story of Ireland
Revolution in Medicine
West Briton
Fringe Medicine
Private Conscience: Public Morality
Drugs, Doctors and Disease
A History of Medicine
Abdication
Poverty and the Industrial Revolution
The Forbidden Game
The Opium War
Natural and Supernatural
The Book of the Back
Natural Medicine
The Diseases of Civilization
The Alternative Health Guide (with Ruth West)
Science and Parascience
The Paranormal: an Encyclopedia of Psychic Phenomena
The Hidden Power
The Power of Dreams
The Unknown Guest
Trance
Downstart

COINCIDENCE

A Matter of Chance – or Synchronicity?

BRIAN INGLIS

HUTCHINSON

London Sydney Auckland Johannesburg

This edition first published in 1990 by
Hutchinson

Reprinted 1990

Random Century Group Ltd
20 Vauxhall Bridge Road, London SW1V 2SA

Random Century Australia (Pty) Ltd
20 Alfred Street, Milsons Point, Sydney NSW 2061, Australia

Random Century (NZ) Ltd
Po Box 40–086, Glenfield, Auckland 10, New Zealand

Random Century South Africa (Pty) Ltd
PO Box 337, Bergvlei 2012, South Africa

British Library Cataloguing in Publication Data
Inglis, Brian *1916–*
   Coincidence: A Matter of Chance or Synchronicity?
   1.   Psychic phenomena: Coincidences
   I.   Title
   133.8

   ISBN 0 09 174160 2

Set in Linotronic Bembo by Deltatype Ltd, Ellesmere Port
Printed and bound in Great Britain by
Mackays of Chatham PLC, Chatham, Kent

Contents

1 Forerunners 1
2 Seriality? 13
3 Synchronicity? 33
4 The Subliminal Component 65
5 Explanations 97
6 The Implications of Research 178
7 Kammerer Revisited 192
8 Jung Revisited 195
9 Where, From Here? 198
Bibliography 206
Appendix 209
Index 211

The accounts of coincidences in this book came initially from the correspondence which reached the Koestler Foundation following the publication of *The Unknown Guest* in 1987. They have been supplemented since from the Koestler Archive in the Edinburgh University Library, and from contributions following references to the Foundation's research in the *Daily Telegraph*, the *Guardian*, the *New Scientist*, the *Spectator*, and Godfrey Smith's column in the *Sunday Times* (a particularly valuable source, this, testifying to the column's popularity). But easily the largest and most varied set of accounts came in following the publication on Christmas Eve 1989 of my article on the research in the *Observer*, and a questionnaire, compiled by Jane Henry of the Open University, for its readers to fill in. There were over a thousand replies, most of them containing accounts of coincidences which had intrigued, amused, startled or disturbed the writers. Many gave several examples; one gave forty.

Contributors wishing to be involved in further research were asked to send in stamped and addressed envelopes. The work is now in progress, and its findings will be presented when the project has been completed. The questionnaire is reproduced here in the appendix (on p. 209); anybody who wishes to assist in the project should make a copy of it, fill it in and send it – along with accounts of their experiences, if desired – with s.a.e., to the Koestler Foundation, 484 King's Road, London, SW10 0LF.

Acknowledgements

My thanks to Bob Morris, John Beloff and their colleagues in the Department of Psychology, Edinburgh University, for their encouragement, and their comments on the text; to the Edinburgh University Library and Harold Harris, Arthur Koestler's executor, for permission to examine the Koestler Archive (and to Harold for his comments on the text); to Godfrey Smith, for helping the project along through his *Sunday Times* column; to Bob Lowe and the *Observer*, for setting up the article and the questionnaire which drew in most of the accounts included here; to Ruth West, Director of the Koestler Foundation, which collected and dealt with the replies; to Jane Henry of the Open University, who compiled the questionnaire; to Douglas Matthews, for his index; and as of old, to Bernard Levin, for casting his caustic eye over the proofs – as also did Ruth, Jane, and Alison Hawkes.

1

Forerunners

As a schoolboy in Orleans, Emile Deschamps was given a taste of plum pudding – then hardly known in France – by M. de Fontgibu, one of the emigrés who had fled to England during the Revolution, and had returned. Some ten years later, walking along the Boulevard Poissonière in Paris, Deschamps noticed a plum pudding in a restaurant window, and went in to ask if he could have a slice. 'M. de Fontgibu,' the *dame du comptoir* called out to a customer, 'would you have the goodness to share your plum pudding with this gentleman?'

Eventually Deschamps, who by the mid-nineteenth century had achieved fame in France as a romantic poet and librettist, related this coincidence to his young friend the astronomer Camille Flammarion. It had not proved to be the end of the story, he explained. Many years after the restaurant encounter, he had been invited to dine in a Paris apartment, and his hostess told him he would be having plum pudding. Jokingly, he said he was sure M. de Fontgibu would be one of the party. When the pudding was served, and the guests were enjoying the dinner, the door opened and a servant announced: 'M. de Fontgibu'.

At first Deschamps thought his hostess must be playing a joke on him. He saw it really was Fontgibu when the old man, by this time enfeebled, tottered round the table, looking bemused. It turned out that he had been invited to dinner in the same house, but had come to the wrong apartment.

Flammarion recalled the tale in his *L'Inconnu* in 1900. We have no way of ascertaining whether the facts were as Deschamps related or, for that matter, were as Flammarion told them nearly thirty years after his death. Yet as the psychologist John Beloff has observed, whatever may be the doubts about its authenticity 'it is likely to remain the *ne plus ultra* of coincidence, with its unique combination of the comic and the preposterous'.

'The little god Chance,' Flammarion commented, 'sometimes

produces extraordinary results.' He was being mildly sarcastic: Chance had become a little god, in this context. Until the eighteenth century it had been possible to attribute coincidences to supernatural intervention. Oedipus's encounter with his father was clearly pre-destined; Joseph's uncannily accurate interpretation of Pharaoh's dreams was made possible because the Lord had given him the power of divination; the portents accompanying Caesar's assassination were signals from the gods; when a witch's spell gave results, it was the devil's work – and so on. But the replacement of the supernatural by what were assumed to be laws of nature led to the development of eighteenth-century rationalism, and later of nineteenth-century posivitism, proclaiming the supremacy of the doctrine that every effect must have a cause. Where no acceptable reason for a coincidence could be found, chance could be invoked; chance, which had acquired its own respectable standing through probability theory.

Flammarion was not denying that even weird coincidences could be fortuitous; he was merely questioning whether 'coincidence' and 'chance' should be as synonymous as they had become. He was not quite the first to challenge the positivist dogma; a few months earlier, in 1899, it had been critically scrutinised by the young Cambridge biologist Alice Johnson – 'a small, quiet kindly woman of extreme integrity', Rosalind Heywood was to recall – who had been working with Henry and Eleanor Sidgwick in the early years of the Society for Psychical Research. Although 'little impressed with the marvellous', she shared their belief that orthodox science needed to come to terms with the reality of telepathy. If telepathy occurs it should theoretically be possible, Alice Johnson thought, to estimate its probability, as compared to chance, at least in the case of some coincidences.

Suppose, for example, somebody forecasts a hand at whist. The odds against the forecast being correct by chance can be estimated, and obviously they are formidable. Some other cause is much more likely, such as a previously rigged pack. But if causes of that kind can be eliminated, investigation could lead 'to the discovery of a cause hitherto unknown, or at least unrecognised by science'; and in a book-length article of some 60,000 words she presented a selection. Her evidence strongly supported the case for a cause, or causes, which orthodox science rejected as a relic of superstition.

Alice Johnson, though, was unknown both to the public and to scientists. Moreover, her article appeared in the Society's *Proceedings*, circulated only to members. Flammarion's was a household name in

France; he had prised astronomy out of the tenacious grip of his fellow astronomers, turning it into the popular hobby which it has since become (with valuable consequences; to this day, many an important discovery is being made by amateurs conducting research along the independent lines he advocated). His voluminous correspondence revealed the affection and trust he inspired, and his book was translated into many languages. And where Alice Johnson had cautiously insisted that she was only trying to clear the ground – to present the problems which coincidences posed, rather than try to solve them, their solution being 'impossible for the present' – Flammarion came out boldly for the adoption of a new attitude to them. What was ascribed to chance, he felt sure, must allow for 'something unknown to us in the forces at work'. An experience of his own suggested this.

When he was writing a description one morning of the curious forms which wind can take, a window in his study blew open, whisking the pages he had just written out of another window, 'carrying them off in a sort of whirlwind among the trees.' As, a moment later, it began to rain, he thought it would be futile to go out and look for them.

What was my surprise to receive a few days later, from Lahure's printing-office in the Rue de Fleurus, about half a mile away from where I live, that very chapter printed without one page missing.

Remember, it was a chapter on the strange doings of the wind.

What had happened?

A very simple thing.

The porter of the printing-office, who lived near the Observatory, and who brought me my proof-sheets as he went to breakfast, when going back to his office noticed on the ground, sodden by the rain, the leaves of my manuscript. He thought he must have dropped them himself, and he hastened to pick them up; and, having arranged them with great care, he took them to the printing-office, telling no one of the affair.

Among those who were impressed by *L'Inconnu* was the Austrian biologist Paul Kammerer. In 1900 he began to collect coincidences, publishing a selection and a commentary in *Das Gesetz der Serie* in 1919. He was impressed less by the significance of individual coincidences than by what he described as 'the lawful recurrence of the same or similar things and events – a recurrence, or clustering, in time or space whereby the individual members in the sequence, as far as can be ascertained by careful analysis, are not connected by the same active cause.'

Most of his examples were trivial: recurring numbers – his brother-in-law, attending a concert, found that his seat and cloak-room tickets each bore the number 9; the following day at a concert his seat and cloakroom ticket were both No. 21. But from his study of them, he came to the conclusion that they were significant. 'The crucial phrase is "*lawful* recurrence",' Arthur Koestler explained in his biography, *The Case of the Midwife Toad*; Kammerer's purpose was 'to prove that what we traditionally call a coincidence, or a series of coincidences, is in reality the manifestation of a universal principle of nature which operates independently from the known laws of physical causation.'

Kammerer was claiming, in other words, that when we say 'it never rains but it pours' – the English equivalent, Koestler observed, of the title of his book – or recall enviously a gambler's 'lucky streak', or lament that 'troubles never come singly', we are recognising, perhaps without realising it, that 'seriality' really is a force in our lives. By analogy, the scattered islands and rocks of an archipelago can indicate the presence of a mountain rising from the ocean bed.

Kammerer's ideas attracted the interest of Carl Jung. For a time, Jung was even tempted to accept that 'clusters' lay outside conventional causality. While he was engaged on research into the history of the classical 'fish' symbol (Pisces), fish cropped up in his life six times in twenty-four hours, a run which for him seemed to have 'a certain numinous quality'. Later, he decided that there was no real justification for regarding it as anything but fortuitous. By then, however, he had become impressed by a different type of coincidence. In the course of his research into the collective unconscious, he had noted numerous occasions when he had experienced coincidences 'so meaningfully connected that their "chance" occurrence would represent a degree of improbability that would have to be expressed by an astronomical figure'. They must consequently, he believed, 'be connected through another principle, namely the contingency of events': the principle of 'synchronicity' – as distinct from synchronism, which simply meant the simultaneous occurrence of events – which he illustrated in an example from his own experience.

A young woman I was treating had, at a critical moment, a dream in which she was given a golden scarab. While she was telling me this dream I sat with my back to the closed window. Suddenly I heard a noise behind me, like a gentle tapping, and saw a flying insect knocking against the window-pane from outside. I opened the window and caught the creature in the air as it flew in. It was the nearest analogy to a golden scarab that one finds in our latitudes, a scarabeid beetle, the common rose-chafer (*Cetonia aurata*), which contrary to its usual habits had evidently felt an urge to get into a dark room at this particular moment.

This passage has sometimes been used, as it was by Koestler in *The Roots of Coincidence*, to illustrate Jung's theory. Up to a point it does; not merely had the beetle arrived at the right time, but its urge to get into the dark room hinted at a purpose of the kind that in earlier times would have been regarded as qualifying it as an emissary from the gods.

For Jung, however, there was more to it. The scarab, he knew, was 'a classic example of a rebirth symbol'. In ancient Egyptian lore 'the dead sun-god changes himself at the tenth station into Khepri, the scarab, and then, at the twelfth station, mounts the barge which carries the rejuvenated sun-god into the morning sky.' Fitting in, as this did, with his theory of archetypes – messengers from the collective unconscious, making its presence felt through their symbols – this provided another layer of meaning.

There was also a third layer. It had been 'an extraordinarily difficult case to treat, and up to the time of the dream little or no progress had been made'; his patient had been too locked into conventional beliefs. Although the dream had slightly disturbed her resolute rationalism, it had needed the arrival of the beetle at precisely the crucial stage of the analysis to break through her mental armour, so that 'the process of transformation could at last begin to move.'

The existence of meaningfully connected coincidences had been recognised earlier. 'If meaningless coincidences are frequent there must occasionally occur coincidences that have meaning,' the philosopher Herbert Spencer had written; 'coincidences of which the elements are related in some significant way.' But Spencer was imbued with positivism – or materialism, as it was coming to be regarded. He assumed that meaningful coincidences must be the outcome of chance, rather than of some 'supernatural cause', which for him appeared to be the only alternative.

By the time Jung came to present his theory, however, it was possible to offer another. The materialist reliance on the sanctity of causality had been challenged: when *Synchronicity* was published in 1952 Jung gave it the subtitle, 'An Acausal Connecting Principle', and it was accompanied by an essay from Wolfgang Pauli, one of the most influential of the quantum physicists and a Nobel Laureate, with whom Jung had been collaborating. The new physics, Jung felt entitled to claim, had finally demolished the stock materialist case.

It was the link between psychology and physics which initially aroused Koestler's interest. As science editor of the Ullstein newspaper chain in Germany in the early 1930s he had established a reputation for making complex issues readable, and when in the 1950s he decided to give up the quasi-political role into which his novel *Darkness at Noon* had thrust him, it was to science that he returned. That Pauli, whose work he greatly admired, should have lent his support to synchronicity impressed Koestler. The hypothesis that acausal factors might be affecting people's lives had, for the first time, been given 'the joint stamp of respectability by a psychologist and a physicist, both of international renown'.

A few years later Koestler found himself, as if through coincidence, confronted with Kammerer's findings, and the seriality theory. His interest had been aroused by Kammerer's work as a biologist, which had appeared to show that Lamarck's theory of evolution should not have been so brusquely discarded in favour of Darwin's. When Koestler found that the evidence of fraud which had led to Kammerer's suicide in 1926 and to his findings being discredited had almost certainly been 'planted' by an unscrupulous rival, he decided to write his biography; and in the course of the research, he read *Das Gesetz der Serie*. Although inclined to be sceptical about the theory of seriality, Koestler made allowances for the fact that Kammerer had been writing before the quantum physicists had confirmed the acausality he was seeking to establish. Einstein, too, had been impressed; he had called the book 'original and by no means absurd'. But what intrigued Koestler, uneasy though he always was about subjective reactions, was that while he was engaged on the research for the biography in 1970 a whole series of coincidences seemed to descend on him, 'like a meteor shower on a summer night'.

By this time, Koestler had another reason for devoting more attention to coincidence. As a child, and occasionally later, he had experienced psychic phenomena. They were an embarrassment to him; from his scientific training, he had longed to find materialist explanations for them, and as a communist, he had felt bound to regard acceptance of them as a bourgeois deviation. But from his study of the research at Duke University in North Carolina in the 1930s, and at other centres later, he had come to the conclusion that the evidence could no longer be dismissed. Yet dismissed it was by the majority of orthodox scientists, who showed no signs of allowing it to be accepted even as a valid field for research.

Coincidence was another matter. Nobody could deny that coincidences happened. If they could be scientifically studied, they might throw up useful evidence about 'psi', the term parapsychologists had begun to use about the forces they were exploring and their effects. Jung had incorporated psi in his theory of synchronicity, and the quantum physicists were turning up evidence which, if it did not actually demonstrate psi, at least weakened some of the traditional materialist objections to accepting it as a possibility.

When Koestler turned to the theory of synchronicity as a starting point, however, he was quickly disillusioned. He called his next book *The Roots of Coincidence*, but the title was a little misleading; it was primarily about psi and its relationship to the new physics. He devoted only a chapter to 'Seriality and Synchronicity', and it was dismissive of both. Jung had complained that seriality, which Kammerer had presented as acausal, was simply another species of causality. Jung, Koestler thought, had without realising it made the same mistake, presenting archetypes as if they fulfilled a causal role.

The Roots of Coincidence, however, led to Koestler being sent several interesting case histories, including one which particularly intrigued him. In London in 1971 'Harold' a young architect, suffering from a nervous breakdown, threw himself under an approaching Underground train. It stopped just on him, but not over him; he was taken to hospital, where he survived his severe injuries. A relation of Harold's wrote to Koestler (who did not know either of them), after reading *The Roots of Coincidence*, with the startling information that it had not been the driver who had brought the train to a standstill, just in time. 'Quite independently, and with no knowledge of Harold or of what he intended to do, some passenger on the train had pulled down the emergency handle. London Transport had actually interviewed the passenger, intending to prosecute him for acting without reasonable cause.'

The passenger's action had saved Harold's life. 'They had to jack up the train to get him out, therefore he must have been well under it. On the other hand a wheel cannot have passed over him or he would have been killed.' The coincidence would have been striking enough if the passenger *had* seen what was happening, and reacted accordingly; but as Koestler pointed out, 'anybody familiar with the London Underground system can confirm that it is quite impossible to see what is happening in front of the engine'. That a passenger had pulled the emergency handle was confirmed by London Transport; but as they had decided not to prosecute, they could claim that they did not know the passenger's name. Tom Tickell, then a journalist on the *Guardian*, tried to trace his identity, but without success.

Koestler found another source of case histories; Sir Alister Hardy, FRS, Professor Emeritus of Zoology at Oxford University, had set up the Religious Experience Research Unit at Manchester College, and many of the accounts which had come pouring into it were of strange coincidences. A letter to the *New Scientist* in 1972 brought in several more, and Koestler published a selection the following year in *The Challenge of Chance*, to which Hardy and the statistician Robert Harvie also contributed.

Alice Johnson had adopted what she described as a provisional classification: '(A) Coincidences suggestive of "Causation"; (B) Coincidences suggestive of "Design"; (C) Coincidences due to "Chance".' Koestler apparently was not familiar with her article, as he did not refer to it; he, too, adopted a provisional classification but of a more subjective type, with particular emphasis on coincidences of the kind that most interested him: the 'Library Angel', where a combination of serendipity and intuition appears to be operating to find missing books or source references; '*Deus ex Machina*', where machinery is involved, sometimes as if with a mind of its own; 'Clustering', on the Kammerer model; the 'Practical Joker', seemingly setting up the coincidences for its amusement. Inevitably there was overlapping, but there were also more serious problems.

Koestler put the London Underground case into the *Deus ex Machina* category, for example, but he had no way of knowing whether there was 'a ghost in the machine'. Had the handle been pulled accidentally? Was the puller drunk? Did he do it out of bravado, or for a bet? Or did he do it as a result of some inexplicable impulse? Unless he, or somebody to whom he explained what had happened, or a passenger who witnessed the episode, came forward, the coincidence would elude classification. Nobody came forward.

Koestler also made a problem for himself by deciding that his 'guiding principle', as he put it, had been a preference for cases which appeared to resist explanation not only in terms of ordinary physical causality, 'but also in terms of telepathy and other categories of "classical" ESP.' Reluctantly he had decided to exclude some of the most dramatic coincidences, 'such as telepathic dreams or premonitions of death or accident'.

As he had come to accept the reality of ESP, this appeared to him to be logical. Suppose that – a commonly reported occurrence – a mother suddenly feels worried about her child, to find later that the child has been ill, or in danger, at the time. If the communication is attributed to telepathy, the onset of the alarm, it can be argued, is no more 'coincidental' than if the mother had been informed of the illness or accident by telephone. Nevertheless it was a curious decision on his part because, as he himself admitted, 'we do not have even the beginning of a methodology which would enable us to decide whether some event with astronomical odds against chance should be interpreted as a manifestation of ESP – or in terms of "synchronicity" or the "clustering effect".'

The case histories in *The Challenge of Chance* presented a powerful argument in favour of the existence of some unexplained process, whether serialistic or synchronistic, causal or acausal, at work in the generating of coincidence; but Koestler knew only too well that they would carry little weight among scientists, the people he would most have liked to impress. They would dismiss the evidence on the ground that it was derived from spontaneous occurrences, 'usually referred to, somewhat contemptuously, as "anecdotal material" because the value of such reports depends in most cases on subjective assessments of the reliability of the reporter; they do not qualify as scientific evidence in the strict sense.' Still, it might be possible to get around this difficulty by exploiting the method academic psychologists sometimes had to adopt, relying on numbers to obtain a sufficient quantity of evidence about spontaneous cases to compensate for the lack of experimental laboratory confirmation; accordingly in 1974 he persuaded *The Sunday Times* to offer a prize of £100 for the best coincidence account, and £5 each for any others which would be printed.

The competition attracted almost 2000 entries. The paper screened them, sending Koestler fifty, from which he selected the winners. But he could not face the prospect of ploughing through the rest of them, to decide on the next step: indeed, he was soon telling his friends he wished never to hear another coincidence story again. He was compelled to read some of those which continued to reach him; his wife Cynthia took on the screening, passing on to him those which she thought he should see and reply to – as he did, punctiliously. But no further use was made of the collection, and after his death it went with the rest of his papers to the Edinburgh University library, where it remains. His name, however, had become attached to coincidences. The Koestler Foundation, set up in his lifetime, continued to receive letters relating fresh examples. The Foundation's aim was, and is, to promote research into areas which lie just outside the boundaries of orthodox science – a wider range than Koestler decided upon for the Edinburgh Chair of Parapsychology that bears his name; and in 1987 we produced *The Unknown Guest*, subtitled 'The Mystery of Intuition' – one of his main interests, as he had shown in *The Act of Creation*. At the end of the book we invited readers to send in accounts of a variety of experiences related to intuition; among them, meaningful coincidences. In they flowed, prompting me to suggest to Koestler's friend and executor Harold Harris – he had been Koestler's editor at Hutchinson, and although by this time in retirement had remained a consultant to the firm – that coincidence could be the subject of the Foundation's next venture. This book is the result.

In certain respects I have departed from Koestler's model; in particular, by making more use of the available historical material, some of which is actually more reliable as evidence than most contemporary accounts: Alice Johnson, for example, went to great pains to obtain attestation for the stories she included.

This raises an issue which, I have found, tends to be brought up when coincidence is discussed: how far can the contributions be relied upon? I will be dealing with this in greater detail in the fifth chapter, but on one point I feel reasonably certain there is nothing to fear; the project has not been inundated with deliberately faked stories. The reason is that as everybody knows, coincidences can be so weird that rationalists long ago stopped doubting. Instead, they began to invoke probability theory as capable of accounting for any and every case. What we do get, from time to time – as Koestler did – are letters explaining to us that investigation of coincidences is a waste of time, for that reason. Invariably the writers reveal their ignorance of probability theory, in this context.

In any case, this has not been a formal research project. The book describes the findings of a pilot investigation, chiefly designed to discover what kind of coincidences people are most interested in, the reactions which they provoke, the interpretations put on them, and so on. The only check employed has been to obtain the permission of all those whose accounts are included to publish them, either under the contributor's own name or a pseudonym (indicated here by putting the name in inverted commas). The planned second stage of the investigation, we hope, can be made more systematic, with the help of the additional data from opinion polls, and other sources.

The main difference of our approach to the subject from Koestler's arises from our decision not to try to exclude, as he did, cases of 'classical' ESP – or, indeed, of other possibilities unacceptable to orthodox science. Accounts of visions of what is happening at a distance, or of dreams accurately foretelling some future event, are necessarily accounts of coincidences. Whether they should be attributed to some undiscovered faculty, to chance or to sheer invention is for readers to decide.

I have to admit, though, to the deliberate exclusion of two categories of coincidence; those reported from laboratory-type trials based on card-guessing and from 'remote perception' tests; and those reported in connection with professional divination. If you cross a gypsy's palm with silver, and get a painfully accurate picture of your past; if a fortune teller assures you that you are about to meet and marry a tall, dark man, and you do; if a medium persuades you that you are in contact with your Uncle Harry, dead these ten years – these experiences must all, if they are not fraudulent, be attributed to coincidence, if psi is not accepted as an alternative. I propose therefore, to include only spontaneous coincidences, leaving out what might be described as the manufactured variety.

The accounts are divided into three groups. 'Seriality?' concentrates on what, for convenience, can be described as Kammerian coincidences: those which excite curiosity, but are not as a rule regarded as of 'meaningful' personal significance. Should you find your cloakroom ticket, your seat ticket, and even the number of the bus which you take home, are all the same, you may regard this as evidence of the existence of unexplained forces at work; but you are unlikely to feel that they are directed at, or for, or against you.

'Synchronicity?' deals mainly with those coincidences in which the personal component features, giving the impression of design. They are of the kind which in the past would have been attributed to divine or diabolic intervention, to Fate or to Providence.

To some extent, admittedly, the distinction is arbitrary. A few people take numbers very seriously. If their cloakroom and concert tickets and their bus all have the same number, they consider this significant, particularly if the number happens to be one which keeps on coming up in their lives, or which they consider lucky, or unlucky. And there is the further problem of what constitutes 'meaningful'. Should a trivial coincidence which happens to lead to an important outcome, a new job or a new love affair, be put in the Jungian section?

The question marks in Seriality? and Synchronicity? are intended as a reminder that these were, and are, no more than hypotheses, attempts to account for certain coincidences without having to fall back on positivism's safety net, chance. Is there any other way to explore this territory? The third section, 'The Subliminal Component', considers one. If it should be found that a disproportionate number of coincidences, more especially those for which chance does not appear a plausible explanation, are related to, or the outcome of, dreams, visions, intuitions, and other subliminal sources, the implication will be that the subliminal mind may be playing a more active part in promoting coincidences than has been recognised.

The fourth section, 'Alternatives', deals with the evidence for chance in its safety-net role, considers its limitations, and goes on to consider other possibilities; the fifth discusses some which have been provided by recent developments in and around orthodox science. But I must echo Alice Johnson: this collection, like hers, 'is nothing more than an attempt to clear some of the ground in a preliminary fashion, and it is intended to suggest problems rather than solve them – their solution being, as it seems to me, impossible for the present.'

2

Seriality?

Kammerer's aim, as Koestler summarised it, was to prove that coincidences

> whether they come singly or in series, are manifestations of a universal principle in nature which operates independently from physical causation. The 'laws of seriality' are, in Kammerer's view, as fundamental as those of physics, but as yet unexplored. Moreover, single coincidences are merely tips of the iceberg which happen to catch your eye, because in our traditional ways we tend to ignore the ubiquitous manifestations of seriality.

The coincidences in this section are those which appear to fit into this category, though it is far from clear-cut.

Talk of the devil . . .
'By a "Coincidence" is meant any conjunction of circumstances that would primarily be regarded as accidental, but in which a special aspect is involved, suggesting a causal relation,' Alice Johnson claimed. 'It is always this special aspect that attracts our attention, not the fact that the conjunction is in itself a particularly unlikely one to occur.' This is not quite true, today; in the simplest form of coincidence, a 'pair', the chances of its making an impression are strongest if it is so inherently improbable that it suggests some cause other than chance – as in the account given by Oliver Wendell Holmes, Professor of Anatomy at Harvard, but best known as the homespun philosopher of the 'Breakfast Table' series, in *Over the Teacups* (1891).

At dinner with two ladies one evening, he had launched into a reminiscence of a case of 'trial by Battel', which he had suddenly recalled having read about some thirty years earlier. In 1817, he told them, Abraham Thornton had thrown down his glove 'which was not taken up by the brother of the murdered man, and so he had to be let off, for the old law was still in force.' Thornton had then emigrated to America; 'he may be living near us, for aught that I know.' With that, Holmes left the room, and found a letter which had just been delivered. It was entirely unexpected and came from the friend of a friend in England; and it enclosed a report of the trial of Thornton for murder. 'The prisoner pleaded successfully the old Wager of Battell', the letter ran. 'I thought you would like to read the account.'

Holmes had not 'looked at the account, spoken of it, nor thought of it for a long time when it came to me by a kind of spontaneous generation, as it seemed, having no connection with any previous train of thought that I was aware of.' The evidence that there was no connection between his revived memory of the event and the letter, he considered, 'apart from possible "telepathic" causation' was 'completely waterproof, airtight, incombustible and unassailable.'

'Perhaps few experiences are more familiar than to meet with a name or a fact in reading or conversation almost immediately after hearing of it, as we think, for the first time,' Alice Johnson noted; (or feeling it; she cited the case the Homer scholar, Walter Leaf, had sent to her. When he was an undergraduate at Cambridge in 1871 Leaf had two teeth knocked out playing cricket. 'I had a good deal of pain, which gave me such a restless night that I was glad, contrary to my usual habit, to get up early next morning and go to early chapel. In the psalms for the morning (lviii, 6) came the verse, "Break their teeth, O God, in their mouths" ').

In *The Challenge of Chance* Koestler, quoting De Maistre's *L'ange distributeur des pensées?*, included some cases in his 'Library Angel' category; but it was primarily designed for accounts of *useful* interventions – say, the provision of a missing, long searched-for source reference. Most such cases, though, create surprise or amusement, but little more; as in the example sent to him by Ivone Kirkpatrick, OBE, who had been reading a passage from Goethe's *Conversations with Eckermann* when he switched on the radio, which happened to be tuned in to a German station; to his astonishment, a man was reading from the same passage.

Concurrences of this kind appear to be common; so common, in one contributor's experience, that her letter would have delighted Kammerer. Since her retirement Mrs Joy Heiseler has settled into a morning routine which consists of listening to the *Today* programme on Radio Four while at the same time I attempt to do the *Times* crossword puzzle. Two years ago I began to notice that as I either read a word in a clue or found the answer, the very word was simultaneously spoken on Radio 4. I don't mean ordinary words, of course. Here are some examples: beggar, serendipity, case-history, enlargement, developed, disgusted, theory, twin, evergreen – I could go on and on.

Mrs Heiseler is no longer amazed, as it is almost an everyday occurrence; hardly 'meaningful', she admits, 'but it does happen anything up to ten times a week, which, I should have thought, was beyond the laws of chance.'

Small world

Also commonly reported, in the Kammerian category, are the encounters which elicit the familiar comment, 'It's a small world.' Sorting through some books with a view to selecting a few to take abroad, F. E. Ansell of Haworth, Yorkshire came across a copy of Jerome's *Three Men in a Boat* which he had bought in the Pokhara Bookshop in Nepal, four years earlier, and put it aside. That afternoon he and his wife drove to Bradford to see a film; and on the way they decided to make some purchases at the local Asian foodstore.

At the check-out we fell into conversation with the manager, whom we are well acquainted with. Out of the blue, he said, 'You've been to Nepal, haven't you?' and when we confirmed that we had, pointing behind us he said, 'This man is from Nepal.' Turning round we came face to face with the first Nepalese person we had seen for almost four years. He was a young man visiting England, working temporarily in the shop.

Had we stayed in Pokhara? he asked. Where? and where did we go? We mentioned the names of some restaurants, and then I suddenly remembered the book. 'The funny thing is,' I said, 'only this morning I came across a book that I bought in Pokhara.' 'At the Pokhara Bookshop? That is my shop!'

Ansell finds it hard to accept that this could be chance. Might it not be that they were 'somehow drawn towards the encounter, or at least that the two events must have been connected in some way, the statistical chance being so remote?'

The feeling that even a 'small-world' coincidence of this kind may be meaningful, in the sense that something other than chance may be involved, is fairly widespread.

On a train travelling south from Edinburgh shortly after the Second World War, Tan Donald fell into conversation with a stranger and found they had several friends in common. They decided to have lunch together; and were allocated to a table at which there were two Indians, husband and wife.

I felt very much at ease sitting beside this gracious and handsome Hindu lady, beautifully attired in her sari and expensively jewelled. I asked her which part of India she came from; she replied that she came from Calcutta, where I had spent several months during my war service. She asked me where I had lived in Calcutta, and I told her that I had been billeted in a large dwelling house in Carrington Street, requisitioned by the army for officers' quarters. When I mentioned Carrington Street she was dumbfounded momentarily, but recomposed herself to tell me that she used to live there as a child. Then with some urgency she asked if I remembered the number of the house. 'Number Seven,' I replied, not daring to expect that this could possibly have been her house. Imagine the amazement and thrill we both felt when we realized that it was the house that at one time belonged to her father.

Donald and the Indian lady would not have met if his chance acquaintance had not suggested they have lunch together, and gone to the restaurant car; and they would not have decided to have lunch together if they had not earlier struck up a conversation and found they had mutual acquaintances. 'If not a "pure chance" meeting,' Donald wonders, 'might not some "strange force" centred on No. 7 Carrington Street in which we had both lived at different times, have brought us together?'

Other contributors, though clearly intrigued by their 'small-world' experiences, regard them simply as curiosities.

In 1988 'David Howe' was conducting some research in London which took him, about once a month, to an agency in a building which accommodated a variety of small-scale arts and business concerns. On one occasion, waiting to see the director of the agency, he was chatting inconsequentially with the receptionist. They could hear the distant sound of a band rehearsing, and she asked him what kind of music he liked. His tastes, he said, were wide. She asked:

'What was the last record you bought?'

'Ah, I've developed a taste in African music.'

'That's one of my interests, too!'

'The last record I bought is by a man from Mali by the name of Ali Farke Toure. I love his music and could hardly believe that his records were available here.'

'Look – you're not going to believe this, but he's in the room next door. If you listen carefully you can hear his voice through the wall!'

The receptionist explained that because of her interest in African music, she knew that the agency in the next door office had arranged for Toure to come to England. 'The number of coincidences that led to the mention of his name while he was barely a few feet away in a building in North London, in England rather than many thousands of miles from me in his small village in a remote part of Mali, seemed quite incredible,' Howe comments. 'However, other than a great pleasure in his music, I can find nothing meaningful in the event.'

'My most unusual coincidence was not meaningful,' Mrs Dee Murchison insists; nevertheless it was extraordinary in a statistical sense – and it could be verified by her friend, Claire, 'whose coincidence it really was.' Claire's son James, travelling to Japan, had taken the Trans-Siberian railway; and on it had made friends with Michael, from Sweden, who was going to visit his Japanese girl pen-friend. Some months later, when James had returned, Michael had rung up to say the girl was holidaying in Europe, and they came to dinner.

A year later, Claire and I went to Japan for an extended holiday. We spent a few days in Kyoto, and one day went on a Japanese Tourist Board tour of several important temples, finishing at lunch time at the craft/tourist centre. Whilst looking around and choosing some presents on the paper-goods floor, Claire told me all about the girl.

I paid for my goods; then, the girl on the till looked at Claire and said, 'I think I know you, aren't you James's mother?'

The girl had arrived to work in Kyoto only a couple of weeks before. 'Bearing in mind that the population of Japan is 115 million, the coincidence was truly remarkable.'

Small-world coincidences can cause a mild *frisson* even in people who are not disposed to read anything into them. When Barrie Heads

took charge of Granada TV's overseas operations, it meant moving
with his wife and family to London.

> After we left Manchester and sold our house it was pulled down and
> a block of flats was built on the land, next to the London–
> Manchester railway line.
>   Denise and I were going to Manchester on the train one day, and
> said to whoever we were with that we'd show them where the
> house used to be. As we passed, we said, 'There's where it was.'
> Another passenger sitting in the carriage said, 'And I'm the man
> who pulled it down.' He was the owner of the demolition firm.

Mrs Hanne O'Rourke, wife of the Irish Ambassador in London,
recalls an experience her uncle had at Buchenwald towards the end of
the war, when the Germans rounded up members of the Danish police
force and took them to concentration camps in Germany.

> The 'toilets' were planks over a ditch, and the men talked to each
> other while sitting there. One day my uncle found himself next to a
> Canadian air force officer who had somehow also arrived at the
> camp. When the Canadian learned that my uncle was Danish, he
> asked from what part of the country.
>   'Aarhus.'
>   'Then you must know my wife, Grethe.' He produced a photo of
> his wife. My uncle did know her. She had been his childhood
> sweetheart.

Confirming the story, her uncle tells Mrs O'Rourke that they
exchanged addresses, but he had lost the piece of paper, and the
Canadian did not get in touch.

An even more remarkable 'small-world' encounter occurred in
1936 to Peter Elstob, novelist, historian and vice-President of PEN.
Twenty years old at the time, he was window-gazing outside
Lillywhite's Piccadilly sports shop when a middle-aged American
who had been standing beside him asked him for some advice . . .
unusual, in a stranger, 'but his American accent explained that.'
Would it be all right to send a tennis racket to the daughter of the
family he had been staying with (hers, he had noticed, was beginning
to warp), or would they consider it over the top? Elstob reassured him.
The American then went on to say he had been unable to find the

address of a young man to whom friends in the United States had asked him to deliver a letter. The man was not in the telephone directory, and nobody he had asked had been able to help him.

He showed me the letter: it was addressed to me. I can still remember the shock, the shiver, the wild suspicion that he must have known who I was. But that was impossible.

It was not a significant coincidence, Elstob comments. All the writer wanted was his address which, as it happened, he had sent a day or two earlier; and he never met the American again; 'I have no explanation other than one in a million chances do come up one in a million times.'

In 1942 Arthur Butterworth, formerly a member of the Hallé Orchestra and subsequently conductor of the Huddersfield Philharmonic Society, was stationed at Taversham Hall, not far from Norwich. 'Taversham Hall itself was at that time, or so it seemed to me, a bleak, forbidding-looking place, all closed down, secretive, faded lace curtains at all the windows, barbed wire round the lawn with the notice "Out of Bounds to All Troops".' To those who were on guard duty at night, there was a *something* about it; they were glad when their two-hour stint was over.

At that time I was – like all other soldiers – looking forward to my own future career; I was on the look-out for books on music so that I might be ready to go to a music college as soon as the war should be over. I sent away to Foyle's for a second-hand copy of *Counterpoint and Harmony* by Professor Kitson, one of those primers long regarded as an essential for music students.

A few days later the small parcel arrived from Foyle's. I opened it while standing in front of the Nissen hut window, and to my astonishment, out of the pages of the book dropped a picture postcard, a sepia coloured photograph of the kind once popular of seaside places in Edwardian times. The picture might have been taken at that moment – perhaps with a Polaroid camera, had there been such things in 1942 – for it showed *exactly* the scene through the window I was then standing in front of.

The card had been sent by 'Tony', postmarked 3 August 1913; Butterworth was interested to see that it was ten years and one day before his own birth date, and mentioned it in his entry for the prizes *The Sunday Times* offered on Koestler's behalf, winning £5. As a result of the publicity he also got a call from Taversham from somebody who had known 'Tony', offering to show him around if he paid a visit – 'a sequel which I have always been sorry I never followed up – so who knows? Something might even come of it now.'

Copycat
A more startling type of 'small-world' coincidence, for those who experience it, is an unexpected concurrence of names. In 1867 the Rev. Charles Bingham was looking at a collection of bibles on display at the Paris Exhibition when he became aware of the presence of another clergyman, who was also examining them. Bingham vaguely felt he had met the man, but could not recall where; and it was obvious from his manner that he was in the same dilemma. They shook hands.

> 'I beg your pardon,' was our common exclamation, 'but I cannot remember your name.' I forget which was the first to reply, but the answer was identical: 'My name is the Revd Charles Bingham' and 'My name is the Revd Charles Bingham.'

Such experiences remain far from uncommon. Koestler's friend the distinguished psychiatrist and author Dr Alan McGlashan tells the story of the outcome of an accident, in which the car which his stepson was driving to his seaside cottage had been run into by another car, near a country village. The village constable, who happened to be nearby, arrived and took out his notebook. 'Your name?' he asked the other driver. 'Ian Purvis.' He turned: 'And your name?' 'Ian Purvis.' The bobby complained, 'This is no time for silly jokes.' But it was not a joke: a car driven by Ian Purvis had run into a car driven by Ian Purvis.

While Barbara Brice was employed at the Admiralty in Whitehall, she received a telephone call from a man who announced himself simply as 'Michael'. As she couldn't think who he might be, she replied that he must have got a wrong number.

> 'But that is Barbara – Barbara Brice?'
> 'Yes.'
> 'This is Michael – Michael!'
> 'Sorry; I don't know you.'

'Oh, Barbara! You work in the Admiralty, don't you?'
'Yes.'
'You have dark hair – you are about five foot six inches tall?'
'Well, yes.'
'We met at Green Park Underground Station yesterday evening.'

This worried her, as she had indeed used the station but had no recollection of meeting anybody there. Could it be amnesia? But when he went on to say, 'You have just come back from a holiday in Austria, haven't you?' she could reply, relieved, that she had never been in Austria in her life, and put the telephone down, 'somewhat shaken'.

Later it occurred to her to look up the Admiralty internal telephone directory, in case there was another Miss Brice.

I could not believe my eyes. While I was working with a Mr CHESHIRE in one department, the other Barbara Brice was working with a Mr CHESHER in another!

Visiting Vancouver in 1968, Peter Fearnhead called in at the American Express office to find if there was any mail for him and his wife; there was none, he was told, but that day's delivery was expected shortly. He went to an adjoining office to book his return journey to England; returning twenty minutes later, he asked again if there was any mail for Fearnhead.

'Yes,' the counter clerk said, 'but I have just given it to a Mr Fearnhead. He's just this minute walked out of the door.' Needless to say we could not find him, despite rushing into the street.

Well, I looked in the Vancouver telephone directory, and there was indeed a Mr Fearnhead. We rang him and, yes, he had got our mail.

Although the Fearnheads had different initials, the name is by no means common. The Vancouver Fearnhead, too, had not only come to the American Express office at the same time as the English one, but had happened to disclose his identity, and as a result been given the letters which he had not asked for. It turned out that the counter clerk, taking his name, had assumed he must have been the same man who had inquired for mail a few minutes before, and handed them to him; as he was the only Vancouver Fearnhead, he assumed they must be for him, from somebody who had got his initials wrong. The outcome was satisfactory; 'He invited us over to his house for a meal and entertained us most hospitably.'

The most remarkable case in this category was related by the eminent American mathematician Warren Weaver in his erudite but entertaining commentary on probability theory, *Lady Luck*. His next-door neighbour, George D. Bryson, was travelling by rail from St Louis to New York and, as he was in no hurry, decided to stop off at Louisville, a city he had never explored. At the station, he asked about accommodation and was directed to the Brown Hotel, where he registered.

Then, just for a lark, he stepped up to the mail desk and asked if there was any mail for him. The girl calmly handed him a letter addressed to 'Mr George D. Bryson, Room 307', that being the number of the room to which he had just been assigned.

It turned out that the preceding resident of Room 307 was another George D. Bryson, who was associated with an insurance company in Montreal but came originally from North Carolina.

The two men eventually met, 'so each could pinch each other to be sure he was real.'

Clustering

Trivial coincidences of the kind which are noted at the time, but quickly forgotten, can take on significance if they develop into sequences, of the same type of experience – as James Joyce recognised. While Leopold Bloom is walking along a Dublin street in *Ulysses*, he happens to be thinking about Charles Stewart Parnell when he suddenly sees John Howard Parnell; 'There he is; the Brother. Image of him. Haunting face.' Then Bloom reminds himself, 'Hundreds of times you think of a person and don't meet him.' But George Russell – better known as A.E. – has also been in Bloom's mind. 'And there he is, too. Now that's really a coincidence: second time. Coming events cast their shadows before.' A coincidence of this kind, Bloom muses, would meet with A.E.'s approval – a reference to the poet's interest in the occult.

There is no clear-cut definition of a 'cluster' in this context, but the term applies as a rule to a succession of loosely related, usually trivial happenings, such as the example Freud gave in his *New Introductory Lectures on Psychoanalysis.*

In 1919 a visitor to Vienna from London, Dr David Forsyth, had left his card. His visit was of special significance to Freud, as he was the first foreigner to call on him after the war ended, and 'seemed to be the harbinger of better times.' Freud's next patient was Mr P. Recounting his sexual problems P described an affair with a girl whom he might have succeeded with had she not been a virgin. She called him 'Herr Vorsicht' – Mr Foresight.

So far, Freud admitted to his audience, the story might appear thin; but he asked them to be patient. P, he went on, happened to have a library of English books. A few days before, he had brought Freud a copy of one of the volumes from *The Forsyte Saga.* And the clustering had continued. Visiting a colleague, Dr Anton Freund, Freud found to his surprise that Freund and P lived on different floors of the same house. At their next session, P 'for the first time in our long acquaintance let slip the distorted form of my name, to which officials, clerks and printers have accustomed me; instead of Freud, he said Freund'. Later in the session P, telling Freud of an *alptraum* (nightmare) he had just had, remarked that somebody had told him that the English for *alptraum* was 'a mare's nest'. Correcting him, Freud remembered that not long before, seeing a photograph of Ernest Jones, Freud's future biographer, P had asked to be introduced to him. Jones, Freud now recalled, was the author of a monograph on nightmares.

In 1966 John A. Ireland, Lecturer in Music at the Bedford College of Higher Education – 'scientist, musician, sceptic', as he describes himself – took some Dutch friends from his parents' home in Manchester to see Chatsworth, the stately home of the Duke of Devonshire, and took them 'over the fence' for a look at the reservoir which supplies the power for the Emperor Fountain. On their way back they had to jump from the top of a dry-stone wall.

In those days I used to keep my comb in a top outside jacket pocket. As I landed, it flicked out and landed amongst new growth. I searched, and found it sitting nearly vertically on a 1954 sixpence – not easy to see; however, I retrieved it and there was general amusement about it falling on a coin which, presumably, had bounded out of someone's pocket on a previous jump over the wall.

They then walked down a path, on which there was a mat of new grass. About 100 yards further on, when he took out his comb to deal with his unruly hair he dropped it.

As it landed on the grassy path it went 'CHINK'. I stopped to pick it up and it had landed, would you believe, on 2s 3½d in change in pre-decimal coinage – a florin, two pennies and three halfpennies in a little pile.

Had they fallen out of somebody's pocket during an amorous adventure? 'Anyway, the five-minute connection of comb and money seems to me an odd one.'

There are some people whose lives are festooned with clusters. Describing himself as 'coincidence prone' Monty Dare, an Essex company director, lists no fewer than thirty 'small-world' experiences he has had since 1946. Thus:

Friend and I report for National Service in the same week, him to RAF Padgate (Lancashire), me to Pay Corps, Devizes (Wiltshire). Twelve weeks later we meet on a traffic island in the middle of Andover, Hampshire, him travelling by bus to Southampton, me travelling by bus to Barton Stacey. Both stepped on to traffic island at same moment, crossing road, changing buses. Talked for two minutes. Never seen each other since.

We have a minor car crash in Kent. Next weekend my brother photographs me in the paddock at Snetterton. When a slide of the photograph is shown, projected on a screen, the other people involved in the crash can be seen, clear and sharp, walking behind me. We never saw them at the time the photo was taken.

Mother in hospital says how much she enjoys David London on the radio. As I am going on holiday the next day, say I'll contact him (I know him slightly; he's a well-known Colchester business man) when I get back. At dinner in the crowded Post House coffee shop, Gatwick, waitress asks if a family can join us at our table. It is David London and his family, just landed from a flight from Minorca.

Invited to a wedding. Get into conversation with couple sitting next to us. Find we are both going on holiday to Australia; both going to Perth; both going to visit the same people in Perth. They turn out to be cousins of our friends there. Never seen them before, or since.

Another variety of cluster which some contributors describe consists of experiences with numbers. 'In 42 years,' Paul G. Ellis, Ph.D., recalls, 'I've lived in approximately 19 homes for periods of 10 weeks (1 university term) or longer. *Of these a disproportionately large number of homes have had numbers involving 3 and/or 1; very few if any have had numbers 6, 8, 9 or 0.*

No.31   (at least 4 times for 2 yrs, 2 yrs, 1 yr and 10 weeks)
No.3   (twice, for 2 years and 1.5 yrs)
No.1   (once, for 6 yrs)
No.134   (once, for 12 yrs)'

On no occasion, Dr Ellis adds, has the numbering influenced his choice of home; he only became aware of the disproportion in retrospect.

Time warps

Coincidences are usually thought of as happening at or around the same time, or in quick succession; but they can link past and present. When Grenville Tudor Phillips died in 1863, Oliver Wendell Holmes noted his death only because he had been the brother of a classmate at college. Holmes was staying with his own brother at the time, in the house where they had been born. While looking at some of his father's books, his eye was caught by a bible which he thought might prove to be an interesting rarity. As he took it from the shelves, 'an old slip of paper fell out, and fluttered to the floor. On lifting it I read these words: *The name is Grenville Tudor.*'

The most likely explanation, Holmes thought, was that his father had been asked by Grenville Tudor's father, who happened to be a cousin by marriage, to officiate at the boy's baptism; the slip had been handed to him to remind him of the name, and he had put it in the bible. 'There it lay quietly for nearly half a century, when, as if it had just heard of Mr Phillips' decease, it flew from its hiding place and startled the eyes of those who had just read his name in the daily column of deaths.' It would be hard, Holmes thought, to find anything more than a mere coincidence here, 'but it seems curious enough to be worth telling!'

The way in which trivial coincidences can cause a scalp to prickle is illustrated in an account by the novelist and biographer Tom Girtin. In 1950 a letter of introduction from his publishers brought about a meeting with Robert Graves in Majorca. Graves was delighted with himself because he had been able to pay a two-month-old grocery bill with 'one and a half inches of verse in the *New Yorker.*' Graves then launched into a monologue about one of his hobby-horses of the time, the origin and significance of nursery rhymes, citing Little Miss Muffett. The metre, he claimed, showed it to be seventeenth century, and so it was! She was the daughter of the seventeenth-century entomologist Thomas Muffett. As it happened, Girtin had just been reading about Muffett in Aubrey's *Brief Lives*; as he had brought the book with him, he was in a position not merely to air his knowledge of the fact that Muffett had written *De Insectis*, but also to point out that he had written in the *sixteenth* century, and to clinch the argument which followed by producing his copy of Aubrey. 'Extraordinary!' Graves commented, po-faced. 'Must have been two people of the same name!'

In 1984 Girtin bought a copy of John Julius Norwich's *Christmas Crackers*.

It included a poem by Robert Graves – four lines, only, and measuring not even the inch and a half that thirty-four years earlier had paid the grocery bill.

I felt a sudden primitive, superstitious terror: on the page facing the verse – and quite unconnected with it – were some notes on that sixteenth-century entomologist who wrote *De Insectis* – Dr Thomas Muffett.

Working in the International Refugee Organisation after the Second World War, Mrs Heather Prescott and a Norwegian colleague were appalled by the accounts of human suffering which the files of displaced persons described.

Having seen enough for one day, Bill sighed deeply and confessed that he, too, had been subjected to a ghastly ordeal, standing naked for two days in bitter cold because one of his mates in the concentration camp in which he had been incarcerated had escaped.

'If ever I see him,' he joked, 'I'll wring his neck.' At an adjacent desk a newcomer to the office, a handsome Belgian, rose from his chair and came towards us. 'Which camp was that?' he inquired. Friendly discussion followed, at the end of which they embraced warmly; the Belgian had in fact been the very man who escaped from the camp, the only one to get away.

In November 1981 a Londoner, Andrew Hudson, was being driven to Manchester along the M1 in a white Ford car by Ian Jardin, a civil servant in the Ministry of Defence. Nearing the Watford Gap, Jardin began to have trouble accelerating; he pulled onto the hard shoulder, and put through a call for assistance, which duly arrived, and they were able to set out again an hour and a half later. The following Easter, Hudson found himself being driven along the same stretch of the M1 by Dr Stephen Satterthwaite of British Steel. Shortly after they had passed the spot where the trouble had occurred four months earlier, Satterthwaite began to have trouble accelerating, pulled onto the hard shoulder, and rang for assistance. Hudson got out to await the arrival of the AA man. As he was standing by the side of the motorway, he saw a familiar-looking car approaching. It was the white Ford, driven by Jardin.

Douglas Stuart, DSC retired not long after the end of the Second World War after spending a lifetime at sea in the merchant service, ending up as Commodore of P&O. On two occasions, one in the First World War, the other in the Second, he survived the torpedoing and sinking of his ships by German U-boats in the Mediterranean. 'The oddity connected with the two events,' his grand-nephew Charles Fitzgerald comments, 'separated as they were by an interval of more than twenty years, lies in the fact that the torpedoings occurred at exactly the same day and month of the year.'

Shortly before the outbreak of the Second World War a new rose, destined to become famous, was introduced in France and taken for propagation to the United States. During the last winter of the war it was decided that the time had come to replace its number with a name, and a ceremony was arranged for 29 April. Although the organisers, the American Rose Society, clearly knew what they were about when they called it 'Peace', they can hardly have anticipated that the date they fixed in advance for the ceremony would be the day before Hitler committed suicide in his bunker in Berlin. Nor, when they agreed to award the Society's Gold Medal to 'Peace', that the day on which the presentation was to be made would be the day on which Japan surrendered.

Such coincidences can come in even more curious historical clusters, one of the best known being the weird parallels between the careers of Abraham Lincoln and John F. Kennedy, elected president of the United States a century apart. Several of the contributors to the

Koestler Foundation's collection cite them. Both men were shot while sitting beside their wives; both were succeeded by a Southerner named Johnson; both their killers were themselves killed before they could be brought to justice. Lincoln had a secretary called Kennedy; Kennedy, a secretary called Lincoln. Lincoln was killed in the Ford Theatre; Kennedy was killed in a Ford Lincoln – and so on. Eventually the search for further echoes was to become almost an industry, with the proliferation of such trivia as 'the names of both men contain seven letters', but the *Daily Express* heading of the day before Kennedy's assassination is more likely to cause a shiver, if come upon unexpectedly: 'The man who's gunning for Kennedy'. It was a profile of Senator Barry Goldwater, seeking nomination as the Republican presidential candidate; in the picture he is holding a rifle.

Fiction into fact

A category of time warp coincidences of a rather different kind, which has often attracted awed attention, consists of cases where episodes in a novel or short story are repeated in reality later, one of the most remarkable examples originating in *Gulliver's Travels*. The astronomers of Laputa, Swift wrote, had discovered two satellites revolving about Mars, 'whereof the innermost is distant from the centre of the primary planet exactly three of its diameters, and the outermost five; the former revolves in the space of ten hours, and the latter in twenty-one and a half; so that the squares of their periodical times are very near in the same proportion with the cubes of their distance from the centre of Mars; which evidently shows them to be governed by the same law of gravitation that influences the other heavenly bodies.'

The *number* of satellites could have been a guess; the effect of gravity could have been estimated. What was remarkable was the realisation that the satellites were so close to Mars – so close, in fact, that they might revolve around it more rapidly than Mars does on its own axis. The prediction in 1726 was eventually to be confirmed by the discovery of the two satellites, a century and a half later. The Laputans had overestimated their distance from Mars; but in the case of the inner satellite, they had not been far out in their estimate of the time it took to circle the planet. The fact that the satellite revolves three times round Mars in the same time that the planet turns round once, the astronomer Sir Robert Ball noted in his *Story of the Heavens* (1893), 'is unparalleled in the solar system; indeed, so far as we know, it is unparalleled in the universe.'

In one of his *Roundabout Papers* (1860) Thackeray remarked 'the imagination foretells things', citing his realisation that from time to time characters he had invented became realities – notably Costigan, from *Pendennis*

> I was smoking in a tavern parlour one night, and this Costigan came into the room alive – the very man – the most remarkable resemblance of the printed skeleton of the man, of the rude drawing in which I had depicted him. He had the same little coat, the same battered hat cocked on one eye, the same twinkle in that eye.

The living Costigan, he found, had also been in the army, and spoke with an Irish brogue; 'How had I come to know him, to divine him?'

In his *Evidence for the Supernatural* (1911) the deeply sceptical Ivor Tuckett recalled a play by Arthur Law in which one of the characters, Robert Golding, was the only survivor of the shipwrecked *Caroline*. Soon afterwards, Law read of the wreck of a ship called *Caroline*; and the only survivor was a man called Golding. 'This is a case of pure coincidence,' Tuckett claimed, 'about which there can be no doubt.' He would doubtless have said the same about the sequel to 'The Narrative of A. Gordon Pym' in 1838 in which Edgar Allan Poe described how three survivors of a shipwreck killed and ate the ship's cabin boy, Richard Parker. In 1884 *The Times* reported on the trial of three survivors of a shipwreck for murdering and eating the ship's cabin boy, whose name was Richard Parker. (This, incidentally, was the coincidence which on Koestler's recommendation won the £100 *Sunday Times* prize.)

The American novelist Morgan Robertson's *Futility* (1898) described the fate of 'the largest ship afloat and the greatest of the works of men'. A special feature was her watertight compartments which closed automatically in the event of an accident. Even if she hit an iceberg, the theory was, she would not sink; there would be no need to carry more than the minimum of lifeboats required by law. She was named *Titan*; on her third Atlantic voyage she hit an iceberg and sank with unprecedented loss of life. In *The Futility God* (1975) an Ohio business man, J. W. Hannah, listed those features of the loss of the *Titanic* which corresponded to the *Titan*. They both sank for the same reason in much the same place. Dimensions, tonnage, the number of passengers and of lifeboats, were nearly the same, as was the operation of the watertight doors. The *Titanic* had not even

reached the drawing board stage when *Futility* was published; there
was no question of his picking up clues about its design.

In *The Ledger is Kept* (1953) Raymond Postgate described an
investigation into the leakage of official secrets from a nuclear research
station. One of the civil servants there, though unpopular – he had
made a nuisance of himself about a picture hung in the common room
– was not suspect; but he was eventually exposed as a traitor. His name
was Blunt.

H. E. Bates, in *The Blossoming World* (1981), recalled an even
stranger case. In one of his novels he had described how a rich and
selfish woman, who has left her husband, sets out spider-like to
captivate and destroy a young man she meets while on holiday on an
island.

> Her name being Vane, I fitted her out, in the story, with an
> expensive set of matching luggage, each piece stamped with a V.
> Two years later, travelling by ship to the same island on which the
> story is set, I saw the set of matching luggage, each piece with its V,
> going aboard ahead of me and then watched, for the next three or
> four days, the woman of whom I had written, rich and selfish,
> proceed to her spider act of destruction.

Resonance
The border between Kammerian and Jungian coincidences is not well
defined. One type of 'small-world' occurrence is hard not to feel as if it
were delivered by design, as if by a letter marked 'personal'.

In *The Challenge of Chance* Koestler recalled the 'meteor shower' of
coincidences which descended on him when he was doing the research
into Kammerer's life and career, but described only one of them which
had been helpful in getting the book off the ground. The last of them
descended later, providing what should be incorporated as a postscript
in any new edition.

Among the distinguished scientists who had attended the Alpbach
symposium described in *Beyond Reductionism* (1968) was Professor Paul
Weiss of the Rockefeller University, who liked the village of Alpbach so
much that he later arranged to take a house there for his summer
holidays. It was not until the second of them that Koestler found that
Weiss had succeeded Kammerer in his job at the Biological Institute in
Vienna, and that he had actually assisted at tests which disclosed that
Kammerer – his enemy – had tampered with the evidence.

In a letter to Koestler, Kammerer's daughter Lacerta had recalled that her father had been very much in love with a Mrs Grete Somerskjold. Some of his obituaries had suggested that his suicide could have been linked with her refusal to leave her husband and go with him to Moscow, where he had been offered a post. Only later had it occurred to Koestler that this might have been 'the fabulous Grete Wiesenthal, (internationally celebrated dancer and Ballet Master of the Vienna Opera), one of the goddesses of my student days'; and he wrote to Lacerta to check whether he was right. She replied that her father had indeed been very much in love with her, 'but her response did not go far enough'. Koestler happened to have been invited to dinner by Professor Weiss on the day the letter arrived; he went hoping that Weiss would be able to provide further information. In this he was to be disappointed: 'Weiss said he had heard rumours about her and Kammerer, but remembered no details.' Dinner over, they sat down to watch the late night news bulletin on television. It included the announcement that Grete Wiesenthal had died in Vienna at the age of eighty-five.

Careful though Koestler was to avoid allowing such personal experiences to influence his judgement, he cannot have found it easy to avoid speculating whether here was an element of Jungian synchronicity which he had found wanting, at least in the form Jung had presented it. Some contributors have used the term 'resonance' to describe what they feel about such experiences: those which may easily be dismissed as fortuitous, yet leave a lingering doubt.

In the 1930s Peter Fleming, journalist and travel writer, was almost as well known as his brother Ian was to become thirty years later. In *One's Company* (1934) he described a journey through Russia and Manchuria to China, in which he encountered a variety of hazards, including those engendered by the simmering civil war between the communist forces and Chiang Kai-shek's army. On his way through remote bandit country in a small group he was spared the fate of three merchants who had been set upon and robbed the day before; but he narrowly escaped being killed by a falling boulder.

The only other thing worth relating about that walk was a coincidence, trivial but striking. I had been telling Gerald, as we went along, about a journey which I had undertaken the year before, as one of an expedition which had pursued a ludicrous course across the central plateau of Brazil in search of the legendary

Colonel Fawcett. We were discussing the strange immortality of the lost explorer – how after eight years one was still continually coming across references to him. Suddenly Gerald stopped and picked up a scrap of newspaper. It was printed in English. The only complete paragraph on it announced the return, empty-handed, of yet another American expedition from the jungles of Matto Grosso; although defeated they were still convinced, the newspaper said, that Fawcett was alive.

The travellers pointed out to each other 'what a small place the world was', Fleming concluded; adding, a little self-consciously (he was embarrassed by clichés, but felt uneasy about deriding them), 'It is always better to observe the rites.' Yet his was a distinctly unusual 'small-world' case. The bizarre nature of the find was strange enough; that it should relate to the preceding conversation was still more remarkable; and the fact that the Fawcett expedition meant so much more to Fleming than a casual conversational topic, as he had been so deeply involved in it, and had written the book about it which had established his reputation, made the episode far from 'trivial', as coincidences go. Had Fleming been disposed to read meaning into it, he could have been excused for doing so. But he was not that kind of man.

Occasionally it is almost as if such coincidences are arranged as a mark of approval – an occult pat on the back. In the early 1970s John Hurt, who had been making a series of films, decided he would like to try to return to the stage, and asked his agent to keep an eye out for a good part. In the meantime he hired a boat and set off for a break. One morning, in need of provisions, he moored and asked the way to the nearest town. When he arrived he rang his agent, to hear that he had been offered the lead in *Ride a Cock Horse*. Looking out idly from the telephone box while they were talking, his eye lit on a nearby weather-worn stone monument: Banbury Cross.

3

Synchronicity?

Providence

In the mid-nineteenth century, as Arnold Bennett reminded his readers in *The Old Wives' Tale* in 1908, 'Providence was still busying himself with everybody's affairs, and foreseeing the future in the most extraordinary manner.' It may no longer be taken for granted that Providence is an active participant in people's lives; when something is described as providential, the implication may be that luck has intervened. Nevertheless a core of belief remains, even among agnostics, that some interventions cannot be put down to luck, or chance. It is as if somebody (god, demon, spirit) or something (Fate, Destiny, Karma, or some yet to be explained influence) is taking a hand, for good, or ill; sometimes for fun.

These are the coincidences which are most often referred to as synchronistic or meaningful. They may not be striking in themselves; often, in fact, the coincidence itself is trivial, and would hardly be remarked upon were it not for its effects, and their repercussions. In their most frequently reported form, they attract attention because they satisfy a personal need. It is this personal element which, colloquially at least, usually establishes whether a coincidence is considered synchronistic, or meaningful. If you hear a word spoken on the radio which you have just read in a book you may be momentarily amused, or startled, but you are unlikely to ponder its significance. It can be a different matter if you find that the word is what you needed to complete that morning's crossword puzzle.

This distinction between meaningful – though he did not actually employ the term – and 'mere' coincidences was recognised by Augustus De Morgan. At the height of positivism's dominance, in the mid-nineteenth century, a few eminent scientists and savants declined to conform: De Morgan among them. He had been appointed the first Professor of Mathematics in University College, London in 1828, when he was only 22; his *Essay on Probabilities* (1838) interpreted probability theory for the benefit of insurance companies, and he achieved international recognition as a logician as well as a mathematician. But he remained curious about matters which most of his contemporaries dismissed as relics of superstition, and coincidences intrigued him. He used to send accounts of them to the *Athenaeum* and other journals; some were to be included in his *Budget of Paradoxes*, published posthumously in 1872.

In August 1861, M. Senarmont, of the French Institute, wrote to me to the effect that Fresnel had sent to England, in or shortly after 1824, a paper for translation and insertion in the *European Review*, which shortly afterwards expired. The question was what had become of that paper. I examined the *Review* at the Museum, found no trace of the paper, and wrote back to that effect at the Museum, adding that everything now depended on ascertaining the name of the editor, and tracing his papers: of this I thought there was no chance. I posted this letter on my way home, at a Post Office in the Hampstead Road at the junction with Edward Street, on the opposite side of which is a bookstall. Lounging for a moment over the exposed books, *sict meus est mos*, I saw, within a few minutes of the posting of the letter, a little catch-penny book of anecdotes of Macaulay, which I bought, and ran over for a minute. My eye was soon caught by this sentence: 'One of the young fellows immediately wrote to the editor (Mr. Walker) of the *European Review*.' I thus got the clue by which I ascertained that there was no chance of recovering Fresnel's paper. Of the mention of current reviews, not one in a thousand names the editor.

Four years later, De Morgan recalled,

I made my first acquaintance with the tales of Nathaniel Hawthorne, and the first I read was about the siege of Boston in the War of Independence. I could not make it out: everybody seemed to have got into somebody else's place. I was beginning the second tale, when a parcel arrived: it was a lot of old pamphlets and other rubbish, as he called it, sent by a friend who had lately sold his books, had not thought it worth while to send these things for sale, but thought I might like to look at them and possibly keep some. The first thing I looked at was a sheet which, being opened, displayed 'A plan of Boston and its environs, shewing the true situation of his Majesty's army and also that of the rebels, drawn by an engineer, at Boston Oct. 1775.' Such detailed plans of current sieges being then uncommon, it is explained that 'The principal part of this plan was surveyed by Richard Williams, Lieutenant at Boston; and sent over by the son of a nobleman to his father in town, by whose permission it was published.' I immediately saw that my confusion arose from my supposing that the king's troops were besieging the rebels, when it was just the other way.

De Morgan was not contending that such coincidences were anything but 'casual', as he described them. Chance, he assumed, must account for them unless 'the doctrine of special providence' was accepted, and even then it would need to be 'carried down to a very low point of special intention'. Nevertheless he felt it was important to preserve an open mind and if necessary change it; to take note of such experiences in case his innate scepticism had to give way, when confronted, as occasionally he was, by convincing evidence.

Samuel Clemens, better known as Mark Twain, was also interested in coincidence; not so much with an open mind, but in two minds. Sometimes he professed scepticism, sometimes he was impressed by evidence which pointed to the existence of unexplained forces, as his amanuensis and future biographer Albert Bigelow Paine observed. Clemens, Paine warned, was not to be trusted as a raconteur; imagination too readily supplanted fact. But one coincidence story he could accept, as he had been involved in it at the time. He had been unable to find an article which Clemens had written years before for the *Christian Union*; Clemens had to leave the office without it. While he was walking down Fifth Avenue,

the thought of this article and his desire for it suddenly entered his mind. Reaching the corner of 42nd Street, he stopped a moment to let a jam of vehicles past. As he did so a stranger crossed the street, noticed him, and came dodging his way through the blockade and thrust some clippings into his hand.

'Mr Clemens,' he said, 'you don't know me, but here is something you may wish to have. I have been saving them for more than twenty years, and this morning it occurred to me to send them to you. I was going to mail them from my office, but now I will give them to you.' The clippings were from the *Christian Union* of 1885, and were the much desired article.

In the 1970s, Koestler's correspondents were to provide a string of further examples of what appeared to be benevolent interventions.

Commissioned by Imperial Airways (the pre-war forerunner of British Airways) to produce a documentary on the new route they were setting up between England and Australia, Paul Rotha needed a photograph to show him what Australian outposts, where small planes called weekly with mail, actually looked like, so that he could visualise the scenario, as he planned it, for the start of the film. Nowhere could such photographs be found. On the train to London from a weekend in Scotland, he stepped out of his sleeper into the corridor for a smoke. Getting into conversation with a man standing beside him, Rotha discovered that he was an Australian postmaster in Queensland, where he had an outpost; he had a photograph of it in his pocket.

The most remarkable case in this category, though, was sent to Koestler by Jeffrey Simmons, the managing director of W. H. Allen, the publishers. Soon after the end of the Second World War one of the firm's printers bound copies of a work by Hank Janson, steamy by the standards of the time, in covers intended for one of the Tarzan series for children, a mistake which led to irate correspondence. It was actually cheaper to pulp the books than to replace the covers; but neither Simmons nor his production manager knew of any firm who would undertake the job. An office boy who happened to come in with a message, however, knew of one.

> I asked our switchboard operator to look up their number and telephone them for me. 'Their representative is here,' was her reply. I thought at first she was joking, but in fact he had walked in literally seconds before I spoke to the operator. He was an old man, and told me that my office was on his beat and that, apart from a short time during the war when he was ill, he had passed the office almost every weekday for years, but had never before called in.

When Simmons asked him why he called now, 'he said he did not know: something just told him to do so.'

The accounts which have been coming in to the Foundation confirm that coincidences of this kind are the ones which excite most interest, whether or not they are regarded as being the result of an occult intervention.

John Burke is a freelance writer, concentrating mainly on historical and topographical subjects but also producing light fiction. In the early 1970s he collaborated with his wife on three 'Victorian Gothic' novels; and for the third of them, having decided on a Fenland setting, they went to spend a week in Wisbech in order to get the feel of the region.

> In our discussions on the story I had realised that a subsidiary character, father of one of the main male characters, would have to be made more substantial than at first envisaged. At that time I did not know Wisbech other than from passing through it (rather, round it); but off the top of my head, having read somewhere that it had once been a thriving port, I invented a local merchant whose interests expanded until he could afford to have a couple of coasting vessels built for him in Sunderland, and built up contacts with Holland and Germany. He bought himself a Georgian house on the outskirts of the town, became Lord-Lieutenant of the County, and ultimately Lord Mayor of London, leaving the firm in the hands of his son (an essential feature for our plot).
>
> On the day of our arrival we had planned to saunter round the town talking and simply soaking up the atmosphere before exploring further afield. Unfortunately the soaking became a physical one: it began to snow heavily, and we sought refuge in the little local museum. I was on one side of the room when my wife called me across: 'Look at this – here he is!'
>
> What my wife had discovered in a large glass case was the character I had invented. Every detail was correct even down to the relevant dates, with only one exception: he did not become Lord Mayor of London – merely High Sheriff!

Taking this as a good omen, they went ahead with *The Florian Signet*, which was published in hardback in the United States as well as in Britain, and translated into French.

In 1958 the journalist and author Tom Pocock was commissioned by 'the dreadful *Sunday Dispatch*', as he recalls it, to write a feature on the wartime experiences of Derick Heathcoat Amory, Chancellor of the Exchequer, who as a staff officer had insisted on taking part in Arnhem, where he had been wounded and taken prisoner. Asked if there were any Dutch people he remembered who could be interviewed, Amory could recall only that there had been a doctor who had whispered instructions how he and others might be able to escape; but he had been too ill even to reply, and could not remember the man's name.

Flying to Amsterdam to see if he could turn up anything which might help the feature along, Pocock found himself sitting next to an attractive girl.

> I told her why I was going to Arnhem, adding that as I would not know who to look for, I would not be seeing any Dutch witnesses. 'But you will,' she replied. 'Tonight you will meet that Dutch doctor. He is my father.'
>
> That evening I met Dr Marinus Pilaar of Apeldoorn. As a young doctor in 1944 he had been helping with the wounded. Surprised to see a middle-aged British officer amongst the young men, he had noted and remembered his name, later recognising it as that of the British Chancellor of the Exchequer.

Not surprisingly, such interventions often relate to satisfying the needs of modern, increasingly mechanised, life. Driving through Redditch early one Sunday morning on his way to take a holiday a Birmingham man, Edward Brookes, realised that his Austin A40 was overheating. The fan belt, he found, had broken and was missing. There was nobody about, but the owner of a nearby house emerged to ask if he was in trouble. There just might be somebody in a Redditch shop which sold car parts, the householder told him, offering to walk back with Brookes to show him where it was. They found the shop closed; but while they were there a van drove up. 'Hullo, Harry, what are you doing here?' the householder greeted him; and asked, jokingly, 'You don't happen to have an A40 fan belt in your pocket?' 'As a matter of fact I have,' Harry replied, producing it – and refusing payment; he was glad to help out.

While he was writing *The Message of Astrology* (1990), a detached survey of recent research into the subject, Peter Roberts 'lost' an entire disk of his text on his word processor. He was understandably depressed at the prospect of so much rewriting, but when some of the 150 men and women who were with him at a conference asked how the work was going he replied with conventional cheefulness. However,

> one of the people who inquired (and whom I hardly knew at all) received a different reply. For some reason which I cannot explain I

told him about my lost disk. It turned out that he was highly knowledgeable about recovering lost data, and sent me a special recovery programme. This did not work, but it contained the name of the company who specialised in recovering data. Within a week I had got it all back intact.

The point, Roberts stresses, is that his helper was 'almost certainly the only person attending the conference who had the specialist knowledge to assist me – and he was the only one in whom I confided.'

Sometimes the 'intervener' displays remarkable zeal. In a letter to the Foundation, Roy Watkins describes how during a holiday in Bala, Merionethshire in 1985 he was hoping to do some research into his Welsh forebears and perhaps find some living relatives. All that his father, who had grown up in Liverpool, could tell him was that the family had once owned farms near Bala which had been flooded when the reservoir was built. The two of them went to the public record office in Dolgellau, but it soon became clear that as Watkins is so common a name in Wales, the task of combing the microfilm records and then pursuing inquiries among all the nearby Watkinses would be hopeless. They retired to have lunch in a pub.

His father, however, wanted to look at some photographs of the village which he had seen in the record office, so they went back. While they were there, a woman walked in with a bundle of papers which contained a will. It turned out to be Roy Watkins's great-great-grandfather's, giving, among other things, details about the family farms. The papers, she said, had lain in the basement since they had been left there by a lawyer in the 1950s, and had not been opened until that morning. She herself had started work in the record office only that day, and the cataloguing of the papers was her first job. Happening to see the name Watkins in the visitors' book, she had thought there might be some connection. Armed with the information from the will, they were able to visit those of the family farms which had not been inundated, finding relatives in two of them.

One account of a need supplied by coincidence could have fitted into Koestler's 'practical joker' category. Bob Treuhaft, of Oakland, California, and his wife the Hon. Jessica Mitford, author of among other books *Hons and Rebels* and *The American Way of Death*, used to play Scrabble; but then they became addicted to a variation, Boggle – sixteen dice bearing letters of the alphabet, and a box to shake them out of, to produce four rows of four letters each, the idea being to use contiguous letters to make words of five letters or more. According to Bob Treuhaft,

> we never travel without our Boggle set and, although it's available now in some of the bigger stores in London, feel that we have to some extent introduced it to England by teaching it to friends and presenting them with sets.
>
> In the summer of 1989 we decided to give a present of Boggle to a young friend. Unable to find one in Kentish Town, where we were staying, I was deputed to pick up a set the next time I was in central London. Next time happened to be a warmish day and as I walked along Regent Street I came to what appeared to be a very big toy shop indeed, unaware at the moment that it was Hamley's. I was about to enter, but it was midday, getting hotter by the minute, and the entrance was so crowded that I decided to pass it by.
>
> As I passed it by, an object fell from above and landed by my feet. I stopped, as did several passers-by; but with typical English reserve none of them made a move. After half a minute I picked up a box which turned out to contain a Boggle set in mint condition (except for a dent in the corner of the box that had hit the ground), bearing a Hamley's price tag.

He looked up to try to find where it had come from, but there was no indication. He walked back to the still crowded entrance; then walked away a few steps; then, box in hand, stood irresolute. 'Mate, if you go back there,' one of the passers-by who had seen what had happened suggested, 'you may have the rest of your Christmas shopping done for you.'

> When I told my wife that the game hadn't cost me anything, it took some persuading to convince her I hadn't shop-lifted it. And I began to think: suppose a store dick had seen me on the pavement with the box in my hand.
> 'Where did you get that, sir?'
> 'Oh, it just fell from the sky.'
> Good morning, Judge . . .

In a few cases, an 'intervener' appears to be using coincidence as an instructor. In 1986 'Peter Kelly' was returning to his home in South London in the early hours after a row with his girl friend during which, he later realised, he had been 'particularly stubborn and needlessly hurtful and destructive'. As he turned into his road, he saw a man throw a brick through the window of a house, then leap into a car and drive off. The letters on the registration plate were PWK – Kelly's initials. 'I do not ascribe any paranormal "force" to this event,' he comments. 'However, it was a dramatic illustration of my own foolishness and, although the relationship didn't survive, the memory of that night remains for me as a lesson which I would perhaps not have learned had the brick not been thrown, or the registration been different.'

Many people must have had the experience of interventions which, at precisely the right time, have saved them from embarrassment, and one such occasion was gratefully recorded in verse by 'Senex' in the *Times of India*, and later included in his *Verses from Senexpur*. 'Senex' was P. G. Wodehouse's brother Armine, a schoolteacher in Poona, who used to contribute light verses and parodies to the paper, and he was recalling an incident at a dinner party. He had been just about to say something which would have caused a husband and wife at the dining-table to rise and leave in a marked manner, when providence intervened to put an idea into the head of one of the guests

> And made him make the one remark
> that meteor-like illumed my dark.

The recollection of what might have happened on that occasion meant that Armine would still wake up rigid with terror.

> All my muscles turned stiff
> At the thought of that 'if' –
> Of that terrible 'if': if I'd done what I meant
> And young Jones hadn't stymied my ghastly intent.

Guardian angel

The intervention coincidences which understandably make the most impression, are those which precipitate an important change in the lives of those who experience them. If they are members of a religious sect they will have no difficulty in attributing it to their guardian angel, or whatever their creed prescribes; but it can be hard for militant agnostics to have to admit that their lives have been transformed by a succession of coincidences, as Harriet Martineau had to do.

Her *Illustrations of Political Economy* (1832), and her advocacy of Comte's positivist doctrines, had established her reputation as a hard-headed materialist; but her health broke down, and for nearly five years she lay apparently dying from an incurable tumour. She had dismissed the possibility of experimenting to see whether mesmerism might have any beneficial effect, her scepticism reinforced by the realisation that if she tried it, her doctor and her family would be antagonised. Then, within a fortnight there were no fewer than three letters of advice to try it; and when her brother-in-law admitted he had been impressed by what he had heard about it, the quadruple coincidence decided her to give it a trial. This led to her being denounced by members of the medical profession, and shunned by most members of her family; but it gave her, she claimed in her autobiography, thirty more years of active life, 'infused with keen enjoyment of mind and heart'.

In 1977 Commander R. N. Stanbury, DSC, who after his retirement from the Navy had become personal assistant to Sir Bernard Lovell at Jodrell Bank, described in an autobiography how throughout his life he had encountered many examples of synchro-nicity, in particular some which occurred after his daughter Elizabeth contracted acute myeloid leukaemia, then notoriously incurable. Eight years later, in *Light*, he re-examined some of the coincidences, beginning with the sudden reappearance, nearly forty years after he had last seen it, of his school Divinity notebook containing a two-page essay on Jesus's miracles, 'coming down heavily on the side of their authenticity'.

This started a chain of coincidences which, he gradually came to believe, could not be put down to mere chance, culminating in what, for him, was the most incredible of all of them. When he and his wife were on their way home from Worthing Hospital, where they had been told that their daughter had only a week or two to live, he picked up a book on the Burrswood Healing Centre. He was a slow reader, and found the book heavy going; but he happened to meet 'a highly-respected business man, whom I had never seen before, and knew nothing about, but who brought up the subject of Burrswood and suggested I should take Elizabeth to a healing service'. He did, 'Elizabeth is now 22, and has not been near a doctor in the last twelve years.'

In the second volume of his autobiography – though not, curiously, in *The Challenge of Chance* – Koestler described a coincidence which had saved his life. In 1934 he was becoming disgruntled with the Communist Party; the caucus of which he was a member had condemned the novel he was writing. Further, he was living in dire poverty. One night, in despair, he stuck scotch tape over the slits in the door and window of his room and turned on the gas tap.

> I had placed my bug-stained mattress next to it on the floor, but as I was settling down on it, a book crashed on my head from the wobbly shelf. It nearly broke my nose, so I got up, turned off the gas and tore off the tape. Of all one's failures, a failure in suicide is the most embarrassing to report. The book that fell on my head was the Second Brown Book, *Dimitrov contra Goering*, with the story of the Reichstag trial. A more drastic pointer to the despicableness of my antics can hardly be imagined.

It was not only that the book had fallen on his head, in other words, that had made Koestler feel despicable. The Bulgarian communist Georgi Dimitrov was a hero figure – and not only to communists – for the way he had stood up to Goering in the trial in 1933, humiliating him from the dock. 'I must either have kicked the shelf,' Koestler commented, 'or it was a case of the Dialectic producing a miracle' – a not entirely facetious notion, coming from him, although at the time he was writing he had yet to avow his interest in psychic phenomena.

Inevitably the Second World War produced a crop of intervention-coincidences which rescued individuals from injury or death. They could easily fill a book: two will have to suffice. Fulfilling his role in the plot to kill Hitler in July 1944, Count Stauffenberg left the briefcase with the bomb in it under the table, where he knew Hitler would be standing. One of the generals in the room happened to notice it, and moved it so that the table support, a heavy wooden plinth, was between Hitler and the bomb. When it went off it destroyed the table, blew the roof off the conference room and killed four people; but Hitler survived – although, as Roger Manvell and Heinrich Fraenkel described it in *The July Plot*, 'his hair was on fire, his right arm partially paralysed, his right leg burned, his ear drums damaged, his uniform torn by blast and falling debris, and his buttocks so bruised that, as he himself described it, he had a "backside like a baboon".' If he had died, the war would almost certainly have ended quickly; as it was hostilities did not cease until the following May.

Many people who saw active service will echo E. M. Greenwood's comment on his own wartime experience. Twice, coincidence saved him from being sent where he would inevitably have ended up a prisoner of the Japanese; on the second occasion, the man who was posted instead of him died in a Japanese prison camp. 'This is probably simple chance,' he admits; 'but when it happens to you, you wonder, like Hamlet, if there's a divinity that shapes our ends, rough-hew them how we will.'

It was not only people on active service who found their lives influenced by such interventions during the war; the shake-up, shifting people from place to place, seems to have encouraged them to proliferate.

In 1941 Mrs Ilona Kearey, unable to find work in London, was about to return to the family cottage in the country. On her last day, depressed, she was alone in the flat where she had been staying with friends, playing their piano.

> After a while, I heard the sound of a cello being played solo in the flat directly above me. I listened, and became convinced I knew that tone. When I was eleven, I had studied the cello for two years, and had made a friend who was ten at the time. We had gradually drifted apart, and it was about eight years since we had last met, our careers being different. I decided to go up one flight and knock on the door. It was opened by my friend, now 22 and successful. I told her my wish to stay in London; she agreed I should stay in her flat.

Mrs Kearey stayed for three years, after finding a war job. They became and remained close friends; when she married, 'I became her son's godmother; she is godmother to my eldest son, and now I am grand-godmother to her son's eldest daughter.'

'Flurries of small coincidences occur at times of emotional intensity,' Clifford Dean believes, 'and though most of these seem to be of little consequence, they enhance my life in a manner analogous perhaps to a passage through a harmonious landscape. It seems to me that certain states of mind actually attract or generate events.' Three years ago, working as an art specialist in a secondary school, finding stress increasing and promotion blocked, he asked himself whether he should drop out of teaching altogether. He had been happy at the start of his career teaching in a rural village and wondered whether it was feasible to return to junior teaching, but had done nothing about it.

I was increasingly miserable and confused, sensing conflict between duty and desire, until one day I suddenly thought, I don't have to do this. I'm not going to play any more. I'm going to cease striving, become receptive, and take what comes.

Within a week, my wife asked when she picked me up from school one afternoon, 'Would you be interested in a job at Winchelsea?' I recognised at once that this was, as it were, a message from heaven, and when she explained further I was even more convinced. She had recently been doing a bit of supply work in this small local school, at which we had long cast covetous eyes, and had found it a pleasant place to work. At some point the phone had rung while the Head was teaching, so my wife had answered it for him. It was an enquiry about a job at the school.

Though we were in the habit of scanning the job vacancies, we had both completely failed to notice this one. At first she regretted that, with a young child to care for, she could not apply, then realised that I might, which I did, got the job and am very happy in it.

If his wife had not been working that day; if there had been somebody else in the office; if she had been out of earshot of the telephone . . .

Such interventions can have even more dramatic consequences. In 1948 Mrs Dorothy Rumble of Fleet in Hampshire misread the time as she was going into the local cinema, thought it was 20.40, not 19.40, and, assuming she would have missed most of the programme, walked back down the steps. Almost immediately she realised her error but felt too self-conscious to return. She walked the mile to her home, but 'then had an insistent feeling to walk round the deserted town again.' On this walk, she met a boy whom she thought she had been speaking to the previous night, so when he spoke to her she responded. It wasn't him; but he, and a friend who was with him, walked back with her to her home.

The boy she thought she had recognised made a date to take her to the film the following night. But he was a National Service man, and found himself on guard duty, so his friend turned up to take her in his place. They started going out together, and he became her husband. If she had not mistaken the time; if she had returned to see the film; if she had not had the impulse to walk around Fleet; if she had not believed she recognised the boy who spoke to her; if he had not been on guard duty . . .

In 1952 Alan Elliott was 32 years old, married, with a young son. He had just returned from two years' field work in Singapore as a social anthropologist, and was working – mainly at the London School of Economics, where he was enrolled as a Ph.D. candidate – to complete his report for the Colonial Office's Social Science Research Council. His contract with the council was due to run out two months later; he had no idea what he would do next.

That April I received an urgent demand from the LSE library to return a book, well overdue. It was one of those days when nothing went according to plan, and I thought of leaving the LSE to another day; but as I had brought the book with me, I felt I should go there. It was one of those decisions which might have gone either way.

Being vacation time, LSE was nearly empty. The library was at the end of the long corridor on the ground floor. Part of the way along the corridor there were pigeon holes for mail for BA and B.Sc. students; but as I did not get much outside mail at LSE, and such as I did get was delivered to the postgraduate students' Common Room, I had *never* collected mail from the ground floor pigeon holes. However, as I passed them I had the idea of seeing if there was anything for me.

In the 'E' pigeon hole were several letters, one addressed to Mr Alan Elliott from UNESCO, in Paris. I had read about the organisation in an article J. B. Priestley had written for *Picture Post*, which had praised it but said it was well-staffed and that job applications were unlikely to succeed, so I had mentally crossed it off my jobs list. My first reaction was that the letter must be for another Alan Elliott, and I nearly put it back. But it was my name, after all; I opened it, and found that to all intents it was the offer of a job. It was the first stage towards working for them for 28 years.

If Alan Elliott had not picked up the letter, the offer would have lapsed. What had happened, he found, was that after he had helped the well known American anthropologist Cora Du Bois while she was on a visit to Singapore, she had gone on to Paris, where she had met an old friend who was head of one of UNESCO's departments; he had asked if she knew anybody suitable for a vacant post; she had thought of Elliott, but knew only that he would be working at LSE; hence the letter, which by a further piece of good fortune had reached LSE only a few days before Elliott happened to be on his way to the library.

I have had other experiences that may fall into the same category, but none as clear-cut and distinct as this. It leaves me with a vague feeling that there are influences at work which, in human terms, are consciously guiding our actions at critical moments. They are not necessarily consistent in so far as they are following any particular set of objectives on behalf of a certain individual. And they are not necessarily beneficent.

The only thing of which I am reasonably sure is that we are participants in situations that we are very far from understanding in matter-of-fact human terms. In a general way I am an upholder of Christian beliefs and a supporter of the idea that God has an important role in our lives. However, the sort of influences of which I am vaguely aware are not at all clearly identifiable with Christian personalities such as saints or angels, or necessarily the devil and all his works. In short, I have no plausible explanation, other than coincidence.

In 1961 Mrs Elizabeth Abrahams had left her husband, taking her seven-year-old daughter with her to a rented flat. It was the Rachmann era; all the tenants were given notice by strongmen with dogs; as she worked full time she could not find anywhere to live without paying key money ('for a bit of rotten lino, old phone books and lamp-shades'), which she did not have.

One morning in the tube to Aldgate East a woman sat next to me and began to tell me all about her life, her husband, canary and the workmen. She got off at Moorgate.

The following morning she sat next to me again, out of all the millions of people on the Metropolitan Line. This time she said, 'You have such a nice face, tell me about yourself.' I burst into tears and told her about my daughter, and that I had nowhere to live. She responded by saying she was a tenant of the Church Commissioners who had a lot of property in Hampstead and she would phone them at once. She kept her word – there was one tiny top flat empty in Lancaster Grove. I moved in a month later.

They remained friends until the woman's death. 'My guardian angel? I should like to think so,' Mrs Abrahams comments. 'I could not have been more desperate.' If it *was* her guardian angel, it stayed with her. A woman collecting for a jumble sale who called at the flat got her a job as a teacher; she became the first woman allowed to teach English in evening classes in Pentonville Jail; at the age of 47 she won a major scholarship to study English Literature, to obtain better qualifications.

> Before my finals in 1974 I bought the *Times Ed. Supp.* for the first and last time. Very boring paper. There was a tiny advertisement in it for work at the Tavistock Clinic, to work with maladjusted children, and I got it.

Library angel

A type of intervention-coincidence which particularly interested Koestler was the 'library angel', as he called it; citing, among other accounts, one which had been sent to him by Dame Rebecca West. While she was doing the research for *The Meaning of Treason*, she decided to go to the Royal Institute of International Affairs to check a reference in the shelves of volumes, only to find that they consisted of abstracts catalogued under arbitrary headings which gave her no help. After hours of search, she went to an assistant librarian to complain: 'I can't find it, there's no clue, it may be in any of these volumes.' She took one out to illustrate her point, and carelessly looked at it; 'It was not only the right volume, but I had opened it at the right page.'

'Library angel' interventions had been reported in the nineteenth century. De Morgan's accounts of the way he found what he needed (see page 34) could be in this category; and Alice Johnson offered a case in her 1899 article. Kate Blyth, an Irishwoman living with her husband in Edinburgh, wanted to track down information about two members of her family who had fought in the Irish Brigade, the 'Wild Geese' who left to fight under King James II, in Europe. Eventually she went with her daughter to the Edinburgh Advocates Library; it was their first visit, and they found themselves by mistake in a room for members only. Suggesting she should wait there, her daughter went to find where they ought to go, leaving her in the large room surrounded by thousands of books. She crossed it 'with no particular end in view', stopping in front of some shelves. The title her eyes fell upon turned out to be a two-volume Army List of the Irish Brigade, published in Dublin in 1860.

Mrs Blyth's account, along with confirmatory notes by her daughter and her husband, was written and sent off the same evening, presumably because the SPR had already established how important it was to pin down episodes of this kind as soon, and as comprehensively, as possible, to avoid the stock accusation of memory playing tricks – an injunction now rarely recalled. It was not, as coincidences go, particularly striking; yet in her letter written a few hours later Mrs Blyth admitted she had 'not yet recovered from the curious shock I then received', and her daughter confirmed that her mother had been 'quite startled and nervous all the afternoon and evening'.

Coincidences of this kind, Alice Johnson noted, must be met much more frequently by omnivorous readers than by persons of more limited intellectual interests; and doubtless the proportion of 'library angel' stories which Koestler received, and have come in to the Foundation since, exaggerates their frequency. Still, unquestionably they are commonly experienced, and occasionally they are striking, as one was for Charles Gibbs-Smith, the leading historian of aviation of his day (he was later to be appointed Lindbergh Professor of Aerospace History at the Smithsonian Institute in Washington).

Gibbs-Smith was engaged upon a monograph of Sir George Cayley, a pioneer of aviation who had experimented with gliders and parachutes in the early nineteenth century; and a student, writing to him, had said that he thought he remembered seeing an article by Cayley in the *Mechanics Magazine*, which appeared in about 1840–42. Gibbs-Smith believed he had 'every conceivable Cayley document'; but he went to the London University Library, which had a set of the magazine, and searched the volumes for some years before and after 1840, only to find that 'as I feared, there was no such article.' However, as he was there he thought that to be on the safe side he had better check the indexes of every volume of the magazine.

To my surprise, in the index to the volume for 1853, I found a reference to an article by Cayley on 'governable parachutes'. I of course knew all about his main work on parachutes – which was done much earlier – and, as I turned to the relevant pages, was wondering why he should use the odd word 'governable' in connection with parachutes.

I then found myself gazing at Cayley's highly sophisticated design for a piloted glider, which none of us historians living or dead had ever seen or checked on. I had accidentally rediscovered one of the most vital documents in aviation history, which is now reproduced all over the world.

Gibbs-Smith related what had happened in a letter to Koestler, who wrote to thank him, with

> a small added twist: a day or two before your letter arrived I read a long article on Cayley, which much impressed me. The point is that – as I must confess to my shame – I knew nothing of Cayley before.

Few accounts of 'library angel' visitations describe such important discoveries; most are impressive chiefly to the researcher, for whom the unexpected appearance of even a minor source reference can cause a glow of satisfaction. Occasionally, though, they are more useful. In a second-hand bookshop in Windsor in 1969, Ivor Grattan-Guinness, editor of the international review *Annals of Science*, casually picked up a book which turned out to be a study of Bonaparte in Egypt. It contained a drawing by Jean Baptiste Fourier, a civilian who had accompanied Bonaparte, and had been made governor of Lower Egypt. 'Fourier later became a prominent mathematician, the inventor of the "Fourier analysis",' Grattan-Guinness recalled in an article 'What are coincidences?' in 1978. 'I was writing a book on Fourier at the time, and the drawing later appeared in it.'

Sitting in a club in Lagos, Nigeria, in or around 1984, Bill Haines read a review of a new book about Jung in one of the English papers; it had a brief description of synchronicity which he found interesting.

> After leaving the chair I went to the library, which in that club consisted mainly of who-dunits and other paperbacks of the more lurid kind. I happened to be standing opposite the 'J' section. Directly in front of me was a paperback selection of Jung's writings. I opened the book in the middle, and I found myself reading the section on synchronicity.

This had made Haines 'a firm believer in the synchronicity principle, much to the amusement of my friends'.

Reaching to pull down an almanac from a bookshelf in 1987, Alistair Cooke found he had in his hand, by mistake, a *Good Food Guide* for 1972. It promptly struck him that as his BBC radio broadcast that week was to be about inflation, it might be a help. It was: opening it at random, he found the description of a London restaurant's three course meal, for between £3 and £4, as 'pricey, though worth the expense' – just the illustration he had needed.

Margaret Forster, the biographer of Thackeray and Elizabeth Barrett Browning, was even luckier. Tidying up her London home in 1989, she accidentally knocked *Rebecca* out of a bookcase. This gave her an idea: was it not time for a biography of its author Dame Daphne du Maurier? She wrote to her publisher, Carmen Callil of Chatto and Windus, suggesting the idea; Carmen Callil agreed, and approached Dame Daphne's agent. The next day, the BBC rang Margaret Forster to ask her to pay tribute to Dame Daphne, who had just died at the age of 81. Two other publishers asked her if she would write the biography before the decision was taken by Dame Daphne's literary executors that there should be an official biography. Margaret Forster, one of the possibles on their list, got the job.

Bernard Levin has contributed two 'library angel' interventions. In 1989, he wanted to find some more details in connection with a story he had read years before about a statue, a monument to Alexander the Great, which was to be so large that it would have a city in its left hand and a river in its right. Wading through the books and encyclopedias which might provide him with the story, he could find no trace of it; but while he was looking through the synopsis which precedes the account of Alexander in Plutarch's *Lives*, his eye caught the reference, 'Crucifies his Physician'. Puzzled, as Alexander was not a cruel man, he turned to the page indicated. There was nothing on it about the episode (the page number in the synopsis, it turned out, had been a misprint) 'but the first paragraph on the "wrong" page contained the story of the statue, just as I had remembered it, but with more detail and the name of the man who had proposed it, and offered to build it'.

Working on *The Times* in the first week of 1990, Levin was telephoned by friends whose schoolboy son was filling in the answers to a general knowledge exam of the kind where outside assistance was permitted. The first on their list of questions that the family had been unable to answer was 'Where did Daphne du Maurier write *Rebecca*?' Bernard told them that he would get down to the search when he got home that evening. On the way home, calling on his literary agents, he saw some books on the table in the waiting room. One was by Daphne du Maurier, about her life in Cornwall. Looking up 'Rebecca' in the index he found a number of single page references, and one, more extensive, of a dozen pages. 'I turned to it; on the first page of the chapter she said, "I began *Rebecca* in Alexandria . . ." (where her husband, later to become a general, had been stationed).'

Several contributors have sent in variations on the 'library angel'

theme. In 1947 Andrew Fyall, waiting to go to university, was
working as a lumberjack, with a German prisoner-of-war as his
'mate'.

> Gerhard, anxious to resume his studies in architecture, had saved six
> shillings (30p) from his daily wage of one shilling and ten pence
> (9p). Could I get him a second-hand book?
>   Incredibly, that evening I had the opportunity to help myself
> from thousands of books, the aftermath to the salvage drive. The
> first book I picked up was on architecture, printed in German. I can
> still see the tears in Gerhard's eyes next morning – a miracle in less
> than twenty-four hours.

Even discussing or writing about the coincidence still gives Fyall 'a
distinctly "unearthly" feeling'.

Anthony Hopkins, invited to play a part in *The Girl from Petrovka*,
wanted to read the novel by George Feifer from which it was to be
taken, but could not find it in London bookshops. Waiting for an
underground train at Leicester Square station, he came across a book
left on a seat; it was a copy of the novel, with some scribbled notes in
the margin. Meeting the author later, Hopkins heard that a friend had
lost Feifer's annotated copy of the book. It was the copy Hopkins had
found.

Two celebrated authors have left grateful accounts of the way in
which the intervention of 'library angels' saved them from public
obloquy and humiliation. In his fragmentary autobiography Kipling
recalled how he had written a short story about a body-snatching
episode in deep snow, 'perpetrated in some lonely prairie town and
culminating in the purest horror'. Not quite satisfied, he set it aside,
intending to return to it. A few months later he had to go to the
dentist; while he was in the waiting-room he picked up a bound
volume of *Harper's* magazine from the 1850s.

> I picked up one, and read as undistractedly as the tooth permitted.
> There I found my tale, identical in every mark – frozen ground,
> frozen corpse, stiff in its fur robes in the buggy – the inn-keeper
> offering it a drink – and so on to the ghastly end. Had I published
> that tale, what could have saved me from the charge of deliberate
> plagiarism?

Conan Doyle had a similar experience. 'I cannot write the name of Maupassant,' he remarked in 1907 in *Through the Magic Door* – the door which led to the room where he kept his books – 'without recalling what was either a spiritual interposition or an extraordinary coincidence.' On a visit to Switzerland he had happened to stop off at an inn on the Gemmi Pass which, he was told, was cut off by snow from the community in the valley below for about three months every winter. 'So curious a situation naturally appealed to one's imagination, and I speedily began to build up a short story in my own mind, depending upon a group of strong antagonistic characters being penned up in this inn, loathing each other and yet unable to get away from each other's society, every day bringing them nearer to tragedy.'

Turning over the idea in his mind as he came back through France, Conan Doyle happened to come across a book of Maupassant's short stories which he had not read before. The first, *L'Auberge*, turned out to be set in the Gemmi Pass inn. The plot depended on the isolation of a group of people through the snowfall. 'Everything that I had imagined was there, save that Maupassant had brought in a savage hound.'

That Maupassant should have picked up the same idea from a visit to the inn surprised Conan Doyle not at all; 'What was perfectly marvellous is that in that short journey I should have chanced to buy the one book in all the world which would prevent me from making a public fool of myself, for who would ever have believed that my work was not an imitation?' On reflection, Conan Doyle felt he could not accept the coincidence hypothesis. It was one of several examples in his life which had convinced him of the promptings of some beneficent force outside ourselves, which tries to help us where it can. The old belief in guardian angels was not only attractive, he thought, 'but has in it, I believe, a real basis of truth'; or was it that the subliminal self has the ability to 'learn and convey to the mind that which our own known senses are unable to apprehend?'

Property restorer
The most immediately popular of coincidences, not surprisingly, are those in which the 'intervener' stages the recovery of lost or stolen property. Jung recalled that several cases were reported in a collection by Wilhelm von Scholz, published in 1924; among them, the tale of a mother who had taken a photograph of her young son which she left in Strasbourg to be developed, but had been unable to collect owing to

the war. Two years later she bought some film in Frankfurt to take a picture of her daughter; when it was developed it was found to be a double exposure, and 'the picture underneath was the photograph she had taken of her son!' Von Scholz had come to what Jung felt was the understandable conclusion that there must be some 'mutual attraction of related objects'; such happenings, he felt, might be arranged as if by 'a greater and more comprehensive consciousness, which is unknowable'.

Coming across the reference in the *Spectator* to the Foundation's interest in coincidences, Mrs Dorothy Woo wrote to tell us of the eventually fortunate outcome of her decision – rash, as booklovers invariably soon find – to allow an edition of a book which she cherished out of her hands, in this case to be circulated among a Church Fellowship group she attended. It was not returned, and when she inquired about it, it could not be traced.

It must have been about six months afterwards, when I was walking home from church one evening, that thoughts of the book returned to me. I remember having a real longing for it. If only I hadn't lost it! A few days afterwards I travelled into the city and dropped into the Overseas Aid shop. I was browsing round when, on a shelf, I saw what looked like a replica of my lost book. There, on the fly leaf, was my name in my own handwriting. I bought it for 40p.

'Could it also be coincidence,' Mrs Woo asks, 'that the copy of the *Spectator* which contained the article was the only issue I have ever read?'

'It has become statistically supportable over the last thirty years (I am 51) that I seem to occupy a personal "domain" of extremely high coincidence, a bubble of skewed probabilities,' Lord Birdwood, chairman of Martlet Ltd, has found. 'Witness to it have been past secretaries who after the first month of working for me become blasé to repeated events which underscore this.' One a week, he thinks is about the average; some trivial, but providing a short circuit of work for him, one of them remarkable.

I left a technical manual in a taxi in the Fleet Street area. It was a prototype, valueless except a thorough nuisance to get a further copy from the Italian R&D centre which had written it. But I knew there was no other copy in the UK. I didn't bother to try to trace the taxi as its uniqueness would have been unrecognised by the driver. Two weeks later I was driving myself through St John's Wood, north out of London. At a red traffic light I saw some children playing with this manual on the pavement. As I watched they got bored and threw it over a hedge into a private garden. I stopped the car, retrieved it, and drove on.

The manual had travelled six miles across London; two weeks had gone by; and the time during which it and Lord Birdwood could have been brought together again was less than thirty seconds. 'Totally puzzling, apparently to save me delay, irritation and possible embarrassment,' he concludes. 'The temptation to read anthropocentric management into the episode is strong.'

Living some years ago in a guest house in Antwerp, Mrs B. Ivory came back one day to find that her portable gramophone and records had been stolen. Later, celebrating Mardi Gras in a crowded hall, she was sitting out waiting for her escort to return when she began to overhear a conservation in Flemish. It was a language of which she had no more than a smattering, but she understood enough to realise that a young man was telling his companion about an English gramophone he had just bought. When her escort, the owner of the guest house, returned, she asked him to inquire, tactfully, where the gramophone had come from. She was certain it must be hers, and so it proved to be; it had been sold by a man who had been staying in the house.

In the summer of 1986, John Bland, editor of *World Health* for the World Health Organisation, recalls

my wife went in to Geneva to have lunch with Mrs X, on a visit from Copenhagen, and an American friend, Ms Y, with whom she had been shopping. They never got their lunch, because Ms Y found she had lost her purse with her passport and over $250 in it. They revisited every shop, but in vain; and my wife drove them back to WHO HQ.

They decided to take the lift to my office. Out of it stepped a man from the Copenhagen office, where Mrs X's husband worked. They greeted each other with surprise: neither knew the other would be in Geneva. Mrs X told him about the lost purse. 'You didn't travel to WHO by bus this morning, did you?' he asked Ms Y. She had, but had forgotten about it. The man from Copenhagen had left WHO that morning by the bus, and had seen a woman hand a purse to the driver, who had grumbled about passengers' carelessness. The purse was recovered, intact.

This incident, John Bland remarks, 'would come under your small-world, problem-solving, guardian angel *and* recovery-of-lost-property categories. But it was, of course, "meaningful"', he adds, 'primarily to the American lady.'

Coincidence can also lead to compensation for lost or, as in the case related to Koestler by Michael Meyer, Ibsen's translator and biographer, damaged property. One morning, in the early hours, a lorry brushed the side of his car, doing considerable damage; but his insurance company would not accept his claim, in spite of the fact that a passer-by had left a note on his windscreen giving the lorry's number and its owners' name and address. The passer-by, however, had apparently thought better of signing the note, as the bottom of it had been torn off; and the lorry owners refused to admit liability.

A few days later Meyer was playing in a cricket match when an acquaintance in the opposing team, whom he had not met for many years, remarked on the condition of his car. As soon as Meyer began to describe what had happened, his acquaintance interrupted to say *he* had left the note, but had not cared to become further involved. 'That, I think, is an amazing coincidence,' Meyer commented. 'What on earth can the odds have been against my meeting that witness under circumstances which could enable him to identify me as the owner of the car?'

Habit breaker

A curious feature of some coincidences is that the 'intervener' appears to have found it necessary to make people do something – often trivial – they would not normally do, or not do something they would normally do, breaking set habits and setting events in train. 'I had just made a particularly difficult decision about a key area in my life,' Louise Taylor recalls,

> and did not feel totally confident about it. I had not had time to read the *Sunday Telegraph* and decided, unusually, to keep it as I felt there might be something of interest in it.
>
> On the Monday, I was telling a friend about my decision, and he told me there was an article in the *Sunday Telegraph* about the area I was interested in. Lo and behold, the article contained information that reassured me about my decision.

Later that week I received details from one of my clients to write a script for an information tape for one of their new advertisers. In the course of the conversation with the advertisers I discovered that they were the company about whom the article had been written (it had not been identified in the article). Since their work is in the area that I had decided I wanted to work in, I was able to use the opportunity to discuss working with them.

The meeting enabled her to move into that area.
'Mrs Raili Kuoppa' relates how she went to a small local town,

which I had not done for months. On impulse I went to a newsagents and bought only a local newspaper, which I never normally do. I opened the paper on a page and my eyes were drawn immediately to a small item detailing a granted planning permission (again, I do not normally read these). This item turned out to be crucial evidence needed for my impending divorce settlement. Without this chance happening I would have had no other means of discovering this vital information – I had no idea of its existence.

Crossed lines

The feeling of being personally aimed at is strong in 'crossed lines' coincidences. Although for some reason Koestler did not include any of them in *The Challenge of Chance*, some unnerving accounts came in to him in his correspondence. In one of them, a London woman described an occasion when she was having a cup of tea with a friend when the telephone rang. 'It's for you,' the friend told her. The caller turned out to be her accountant. How did he know where she was? He did *not* know where she was; he had actually dialled her correct number, and come through to a wrong one with no resemblance to hers, except that both were on the same exchange.

In Koestler's *Sunday Times* collection, an Essex police constable, Peter Moscardi, related how when his station's telephone number had been changed, he inadvertently gave a friend a wrong number. Passing a factory while on night duty shortly afterwards, he noticed that a door was open, and a light on in the manager's office. Suspicious, he went to investigate. Nobody was in the office, but while he was there the telephone rang; it was his friend, ringing the wrong number which had been given him – the manager's ex-directory number.

When 'Jean Randall' answered the telephone in her office one morning, the call was from a taxi driver for David Gallagher. Nobody of that name worked there, she replied. 'But I took him home from there last night,' the driver said, bemused. 'He left his chequebook in my cab. Tall guy, dark hair. Said he came from Ireland originally.' '"That," I told him, "is not David Gallagher. It is a man called David Gresham. He was in your cab last night, because I made the booking."' It happened, though, that a friend of Jean Randall's was married to a David Gallagher. She rang her; had her husband lost a chequebook? He had, and had no idea where it could be. 'As it was a fluke that I happened to be in the room to answer the telephone at all,' Jean Randall comments, 'and an entire fluke that both Davids were known to me, I can only conclude that the chequebook was meant to get back to its owner.'

Lady Redgrave has contributed an even stranger 'crossed line' experience to the Foundation. After her husband, Major-General Sir Roy Redgrave, retired, she worked in a London estate agency where one of her colleagues, Claire Townley, was to marry an Italian/American banker, Jay Runnowitsch, whom she had met in the course of her work. Claire had left the agency in 1984.

One afternoon during the spring of 1985, the telephone in my office was answered by the negotiator sitting at the desk in front of mine (where, by the way, Claire Townley herself used to sit) and I heard her say: 'This is Carlyle & Co . . . Sorry, we seem to have a crossed line.' The person at the other end then said: 'Since you are Carlyle & Co., I would like to speak to Lady Redgrave.' It was Jay Runnowitsch. He then explained to me that the telephone had, in fact, rung on *his* desk; that he had not made an outgoing call, and that he had picked up the telephone only to hear my colleague replying 'Carlyle and Co.'

While he and I were chatting, and remarking on what a coincidence it was to get a crossed line with somebody one knew, I noticed a Range Rover drawing up outside the office. 'Hang on a moment,' I said to Jay, as in walked none other than Claire, whom I had not seen for several months. She was absolutely stunned to be told her husband-to-be was on the line.

What had happened, Claire Townley explained, was that driving along the Fulham Road she had 'had a sudden urge to visit her former office, and decided then and there to drop in, on the spur of the moment.'

The Scots psychiatrist James McHarg relates an experience which, if not strictly one of the 'crossed line' coincidences, has an affinity with them. He was having lunch one day at his brother-in-law's home in the country when the telephone rang. As he happened to be nearest to it, he was asked to answer. 'Is that Ward 2?' the caller asked. Told it was not a hospital, nevertheless he said he wanted to speak to Dr McHarg. Recognising him as the husband of a patient, desperately concerned about his wife's illness, McHarg asked him how on earth he knew the number. 'I was not sure of the number of the hospital,' he replied, 'but this was the number which came into my head.'

Lovers' ally

'Chance furnishes me with what I need,' James Joyce once claimed. 'I am like a man who stumbles along; my foot strikes something, I bend over it and it is exactly what I want.' In Nassau Street in Dublin on 10 June 1904, 'chance furnished him with Nora Barnacle', Brenda Maddox has commented in her biography, *Nora*, adding that part of Joyce's genius was his ability 'myopically to pick from a crowd the woman essential to his art.'

Joyce was in fact mocking 'chance'. He was a firm believer in the reality of unrecognised forces at work to provide him with what he needed, including Nora. And clearly some contributors to the Foundation's collection regard love at first sight as an intervention-coincidence. 'I opened the door to her and *knew instantly* that this was the girl I was going to marry. We have been happily married for nigh on 42 years,' one of them recalls. This, he adds, might not be the kind of coincidence we were looking for, 'but if it wasn't a coincidence, what was it?'

To that question there may be different answers; but belief in the old tag 'love will find a way' survives, and coincidences are taken to be one of its routes. Their most often reported form was encountered by Saint-Saëns; in his early days as a composer in Paris, he told Flammarion, while he was at work the vision of his girl would suddenly flash into his mind, and he would know that in a few moments she would be ringing his front-door bell. 'The first few times I believed in chance – but the twentieth time?'

Flying out to the South of France to interview Graham Greene in the summer of 1988, Graham Lord, literary editor of the *Sunday Express*, found that Greene had booked him into a hotel in Antibes; but because a friend, Julian ('Jules') Lewis had decided to come with him, they cancelled the booking in order to stay instead at Jules' favourite hotel, the Auberge du Colombier in Roquefort-les-Pins.

At the hotel Jules and I were lying by the swimming pool when there was a telephone call from London for 'Mr Lewis'. It turned out to be another Mr Lewis who was also lying by the pool, and he turned out to be an old school friend of Jules' whom he had not seen for thirty years. They started reminiscing about their schooldays, and I was introduced to the other Mr Lewis's wife, another 'Jules' Lewis (Juliet), whom I knew immediately was going to be very important in my life. It was love at first sight. Eight weeks later she left her husband, and I left my wife, and we have since lived together with astonishing happiness. For both of us it was like coming home.

The Auberge du Colombier, Lord points out, is named after a dovecote in the hotel grounds, and doves, of course, are emblems of love and peace. 'Just chance,' he wonders, 'or meaningful synchronicity? I have discussed the case with Sir Laurens van der Post who is, of course, a great believer in the Jungian theory of synchronicity, and he seems to think that it is greatly significant. But I honestly don't know.'

Lovers are evidently often intrigued in retrospect by the way in which they seem to have been brought together as if by an intervener who contrives to stop them doing what they would otherwise have been doing. In *The Tao of Synchronicity* Jean Shinoda Bolen relates 'the complex series of coincidences' which led to her marriage. Deciding that a phase of her life was over, she had arranged to leave San Francisco for New York. Before she left, she intended to go to Los Angeles for Thanksgiving, but, two days before Thanksgiving, she found that she had been put on the roster for duty at the clinic where she was working. She stayed in San Francisco and therefore could attend a party given by one of her room-mates. 'As a consequence I met Jim Bolen' – who had also planned to be in Los Angeles for Thanksgiving, but had been prevented by work. They married six months later. There was more to it, she came to believe, than the coincidence that they met at a party which neither of them expected to attend; 'Our inner readiness for such a meeting through which love would grow rapidly into marriage had required a number of twists and turns and other relationships to reach this significant intersection.'

Occasionally it is as if the 'intervener' has gone to the utmost trouble to bring lovers together, without their being aware of it, let alone planning it. 'Mr D and Mrs S', engaged in an illicit affair, had agreed to go up separately from the country to London and to meet there for lunch at the Connaught Hotel. Anxious to pick up a cassette she had ordered from a shop in Great Newport Street, 'Mrs S' found her taxi driver was interested to hear about the shop, wondering if he, too, might begin to use it. When they reached it, and she asked him whether he would mind waiting while she collected the cassette, he said he would come in with her, to browse.

'I emphasise the importance of the cab waiting,' writes 'Mrs S' in her account. Had she paid the driver off, she would have walked north to Oxford Street to pick up another one. As it was, the cab was facing south. On its way to her next destination it got held up in a jam in Soho.

I sat in the taxi looking across at the nearest car in Old Compton Street and did a mental double-take: the car and the registration seemed oddly familiar. It was, of course, 'D'. He had taken the wrong route, and should have been nowhere near Soho.

'How can one explain why we should have been in the same spot, at the same time,' she asks, 'prior to our first planned meeting in London?'

Many years ago, Mary Russell recalls,

I had a temporary job in Kensington. A college friend wrote to ask if she could stay with me for a few days. In fact, she was planning an illicit meeting with her boyfriend, who would travel down from the North of England on the Wednesday.

She arrived from Dublin a couple of days before so that she could spend Tuesday looking at the shops, and I took her to Harrods. While she was looking at the display, a huge pantechnicon pulled into the kerb, and a hitch-hiker climbed out of the cab. It was the boyfriend.

He had arrived a day early in London because he had been able to get the lift in the pantechnicon all the way from Manchester. Although they had not arranged to meet till the following day he had arrived at precisely the right time and place to find her, a day early.

In 1964, about to take a holiday in a country behind the Iron Curtain, 'Jack Bentley' spent a day in London on the way.

Passing a ladies' lingerie shop, on a sudden and unexplained impulse I went into the shop and bought two pairs of ladies' stockings. I should mention that this was totally out of keeping with anything I had ever done before or since when going on an unaccompanied holiday.

The first week of the holiday, nothing occurred: I did not even think of my purchase. The second week, on the first evening, I met the lady courier who was to take charge of our group. The meeting was electric for both of us. The coincidence then became apparent: she had been unable to get such stockings; they were the correct size, and her favourite colour.

The outcome was a powerful relationship which endured for several years.

As usual, the 'joker' occasionally puts in an appearance. When Laurence Eveleigh and his wife Diana were newly married shortly after the end of the war, they were walking along an almost deserted beach on the Isle of Wight when they came across a couple of dinghies drawn up side by side. 'When we came up close to them,' he recalls, 'we could read across the transom of one the name "Diana", across the other, "Laurie"' – as he is usually called. 'It was both baffling and eerie, and yet it struck me as a kind of joke.'

Occasionally the joke is at a lover's expense. In New York on business in 1980, Ian Livingstone, creator of the Fighting Fantasy Gamebook series, was invited by a friend to spend a week in Cape Cod. On the second night there, they went to the local bar, where they met two girls, and Ian ended up talking to Jane.

The four of us spent a lot of the remainder of the week together. Although Jane was English, she was spending an indefinite time in the USA, and we did not bother to exchange addresses. The next holiday I had was in Corfu in late August. There I met an Irish girl, Elizabeth. At the end of the holiday we did exchange addresses, as she was living in Manchester; my parents also live in Manchester. At the end of October I phoned Elizabeth, told her I was coming to visit them, and suggested we go out for a drink. She agreed. So it was that on a wet, early November night I rang the bell of a flat in Manchester. The door opened and there, looking as aghast as I was, stood Jane. Elizabeth and Jane shared the flat.

The joker has, in fact, quite a line in malice. 'Over fifty years ago – when I was a very young man – I had an intense affair with a beautiful woman somewhat older than myself,' Michael Relph nostalgically recalls. She told her husband she was leaving; drunk and emotional, he stormed off threatening to take his life. Back at Relph's flat she seemed unmoved, 'but I found the responsibility too great. I told her that at all costs she must find him and stop him committing suicide.' She left the flat to look for her husband where she knew she would find him – 'at his lawyers.' Such was Relph's distress over losing her that he decided he must go somewhere with no associations which could remind him of the ignominious end of his first love affair; and this prompted him to visit a distant relative, a bank manager in a small Sussex town.

Surprised, no doubt, to be contacted by me he invited me to luncheon with his family. As he took me across the deserted market square to his local pub for a pre-lunch drink, my gloom lifted a little in the knowledge that there was nothing here to remind me of my lost love and no possibility of a chance encounter.

A hotel stood centrally in the square and at its entrance a car drew up. The two people who got out as we approached were my lover and her husband. We were the only people in the little square and confrontation was inevitable. My relative's presence forbade anything but a formal introduction before he and I went on our way, and the two people whom I thought to have destroyed my life went into the hotel for lunch.

Many years later, when the romance was briefly rekindled, she told Relph how much she, too, had dreaded such an encounter: the meal that followed had been fraught, and the marriage had not long survived.

She and her husband had only decided to eat at the hotel because they had taken the wrong road. Neither of us had ever been in the town before, and had she or I been one minute earlier or later, we would have missed one another.

The joker was lying in wait for Mary Taylor, a few years ago.

It 'came to me' – for I cannot use such a term for this as 'I decided' – that I would go to London and take my son to the Chinese Exhibition then at the British Museum. I drove to my sister's in time for lunch to join my son. As we were sitting drinking coffee it again 'came to me' that we must set off for the exhibition at that moment. We did.

Her son, then aged nineteen, had not seen his father since he was eighteen months old. In the exhibition, he and his mother became separated.

He returned to me, ashen white, and said, 'Don't think me silly but I have just met my father. I know it is him. We just came face to face and I knew. He just said, "Are you going this way?" and passed by.'

I went across with my son and realised that it was indeed my one-time lover, and that he, too, from the expression of shock on his face, had recognised my son. (They are actually very similar in appearance, and were even wearing identical spectacle-frames.)

We all went for a drink, and the man told us that he had been in London for a meeting and had suddenly had a compulsive urge to leave it and go to the exhibition, taking a taxi to reach it.

4

The Subliminal Component

Trance

The coincidences which tend to make the greatest impression are those that have their origin in a dream or 'altered state of consciousness' (as some psychologists call conditions ranging from reverie to trance) and an event in the outside world. In its simplest and commonest form, a name comes into your head and the next moment you hear it on the radio, or see it in a book.

Theodore Roszak, author of *The Making of a Counter Culture*, and Professor of History at the California State University, Hayward, recalls such an occasion when he was visiting New York with his wife and daughter.

> One afternoon as we were walking along Central Park West I absent-mindedly began humming a tune. Two blocks farther along my wife turned to ask me if I noticed whom we had just passed. I hadn't. I looked back to see two figures walking away behind us. 'Who was it?' I asked. She answered, 'John Lennon and Yoko Ono'. I looked again and agreed it was them. Then my wife asked, 'What's that song you were humming?' I hadn't thought about it until she asked. Then I realised it was *I Want to Hold Your Hand*, one of the Beatles ballads. As far as I'm aware, I had never hummed the song before; it wasn't in my repertory of favourites.

Had the tune been one he often hummed, the coincidence would have been forgotten: it is the degree of improbability, on such occasions, which can lead to speculation about the powers of the subliminal mind. Do they enable it to pick up information which, if the conscious mind's activity is temporarily suspended, or lulled in the state of absent-mindedness, it can transmit to consciousness? Information, furthermore, of a kind not within the reach of the conscious mind?

If the subliminal mind has such a faculty, its existence is clearly of the greatest significance for any investigation of coincidences. Historically, it is only recently that its existence has been doubted. The reason men and women in the Bible or in Homer do not note curious coincidences is that they did not think of them as chance events; they were assumed to be pre-arranged. When the prophets went into a trance and demonstrated second sight or prevision, the assumption was that the faculty was provided by the gods, or spirits. The gods also provided the information which so often came in dreams – and the correct interpretation, where it was needed, as in Pharaoh's dream of the seven lean kine eating the seven fat kine, and the seven thin ears of corn eating the seven fat ears. When Joseph was able to predict correctly that seven years of plenty would be followed by seven years of famine, it was no coincidence; clearly the Lord had warned him what to expect.

After the Renaissance, it gradually came to be accepted that people might see, in dreams or in trances, what was happening at a distance or in the future without divine or diabolic aid, through 'second sight'. It was a faculty which anybody might possess, but which only a few were able to tap. More commonly, in regions such as the Western Isles where its possession was relatively familiar, it tapped them. 'It is an involuntary effect in which neither hope nor fear are known to have any part,' Samuel Johnson observed on his visit to the Isles with Boswell. 'Those who profess to feel it do not boast of it as a privilege, nor are considered by others as advantageously distinguished. They have no temptation to feign.'

Dreams

Even where the possession of second sight was uncommon, as in England, it continued to be accepted as occasionally occurring in dreams, some of them attracting attention. In 1812 John Williams, a manager of some mines in Cornwall, had a dream in which he saw the prime minister, Spencer Perceval, assassinated in the lobby of the House of Commons; it turned out to be a remarkably accurate portrayal of what was to happen a few days later – even to the clothes the assassin was wearing. Williams told several people about it; he wondered whether he should warn Perceval, but was persuaded that this would only expose him to ridicule.

In 1827, a report of a dream was to make even more of a sensation, when it was brought up in a murder case. Maria Marten had left her home to work for a farmer, William Corder, and although from time to time her parents heard from him that all was well, they began to grow worried about not hearing from *her*. One night, ten months after her departure, her stepmother told her husband, Maria's father, that he ought to examine a red barn which stood on Corder's land. She had dreamed that Maria had been murdered, and was buried there. At first Marten refused; but when her dream recurred, he agreed to investigate, went to the barn, and found his daughter's carelessly-buried corpse.

Three years later, however, a book appeared which was to lay down the positivist dogma on dreams. In *The Philosophy of Sleep* an Edinburgh physician, Robert McNish, set out what was soon to become the new orthodoxy, while at the same time cautiously covering his retreat from the old. There had been a period, he admitted, when miracles occurred – 'when futurity was unfolded in visions'; the times 'when God held communion with man'. But thanks to man's growing maturity, there was no need for such intervention. The world was now 'governed by the fundamental laws originally made by God for its regulation'. It was consequently inconceivable that knowledge of forthcoming events should be transmitted through dreams; this would require a miracle, and that was absurd, because 'miracles are, in their very nature, opposed to the laws of creation'.

McNish cited examples, including an experience of his own, to show how unwise it was to accept the miraculous interpretation. He had had a fearful nightmare about the death of a near relation, whom he thought to be in perfect health. A letter soon afterwards informed him that his relative had died of a heart attack 'the very day on the morning of which I had beheld the appearance in my dream!' What was the explanation? Chance coincidence.

The fact that chance could be invoked as the explanation meant that second sight in dreams could still be reported, and accepted, so long as it was not thought of *as* second sight. For all his fascination with ghost stories, Charles Dickens liked to think of himself as free from all forms of superstition; he could describe an example of prevision in a dream to his biographer-to-be, John Forster, as a curiosity:

I dreamt that I saw a lady in a red shawl with her back towards me (whom I supposed to be E). On her turning round I found that I didn't know her and she said, 'I am Miss Napier.'

All the time I was dressing next morning I thought – what a preposterous thing to have so very distinct a dream about nothing;

and why Miss Napier? for I never heard of any Miss Napier. That
same Friday night, I read. After the reading, came into my retiring
room Mary Boyle and her brother and *the* lady in the red shawl,
whom they presented as 'Miss Napier!'

These were 'all the circumstances,' he assured Forster, 'exactly told.'

An even more striking example of a prevision in a dream was to be
described by Frederick Greenwood, the highly-regarded editor of the
Pall Mall Gazette, whose *Imagination in Dreams* (1894) remains one of
the shrewdest and most balanced surveys of the evidence about
dreaming, as it stood at the time. One night he dreamed that, on a
business call, he was shown into a drawing-room, and walked over to
the fireplace to lean there, 'in the usual English way', with his arm
upon the mantelpiece. After a few moments, 'feeling that my fingers
had rested on something cold, I looked, and saw that they lay on a
dead hand: a woman's hand, newly cut from the wrist.' Although he
woke in horror, the dream slipped out of his mind until, later that day,
he had to make a business call and was shown into a drawing-room; on
the mantelpiece was 'the hand of a mummy, broken from the wrist',
and a woman's hand, at that.

Coincidence? 'Visions of severed hands on mantelpieces are not
common,' he remarked. 'With or without previous dreaming of it,
few men have actually seen one, even when taken from a mummy
case, in that precise situation.' Confronted with cases like this,
Greenwood complained, scientists declined to listen to the argument
for second sight on the ground that dreams could not be taken
seriously. He had no explanation for them, himself; but he felt that
some dreams, like some forms of intuition and inspiration, 'seem to
proceed from some independent agency external to mind.'

By that time, however, the positivist interpretation of such dreams
was sufficiently entrenched for such speculation to be ignored. It was
not until 1927, with the publication of J. W. Dunne's *An Experiment
with Time*, that it was seriously challenged. Dunne presented a series
of his own dreams in which he had witnessed something, or some
event, which he was shortly to come across when he awoke – usually
on the same day. This was not second sight, he claimed; not, that is, in
the traditional sense of a psychic faculty. But neither was it chance
coincidence. It was the consequence of displacements in time which,
he was sure, could be accounted for within the accepted laws of
physics.

A few of the dreams were dramatic. When he was in a remote part of South Africa in 1902 he dreamed that an island with 4000 inhabitants was just about to blow up. He tried desperately 'to get the incredulous *French* authorities to dispatch vessels of every and any description to remove the inhabitants'. When he opened the *Daily Telegraph*, which came in with the next batch of papers, he read of the volcano disaster in Martinique, where a mountain had exploded with – a headline claimed – a probable loss of 40,000 lives (the loss was in fact neither 4000 nor 40,000; but the similarity of the figures was curious).

Many of the coincidences, though, were trivial. He dreamed about a secret loft, which he used to escape from a house; the next day he read a novel in which one of the characters did the same. The fact that the glimpses of the future were often of trivial matters, though, did not disconcert Dunne. On the contrary, he thought this supported his case that the mind can shift in time – but without discrimination, so that it may pick up and, in dreams, display fragments of what is to come. Dunne wrote down his dreams immediately on waking, but he did not have them attested, which critics regarded as remiss of him.

In some ways an even more remarkable succession of dreams of the future was to be presented by John Godley in *Tell Me the Next One* (1950). Over a period of three years, while he was an undergraduate at Oxford after serving as a pilot in the Fleet Air Arm during the war, he dreamed the names of ten horses which, in the dreams, won their races. In each case, when he remembered the dream, and found by consulting the papers that the horse was running, he put money on it. Eight of the ten duly won. Attestation was particularly good, as the title of the book helps to explain. As soon as his friends realised his dreams might provide them with a source of income, they begged him to let them know the next time he had a racing dream who the winner would be, and he had plenty of written as well as verbal testimony to support his account. Eight winners out of ten, too, was all the more impressive a record because, strictly speaking, the two losers need not have been included in his list. In one case, he knew the horse was running and had actually put money on it; in the other – unlike all his dream winners – the horse did not run on the day immediately following the dream, but the day after.

There were some minor discrepancies, notably in the actual names of some of the horses. In his dreams they were named Tubermore, Monumentor, The Bogie; consulting the lists the next morning he settled for the nearest equivalents, Tuberose, Mentores, and The

Brogue. But this, curiously, confirmed what Dunne had found and reported about his own precognitive dreams: that they were often slightly inaccurate, though close, in details – such as the 4000 he thought would be killed in his dream of the exploding island. In Godley's case, too, it further confirmed that he was not being guided in his dreams to known 'form' horses. He did not know the names of the horses he was to back, let alone that they would be running that day.

The sequence of dreams might be Kammerian, but the outcome was Jungian; it changed the course of Godley's life. On 13 June 1947, after he had dreamed a 'double' – Baroda Squadron and The Brogue – he decided to ring the *Daily Mirror* to offer them the story, and got them to promise to use it, if the horses he named won. The paper duly splashed it; it was picked up by other papers in different parts of the world; and a few weeks later the *Mirror* offered him a job on the paper for a trial period. At about the same time Godley was informed he had passed out top in the Foreign Service examinations. But

> I threw over the Diplomatic in favour of the *Mirror*. The trial went well, and I stayed eighteen months with them; from the *Mirror* I moved to the *Sunday Express* and I have been writing in one form or another ever since.

When his father died, and John Godley became Lord Kilbracken, his considerable talents as a writer had to some extent to be subordinated to looking after the family estate in Ireland. Still, as he recognised, there could be no possible doubt that his destiny was settled when Baroda Squadron won the four o'clock at Lingfield.

Of the dream coincidences which have come in to the Foundation, some suggest mind reading. When Sebastian Earl was around fifteen years old, living in Kensington, he was close friends with a schoolmate, Adam.

> One night while drifting off to sleep I was startled by the sentence 'Why do crazy rabbits jump into electric chairs?' popping into my thoughts. I was so amazed by the oddity of this that I told it to Adam the next day at school. He was very shaken; he explained that he had read that sentence in the book he had been reading the night before.
>
> I did not really pay the matter much attention until some months later when, having remembered how much Adam had recom-

mended it, I bought the novel *One Flew Over the Cuckoo's Nest*, by Ken Kesey. I had more or less forgotten about the incident with the sentence. But when I came across it myself while reading the book the full impact of the coincidence struck me. The actual sentence in the novel is not identical, but to anybody who has read the book the sentence (and its significance to the theme of the novel) is readily apparent.

Not that the coincidence itself is remarkable for its significance, Earl admits; but 'what it *is* remarkable for is the fact that there is no so-called "scientific" or "logical" theory that can explain why I "picked up" what my friend was reading in Wimbledon while I was in Kensington.'

In the late 1960s Ian Hunter, artist and lecturer, and his wife went on a camping holiday in Italy, leaving their eight-year-old daughter with an aunt.

One night in a camp site near Florence I had a prolonged nightmare, in which I vividly perceived my daughter covered in spots and blemishes, showing great distress. By morning, my night-time resolve to phone home had evaporated into a 'don't be so silly'.

On returning to England a week or so later we collected our daughter, who by then was virtually recovered from a severe attack of measles, the worst phase of which occurred at the time of my nightmare. When we had left her, she had been in perfect health.

Had he picked up a message from his sister-in-law, who claimed to be psychic? 'Whatever the explanation, it seemed far too precise a coincidence to be mere chance.'

In 1987 Geoffrey Simmerson and his wife Margaret, planning a route to drive from London to Scotland, decided to go through Manchester, as they assumed that on a Sunday morning the traffic would not be heavy. On the Saturday night Margaret dreamed that after they had set off she realised they had left the luggage behind; Geoffrey would continue on, they decided, while she went back to collect it and follow on in her car. She telephoned him from London to say she was just setting off, but couldn't go via Manchester as there was a big factory fire, and the M62 had been closed. Waking up, she told her husband of the dream; he got up to go to the bathroom, switched on the radio, and heard a traffic report that there had been a big factory fire in Manchester; the M62 was closed. This, Geoffrey Simmerson comments, 'still has me foxed'.

Presumably because 'picking up' what is happening at the time is more readily accepted than 'seeing the future', prophetic dreams excite more awe, especially if what is seen is bizarre. For several years, Bari Hooper has followed Dunne's example and kept a book beside his bed for recording his dreams. It is full of grammatical errors, he admits, as he often records them when he is only half awake; this one, dreamed in the early hours of 27 October 1982, is from the book 'without embellishment'.

I was walking along a road which led to a small lake or pond with shingly banks, the whole enclosed within a low sinuous concrete wall. On the banks sloping around the water were several aquatic birds, including a very large one which I thought might be a young albatross. The thought occurred to me that I might take this bird away and care for it, as I suspected [that] it was not being properly looked after. I decided against this when a man came and weighed the bird in a kind of bag on the side of which was recorded the bird's weight at different times. Realising that this man was keeper of the birds, I wandered away, knowing them to be in safe hands. When I returned later, the young bird had grown even bigger, with a more rounded body than that of an albatross. But to my horror I saw that its upper beak had been sawn off. The bird was still alive and did not seem to be distressed. As I looked at it my eyes took on an X-ray vision, and I could see the bird's bone structure. As I gazed at it, the keeper returned and fitted an artificial beak to the bird. The dream then faded.

'Undoubtedly a curious dream,' Bari Hooper comments, but of no special significance to him until the next day, when the following item appeared in *The Times*.

MAIMED PELICAN GETS NEW BEAK

Laguna Niguel, California (AP) – A brown pelican named Pinocchio feasted on raw fish after his sawed-off upper beak was replaced by a new fibreglass one.

Pinocchio, one of 11 pelicans found with their beaks hacked off, is being hand fed at first until he adjusts. The other maimed pelicans will receive similar treatment if it proves successful.

Another macabre dream that disturbingly foreshadowed a future event has been reported by Anthony Burgess. 'I dreamt, or nightmared, Ian McEwan's new novel 15 days before reading it,' he has claimed in his *Observer* review of *The Innocent*; adding that it sometimes happens, 'especially to those ancients brought up on J. W. Dunne's *An Experiment with Time*, that a dream inexplicable in terms of past experiences will yield its secrets in the future.'

> In my nightmare, collaborating with a woman not my wife, I killed a man I did not know, chopped him into pieces of the right size for plastic bags, put these out for the garbage collectors, then toasted my accomplice in a triumphant schnapps or akvavit. It then dawned on me that I was advertising guilt to the world, and I spluttered into a panicked awakening. A dream, thank God. Then it was a matter of awaiting the material in newspaper or novel. I did not have to long to wait.

In the novel Leonard and Maria, about to be married, find her former husband Otto, a violent sot, in her flat. In the ensuing fight, Otto is killed. They saw up the body, and Leonard carries the pieces away in two suitcases.

Harbingers of gloom

On 28 June 1914 Monsignor de Lanyi, Bishop of Grosswardin in Hungary, dreamed that he received a missive from his former pupil the Archduke Franz Ferdinand. It contained a letter informing him that the Archduke and his wife would be assassinated, that day, asking for his prayers; and a picture, which in the dream appeared to merge into a film of the actual assassination. Waking in a state of terror, de Lanyi wrote an account of what he had seen, and drew a picture from memory, before relating the story to his mother and a guest who was staying at the palace. Later in the day, the news came in of the assassination at Sarajevo which was to spark off the First World War. A journalist who saw the picture subsequently confirmed that it closely resembled the photographs of the scene which had been published in the following morning's papers.

Whenever anybody famous is killed, or is in an accident, accounts appear of dreams which appear to have presaged the death. Usually they lack detail; but an exception has been recorded by Professor W. H. C. Tenhaeff of the University of Utrecht. In 1939 an acquaintance wrote to him about a dream in which she had seen a long road, with a meadow beside it, a level crossing, and a lorry stationary behind a gate. A car came at speed along the road; as it approached one of its tyres burst, and it swung across into the gate, and the lorry. One of the occupants of the car, who in her dream was killed, she recognised as Prince Bernhard: 'I saw him lying there'.

Two days after receiving the letter, Tenhaeff heard on the radio that Bernhard had been involved in a car crash. It later transpired that the accident had happened on a long stretch of road, beside a railway and meadowland. There was a gate; and lorries were nearby loading sand. The prince's car had struck one of them; he had been lifted out, and laid on the road. Although there were discrepancies – at the actual crash there was no level crossing, a tyre had not burst, and the prince survived – the dream proved to have been eerily close to the event.

A dream of a death may be startling because the person who dies has not been in the dreamer's mind for some time. Harold Rose, B.Sc., Ph.D., a retired industrial scientist, has occasionally had dreams which his wife, 'far more down to earth than I am', dismisses as chance coincidence; but one is harder to explain away. In 1984 they had been briefly acquainted with Fred Kormis, well known for his Holocaust Memorial sculptures and the British Museum series of medallions of distinguished people. They have four of his bronze maquettes on biblical themes in their house; but they had not subsequently seen or heard of him when, two years later,

> I woke one morning, and because I thought my wife would immediately dismiss the subject of my dream, I impressed her with the fact that, wishing Fred Kormis the best of health, I had dreamt that morning, just before waking, that he had died. Two days later the obituary of Fred Kormis appeared in *The Times*.

When he checked with the director of the art gallery with which the sculptor was connected, he found that Kormis had, in fact, died on the morning of the dream. 'I have no explanation to offer,' Dr Rose admits. If Kormis had been a close relative or friend he could have understood, but, 'apart from the rare occasions when I might have mentioned his name to an occasional admirer of the maquettes', neither he nor his wife had had any contact with Kormis since their meeting in 1984.

It is not uncommon for people to dream of their own death, but John Wade reports an unusual example. Wade – a member of the Inner

Magic Circle, familiar to television viewers – was asked in 1986 by friends in the Society of American Magicians if he would help a writer who was coming over from New York in the course of her research for a book on magic. As she wanted to see his act he drove her to Eastbourne, where he was doing a concert. On the way back, in the Ashdown Forest area, a stag jumped into the road ahead of them; she reacted very dramatically, with a fit of hysterics, even though there was no real danger of hitting it.

> She explained that it had always been a nightmare of hers that she would be killed in a car hitting a stag. I pointed out that the dream had therefore been broken, as we were both alive, as was the stag. She cheered up a bit but was very tearful for the rest of the journey.

A year later, discussing mutual acquaintances with an American friend, Wade heard that she had been killed in a road accident. She was in a car which hit a stag.

Some dreams leave a sense of foreboding which appears to be justified by the reports of a disaster not actually witnessed in the dream. As there are few days when no disaster is reported in the newspapers, most such coincidences can readily be accounted for by chance; but occasionally an unusual and particularly vivid dream, of the kind Barbara Brice had on 4 August 1988, stands out. In the dream she picked up her evening paper, the *Bath and West Chronicle*; to her surprise found that it was dated 28 August and that the front page was blank where the headlines and main story should have been.

> In my dream I went downstairs and took a look at other people's newspapers. They were quite normal, dated August 4th. I am not normally a prey to superstition, but this really worried me. I was convinced that something awful was going to happen on August 28th – possibly to me or one of my family. I was so struck by my dream that I immediately wrote down a description of it, and sent it to a friend (who could vouch for the details). When the 28th approached I was apprehensive that I or one of my family or friends would be involved in an accident of some kind. Fortunately for us, none of us was travelling that day. But it was the day when two planes collided over an airfield packed with people, in France, where many lives were lost – making headlines for that day.

In some cases, the dreamer wonders – as John Williams did after his dream of Perceval's assassination (see page 66) – whether to give a warning. In *The Invisible Picture* (1981) Louisa Rhine included the case of a woman who, in a nightmare, had seen a plane crash on the shore of a lake near where she lived, causing a nearby cottage to burst into flames, killing the pilot. The dream left her with the powerful impression, the next morning, that if the crash happened the fire engine was going to take the wrong, long route and would arrive too late. All day this preyed on her mind; and when that evening she heard a plane going over, she felt so certain that it was going to crash that she asked her husband to call the fire brigade and warn them. He reassured her the plane sounded all right. But it was not. It crashed, just as she had seen in her dream; the fire engine did take the wrong road; and although little damage was done to the cottage, the pilot – the sole occupant – was burned to death in the wreckage of his plane.

Hallucinations

Dreams are hallucinations, in that they give the impression at the time that what is being seen and heard is real. In hallucinations while awake, too, what is seen and heard, and sometimes felt, is taken to be real. 'Every hallucination is a perception, as good and true a sensation as if there were a real object there,' William James explained in his *Principles of Psychology* (1890). 'The object happens *not* to be there: that is all.'

Some people go through life without ever experiencing hallucinations and regard them as symptomatic of insanity; but as Francis Galton found, when he was doing the research for his *Inquiry into the Human Faculty* (1883), a surprisingly high proportion of the scientists and savants he knew admitted they had 'seen' or 'heard' something that was not there. Edmund Gurney and Frederic Myers, investigating at the same time, came to the same conclusion: that sane men and women can, and occasionally do, have hallucinations. Recently, Julian Jaynes of Princeton University has presented a plausible explanation for them, suggesting they were an evolutionary expedient to promote the development of the conscious mind. Nowadays, they often appear to be an expedient to allow promptings from the subliminal mind to break into consciousness. Sometimes, as in schizophrenia, they indicate mental or emotional disturbance; but they can happen to sane people as if to pass information to them which has eluded their conscious minds. And they are particularly closely associated with deaths, in the form of 'crisis apparitions' – hallucinations of people who are later found to have been dying, or in grave danger, at the time.

It is enough, Schopenhauer claimed,

for a person to think of us with strength and intensity to conjure up in our brain a vision of his form, not only through imagination, simply, but in such wise that this vision presents itself to us as a corporeal image, that we should not know how to distinguish from reality. The dying, in particular, manifest this power, and appear in consequence at the hour of death, to their absent friends – to several at once, and in different places.

Such cases had been 'so often affirmed and attested in various quarters,' Schopenhauer insisted, 'that I consider them certain beyond a doubt.' However often they were affirmed and attested, they could be, and were, attributed by positivists to chance. As hallucinations of any kind came to be regarded in the course of the century as symptomatic of incipient or actual lunacy, there was an understandable reluctance to report them; or, if they were reported, the tendency was to follow the cautious course Lord Brougham took in his autobiography – not, in general, a reliable source, but in this instance he was quoting from the diary he had kept as a young man.

Travelling through Sweden in 1799, tired and cold, he had stopped at an inn and was taking a hot bath before going to bed. Lying in it, enjoying the warmth, he looked around at the chair on which he had put his clothes. Sitting on it was G, an old friend from his student days in Edinburgh. As students, they had discussed whether there is life after death, and had 'actually committed the folly of drawing up an agreement, written with our blood, to the effect that whichever of us died the first should appear to the other.' G had left to join the Indian Civil Service, and they had lost touch; Brougham had almost forgotten him. 'How I got out of the bath I know not, but on recovering my senses I found myself sprawling on the floor. The apparition, or whatever it was that had taken the likeness of G, had disappeared.' Recalling their compact, Brougham confided to his journal that he could not help thinking that G must have died, 'and that his appearance to me was to be received by me as a proof of a future state'. Although he tried to brush the idea aside, 'so painfully vivid, so unfading was the impression, that I could not bring myself to talk of it, or to make the slightest allusion to it.' When he returned to Edinburgh, it was to hear that G had died on the day he made his appearance.

Brougham, however, because he was a staunch rationalist, could not bring himself to accept that he had encountered an apparition: it must, he decided, have been a dream. And, he added, it must have been a coincidence. In other words – chance.

Whether an experience of that kind should be put down to a dream or to a waking hallucination is often hard to judge, because the transition from being awake to being asleep, or from sleeping to waking up – Myers christened the stages 'hypnagogic' and 'hypnopompic' respectively – can be productive of particularly vivid images, so that what starts as a dream sometimes appears to merge into a hallucination, as in the remarkable case related in John G. Fuller's *The Airmen who Would Not Die* (1979). In 1928 two RAF officers, Rivers Oldmeadow and G. L. P. Henderson, were returning to Britain on a liner from South Africa when one night Henderson came into Oldmeadow's cabin, saying,

> 'Rivers, something ghastly has happened . . . "Hinch" has just been in my cabin. Eye patch and all. He woke me up. It was ghastly. He kept repeating over and over again, "Hendy, what am I going to do? What am I going to do? I've got this woman with me, and I'm lost. I'm lost!" Then he disappeared in front of my eyes! Just disappeared!'

Three days later, the daily bulletin on the ship's board reported that Captain Raymond Hinchliffe was missing after an attempt to fly the Atlantic. They had known him, but knew nothing about his flight, let alone that he was bringing a woman with him. They found when they got back to England that Hinchliffe had needed funds to enable him to fulfil his ambition to be the first pilot to fly the Atlantic from east to west. Elsie Mackay, daughter of Lord Inchcape, provided the money; and she was ambitious to become the first woman to make the crossing as co-pilot. She persuaded Hinchliffe to take her, but as she did not dare to let her father know, this was not made public. The aircraft took off successfully; and that was the last that was seen or heard of them.

A transition from dream to waking hallucination is also suggested by an entry in the diary which Roy Jenkins kept while he was president of the European Commission, from 1977 to 1981. The published volume records that one morning he woke up, in Rome,

> having had a vivid dream about Tony [Crosland] being present and his saying in an absolutely unmistakable, clear, rather calm voice, 'No, I'm perfectly all right. I am going to die but I'm perfectly all right.' Then about 8 o'clock we had a telephone call from the BBC saying that he had died that morning, curiously enough at almost exactly the same moment that I awoke from my dream about him.

Jenkins and Crosland had been friends and colleagues in the Labour government. That Jenkins, who knew that Crosland's death was imminent, should dream about him was natural enough. The diary entry, though, brief as it is, had features which lift it a little out of the ordinary run of such dreams, towards hallucination. It was not just that it coincided 'almost exactly' with the time of death; it was vivid, and in it, Crosland spoke of his impending death as if he were actually in the room.

In one of the contributions to Ben Noakes's *I Saw a Ghost* (a collection more interestingly varied and less lightweight than the title suggests) the cartoonist Ronald Searle describes a night in 1979 while he was living in Switzerland, when, 'between sleeping and waking', Laura Perelman appeared before him. Laura and her husband, humorist Sid Perelman, were old friends of Searle's; she had died in 1970 but 'here she was, nearly ten years later, very much alive, and looking me straight in the eye.' In her familiar American drawl she said 'Rahnald, Sid's dead', and then disappeared. The next morning, before the breakfast coffee, a call came from Searle's sister-in-law in London to say she had just heard on the radio that Sid had died during the night.

It was also between sleeping and waking, one afternoon on a liner returning to Britain from South Africa, that Laurens van der Post had a vision of himself in avalanche country, filled with the foreknowledge of imminent disaster.

> Suddenly, at the far end of the valley on one Matterhorn peak of my vision, still caught in the light of the sun, Jung appeared. He stood there briefly, as I had seen him some weeks before at the gate at the end of the garden of his house, then waved his hand at me and called out, 'I'll be seeing you'. Then he vanished down the far side of the mountain.

The next morning, when van der Post looked out through his cabin porthole,

> I saw a great, white lone albatross gliding by it; the sun on fire on its
> wings. As it glided by it turned its head and looked straight at me. I
> had done that voyage countless times before and such a thing had
> never happened to me, and I had a feeling as if some tremendous
> ritual had been performed. Hardly had I got back into bed when my
> steward appeared with a tray of tea and fruit and, as he always did,
> the ship's radio news. I opened it casually. The first item I saw was
> the announcement that Jung had died the previous afternoon at his
> home in Zürich. Taking into consideration the time, the latitude
> and longitude of the ship's position, it was clear that my dream, or
> vision, had come to me at the moment of his death.

One hallucinatory coincidence, at least, in Ben Noakes's collection
was reported by somebody who was fully awake. In 1958 Colonel D.
Pritchard was with some friends in the pavilion bar at Lord's cricket
ground awaiting the start of a Test match when he noticed Douglas
Jardine – captain of the England team on the notorious 'Bodyline' tour
of Australia – standing at the bar a few yards away. They knew each
other quite well; as a boy, Jardine for a time had been brought up by
one of Pritchard's aunts. 'We caught each other's eye, and raised our
glasses in recognition.' When Pritchard went over to talk to him,
however, he was no longer there. 'I thought nothing of this until, just
before the start of play, it was announced on the loudspeaker he had
died the day before, in Switzerland.'

In one case sent into the Foundation the apparition was encountered
by two people, both fully awake. Sonia Colvin-Snell had returned to
her home country, New Zealand, in the late 1970s and found work in a
library which was about to move to new premises, with all the chaos
this entails; she was lucky to have the support of, among others, two
girls who were particularly helpful, and she was sorry when they
decided to leave for a working tour of Australia. In 1980 she received a
long letter from one of them, describing how on a visit to Ayers Rock
they had encountered her 'double' – as they later thought she must
have been; at the time, they assumed it was Sonia. She was sitting
sketching, just as she often did; replied when they called her name; and
'looked, talked, and laughed just like you.'

When I read these words, I could only laugh out loud. I was lying comatose (at Death's Door, as another friend put it) in the intensive care unit at our local hospital.

Ayers Rock has a history of such strange experiences and Sonia Colvin-Snell, who is herself ready to accept them as 'perfectly natural', regrets only that she has never since had the opportunity to discuss the encounter with the two girls.

Visions

Although there is no hard and fast distinction between a hallucination and a vision, it is possible to adopt one for simplicity's sake: somebody seeing a vision may immediately be aware that it *is* a vision, and not 'real'. Thus in *A Hind in Richmond Park* (1922) the author and naturalist W. H. Hudson described an occasion when, walking home in London, he suddenly saw the face of a girl he knew who lived with her parents in the country. 'It was the face only, the vivid image of the face, so vividly seen that it would not have appeared a more real human face if the girl had actually come before me.' The girl's mother told him later that at about the time he had seen the vision, the girl had suddenly broken out in a rage against her parents. There had earlier been a possibility that Hudson would adopt her, but complications had led to the abandonment of the project. Now, in her frenzy, the girl told her parents that she had 'made up her mind to leave them, and if she had no money to pay the railway fare, she would walk and live on charity until she came to where I was.'

When J. W. Dunne formulated his theory of time to account for the way he could see into the future in dreams, he realised that if the theory was sound it should be possible to see into the future while awake, in the form of a vision. He decided to experiment. He would pick up a book which he was just about to begin to read, concentrate upon the title, 'and then wait for odds and ends of images to come into the mind by simple association.' He met with varying success, but in the middle of one of the trials he picked up a curious image of an umbrella with a perfectly plain, straight handle. 'This umbrella, folded, was standing unsupported, *upside down, handle on the pavement*, just outside the Piccadilly Hotel.' Happening to pass along Piccadilly in a bus the next day, he saw an eccentric-looking lady walking along the pavement holding a closed umbrella of the kind he had pictured in his mind, using it as if it were a walking stick; 'but she had it *upside down*. She was holding it by the ferrule end, and was pounding along towards the hotel with *the handle on the pavement.*'

In *Flight Towards Reality* (1975) Air Marshal Sir Victor Goddard, who at the end of the Second World War was Chief of the Air Staff in the Far East, recalled how in 1935, flying back from Scotland to his base in England, he descended out of cloud to check where he was and saw, beneath him, an airfield he recognised as Drem.

> The airfield was clear, new-mown and clean, the nearest hangar doors were open and on the tarmac apron, wet from recent rain, stood, parked, four aeroplanes – three biplanes (Avro 504s) and then a monoplane of unknown type. Emerging through the hangar doors there was a second monoplane being pushed by two mechanics, one on the tail, one on the starboard wing. All five machines were brilliant yellow chrome. The mechanics who were there, attending them, were all in dungarees of blue.

But Drem, he knew, was disused. He had visited it, and found it had reverted to farmland. Moreover, in 1935 no RAF aircraft were yellow; there were no monoplanes in service; and airmen wore brown dungarees; 'but what surprised me most of all in this surprising vision was the indifference of the airmen to my zooming over them at thirty feet. Not one of them looked up.' Baffled, he flew on south, and landed safely. He described the vision to his Wing Commander, who warned him to 'lay off the whisky'. He had not had any whisky; but as he had no desire to be reported as 'prone to mental aberration' he did not press the point. And a posting to the Air Ministry, charged with setting up an intelligence branch to monitor the preparations for war other Western air forces were making, meant that he was unaware of the planning which led the RAF to bring Drem back into service in 1939.

> Drem airfield, already then rebuilt, reopened as a flying training school with yellow Avro 504s and Magisters. The Magister was new; it was a trainer monoplane; it was the spitting image of the monoplanes I saw, that stormy day, four years before at Drem. None of that type existed back in 1935 – not in our normal consciousness. Meanwhile, our airmen's dungarees had also been transformed; no longer were they brown, but blue.

In *Beyond Explanation* (1985) Jenny Randles has related how in 1981 British Rail had a call from a woman who claimed to have had a vision of a fatal crash in which a freight train had been involved. So clear had it been, she said, that she not merely saw the blue diesel engine, but could read the number: 47 216. Two years later, an accident of the kind she predicted occurred, all the details matching – except one: the engine's number was 47 299.

That would have been that, but a train spotter, Howard Johnston, happened to have noticed that 47 299 was not the engine's original number. It had been renumbered, a couple of years before, from 47 216. Diesels, he knew, were ordinarily renumbered only after major modifications, which this one had not undergone. When curiosity prompted him to ask why, he was told about the prediction. Apparently British Rail officials had been sufficiently impressed (they had checked with the local police, and found that the woman who had provided it had given them some useful information from her visions) to try to ward off Fate by changing the number. The ruse had failed, and 'they had officially logged it all as an "amazing coincidence".'

In 1988 Tracy Barnes had 'a brief but extremely intense affair' with 'David' in Australia, before he returned to Paris, where he lived.

> In the month after he returned to Paris I was very busy, but I remained impressed (in the real sense of the word) by my time with him. In the week we spent together we seemed to leap formalities which in other relationships had taken years to overcome. This sudden level of deep intimacy was, at times, quite disturbing.

Travelling from Sydney to Melbourne on the evening train, a long and uncomfortable journey, as the train was full,

> I began to experience what I would call extremely strong 'images' of David. I visualised his face with great clarity. Soon, my head began to ache with the intensity of the experience, and I began to feel nausea. I walked out of the carriage and down to the toilet – as much in the desire to be alone as anything else (I felt that I must look half mad and distracted). I sat on the toilet lid with my head in my hands and I remember screaming his name into my cupped hands (lest they take me away) in a bid to exorcise this 'pain' or 'pressure' of his presence.

On her return to the carriage Tracy Barnes decided to record her experience, with a note of the date and time. A week later a letter arrived from David, to the effect that he had woken up that morning with a splendid vision of Tracy smiling, bending over him, her hair hanging loose, her hand to his forehead. Checking the date, she found that, allowing for the time difference, her vision and his would have approximately coincided.

A few people report having visions of an everyday kind. Veronica Milsted sees 'pictures' in her mind of clothes which she later finds in second-hand shops.

The clothes are exactly as in the picture . . . Some, I have seen in a picture in my mind weeks before I find them. I know that they are 'in' simply by a feeling I have to go into a particular shop at that time. Some, I find shortly after I see the picture (within the week).

Sometimes I have to go into all the shops and feel for 'what is there'; I have often thought 'there isn't anything', only to turn and see the item as I am leaving.

Voices

'I have had a remarkable experience,' Socrates told the jury which had just condemned him to death. 'In the past the prophetic voice to which I have become accustomed has always been my constant companion, opposing me even in quite trivial things if I was going to take the wrong course.' The voice had often interrupted him even when he was in the middle of a sentence; yet on this occasion neither when he was leaving to come to the court, nor in the court itself, 'nor at any point in any part of my speech, did the divine sign oppose me.'

Socrates' 'daemon' spoke to him only to oppose him; but sometimes, he realised, it was trying to convey warnings, as on the occasion when its message turned out to relate to a murder which duly took place. Joan of Arc's 'voices' could be more specific in some of their predictions; that they told her when, where and how she would be wounded, was noted down at the time, and their accuracy later confirmed. Many present-day accounts of coincidences are of inner-ear voices which have given a timely warning of danger, as in the case which the singer Tito Gobbi related in his autobiography. Driving one day up a mountain road with a cliff on one side and precipice on the other – and probably, he feared, driving too fast – he suddenly heard his brother Bruno's voice,

so distinctly that he seemed to be sitting beside me, saying 'Stop –
instantly'. Instinctively I obeyed, coming to a halt on a wide grass
verge, practically the only spot of any width in the whole path. A
few minutes later, round the narrow bend came an articulated lorry
out of control.

So natural was Bruno's voice that 'extraordinary though it may seem,
I was surprised not to find him sitting in the car. For in those few
minutes the reality of Bruno's voice speaking to me was more intense
than the reality that he had been dead for several years.'

During the Second World War Philip Paul was walking to work
during the Blitz when a voice told him to stop. For a while he ignored
it, he has recalled in *Some Unseen Power*.

But the warning persisted. So, putting a foot on a pile of rubble, I
pretended to tie a shoelace. At that moment, the high wall ahead
collapsed into the alleyway, filling it ten feet high and burying the
walkers a few yards ahead of me.

In 1961 Mrs Joyce Donoghue's three-year-old son was prescribed a
newly marketed sedative, which her GP assured her was safe. It did
not work, but she left the remaining tablets in the medicine cupboard
in case one of the other children might benefit. The following May,
when she was pregnant, she looked in the cupboard during a sleepless
night, and seeing them, decided that as they had been pronounced safe
for her son they would surely be safe for her.

I filled a glass of water and was about to swallow two when a voice –
from within, I felt – said, as clearly as could be, 'They were not
prescribed for you so don't take them'. It was a voice of authority. I
threw them away and made a hot drink.

It was not until several months later that she read about thalidomide
babies, and even then, for a time, she did not make the connection, as
the bottle in the cupboard bore the trade name, Distaval. When she
realised, she threw the tablets away. The son who was born later that
year has since become an artist; 'I could have destroyed his gift and
sentenced him to a handless existence. The voice was timely.'

'Voices' can be timely in more mundane ways. In 1973, Eric
Laithwaite, Professor of Electrical Engineeering at the Imperial

College of Science in London, was conducting some televised lectures for children at the Royal Institution. In one of them, he was demonstrating that because a result is not repeated in similar circumstances, this does not mean it never happened; and he was illustrating the point with the help of a gadget which caused a ball to jump a couple of inches once in thirty-six times. He switched it on twice: no jumps. The third time, he heard 'an inner voice, clearly a man's voice' which told him 'You know it *goes*, next time'. In astonishment, he replied – mentally – 'Does it?' The voice said, 'Of course! Why don't you tell the children?' He told them, 'But *this* time . . .' He switched on the current, his hand held out in readiness; the ball 'leapt neatly into it.'

Sometimes, the coincidence 'joker' light-heartedly intervenes. In Naples, in the last two weeks of the war, 'A' took a lady friend to a concert; later, they spent the night together.

At some point, when I was fast asleep, she spoke to me. I was 'miles away', and struggling back to verbal consciousness I said, 'What, Muriel?' Alas! It was not her name, and argument ensued.

A fortnight or so later, in the mail was a letter for me – one of those blue letter-card things, from a friend in the UK. It was not the usual crammed epistle, but a few lines only. 'Please write directly you get this; I'm very worried; I heard your voice last night, you spoke to me; please reply at once.'

I wrote immediately and put it in the box. Later, wondering when the letter had been written, I checked the date; Sunday before last. So where had I been on the Saturday night? Oh, yes, that concert, and oh yes, oh dear, that was the night when . . .

I re-read the letter: 'I'm very worried; you spoke to me; please write. Muriel.'

The letter itself, A comments, 'says, better than I can, why "I think it meaningful."'

Odours

Hallucinations of smell are occasionally reported as giving notice of the impending arrival of somebody who was at a distance. The novelist and biographer Michael Harrison once woke up in Colchester in the small hours of the night breathing a scent made by Floris of Jermyn Street which was firmly associated in his mind with a girl he was in love with; it must mean, he decided, that she had returned from London. When he called her next morning, it was to find that she had decided to drive back to Colchester on the spur of the moment, and had arrived at about the time he awoke.

Another writer, Elma Williams, recalls how she was sitting at her desk one afternoon when she had 'the overwhelming smell of cigar smoke'. There was nobody else in the house; when she checked the windows, they were closed. A few minutes later, when her husband came back from work, he went directly to the drawer in which he kept his cigars and lit one up – 'a very unusual occurrence (it's an after-dinner treat, normally)'. He had had a very trying day, he explained, 'and he'd promised himself a cigar immediately he got home. He'd been relishing it for the past ten minutes or so.'

Community of sensation

Experiments conducted in the nineteenth century appeared to demonstrate that certain individuals, when hypnotised, were able to feel what the hypnotist felt: if he pinched himself, they would yelp. This came to be described as community of sensation; and there have been many reports of its spontaneous occurrence, particularly in twins: when one has an accident or illness, the other may report feeling pain or other mimicking symptoms.

Occasionally more dramatic coincidences have been related. In *Memories, Dreams, Reflections*, Jung recalled an occasion when he was woken up one night by a dull feeling of pain, 'as though something had struck my forehead and then the back of my skull'. One of his patients, he heard the next day, had committed suicide. He had shot himself; 'Later, I learned that the bullet had come to rest in the back wall of his skull.'

In a talk in London in 1989 the psychiatrist James McHarg recalled that he has occasionally had patients who described symptoms for which he could find no justification; later, he found that they matched the real symptoms of relations. Some of the contributors to the Foundation's collection have had sympathetic symptoms of this type. 'At times of crisis or stress amongst my family (my parents, my siblings), I experience physically, the suffering for a few minutes,' Kate McVicar writes, and goes on to list occasions on which this has happened, among them:

Waking at 4.00 am with an extremely painful throat, I sit up and waken my husband, as the pain is frightening. It disappears completely only after I have made sure it is not a left-over from a valid dream. The next day I phone mother, with whom I have a particularly close 'ESP' relationship. When I ask how she is she tells me that she has spent a very fraught night with an extremely painful throat.

Mrs McVicar had not been aware that her mother, who lives three hundred miles distant, was unwell. In another case,

I awoke again, in the middle of the night, with hot and cold 'sweats', a pain in my chest and discomfort in my left arm and underarm. The sensations were alien to any that I had experienced and I thought that I was suffering a mild heart attack. I immediately thought of my mother. When I phoned her, she said all was well. The next day my fit, healthy father had a major, first heart attack.

'Laura Cameron', recalls that she was putting some plants in her garden, with her husband

when I suddenly felt as if I had been kicked. I dropped everything and begged my husband to get in his car, and go out and look for my daughter, who was out riding. The feeling was so intense we both went to look, in separate cars. We found the horse, first, and eventually my daughter, who had been badly thrown.

Jennifer Lane had two such experiences within twenty-four hours:

I was sitting in an armchair overlooking the garden at about 4.30 when momentarily I felt extraordinarily weak – 'what's the matter with me, I can hardly move?' Later, I rang my daughter Lizzie; when I told her this she burst into tears. Suffering badly from flu, feeling very grotty, she had been concentrating hard on thoughts of me, hoping I was picking them up, and thinking of her with love.

The night before, at about 9 pm, I had an inexplicable backache, which soon went. At the same time Liz was suffering from severe backache, and again thinking of me.

The ghost in the machine
In *The Concept of Mind* (1949) Gilbert Ryle, Professor of Philosophy at

Oxford, derided the Cartesian distinction between mental and physical as involving a ghost in the machine. Koestler appropriated the phrase for the title of one of his books, and later used it as one of his categories of coincidence. He confined it, however, to cases involving machines which had no ghostly content. Cases in which 'ghosts' appeared to have affected matter were in a separate category, 'Poltergeists'.

Anomalous physical phenomena of this type have a history going back to Belshazzar's feast and 'the writing on the wall'. But in their role as coincidences, Alice Johnson was clearly uneasy about them; one of the more remarkable cases was included in her long article only because it was connected with a well-authenticated premonition.

Waking up on the morning he was due to be hanged in 1885 for a particularly vicious murder, John Lee informed the warders in charge of him that he had dreamed of being led to the gallows.

I thought the time was come, and I was led down through the reception out to the hanging place; but when they placed me on the drop they could not hang me, for there was something wrong with the machinery.

In the dream he had to be taken back to his cell. Later that morning, according to Lord Clinton in his official report on the affair, Lee escaped hanging because the 'drop' refused to budge. It had been tested five times the previous day, and had worked satisfactorily; it worked again after the attempted execution; but it refused to work when Lee was on it, and he was returned to his cell. (He was later reprieved, much to the indignation of *The Times*, which denounced the Home Secretary's decision in an editorial which provoked a shoal of letters, for and against.)

'In cases of physical phenomena,' Alice Johnson warned, citing the faulty trapdoor, 'we have, of course, first to consider whether the conditions sufficiently exclude the agency of ordinary known causes.' She was sceptical about such phenomena, as was Richard Hodgson, who had gone to Boston to take charge of the American Society for Psychical Research. Still, he felt compelled to report one account of a coincidence which had been brought to his attention, because it was so well authenticated.

The woman who had sent him the account had dreamed that her uncle – her mother's brother – had died; she had gone to the funeral but, to her intense annoyance, found that she had arrived too late.

In the midst of this distressing scene I awoke hearing a loud crash, as of something falling. This was a decided reality, but I could discover nothing in my room which had been disturbed. In the morning I related my dream, and felt as though I should hear some news that day.

The noise I had heard was accounted for by the falling of a weight in a tall clock which stood in the hall. Two days passed, and on the morning of the third day the paper contained a notice of my uncle's death (my *father's* brother) stating that he died on the night I had my dream. It was then too late for me to go to the funeral; for some unknown reason I had not been notified by the family.

When Hodgson asked her for attestation, her sister and a friend who had been staying in the house both claimed that she had told them of her dream the next morning. 'The sound I did not hear,' her sister wrote, 'but I was present when it was discovered that the weight of the hall clock had fallen down'; and the friend testified that she had heard the noise made by the fall of the clock-weight.

Although Alice Johnson thought the case for some form of telepathy being responsible for the dream was strong, she could not bring herself to accept that it had anything to do with the clock-weight, which, she contended, 'had only a very remote connection, if any, with the dying person, and it is hardly possible to regard its fall as anything but a mere coincidence.' But Flammarion found that accounts of the connection of physical phenomena, so familiar in classical literature, with dramatic events at a distance, were still far from uncommon – among them, many variations on the theme of the old song, 'The clock stopped, never to go again, when the old man died'.

Relating the story told by Louis de Sales about what happened on the night his brother, St Francis de Sales, Bishop of Geneva, died – the bell in the family chateau at Thuille began to sound, and would not stop even when the cord was detached from it – Flammarion commented that he had collected 'a goodly number' of such occurrences, which

were *first* called miracles, produced by God's will, when they were connected with the lives of the saints. *Secondly* , they were called diabolical pranks when they occurred outside the Church, and *thirdly* they were generally denied.

All three interpretations, he asserted, were wrong. 'We must today investigate the occurrences in full liberty of thought and make use of them in the study of Man.' A typical example came from the memoirs of Alexandre Dumas the elder. Visiting M. Villenave, a collector of rare books and works of art, he had remarked how beautiful he found a pastel of an old friend of Villenave's when she was young. She had indeed been beautiful, Villenave said. He had not seen her for years, but they still corresponded regularly. On a second visit, Dumas found Villenave in an agitated state. Two nights before, the pastel had fallen from the wall. The circumstances were such, Villenave commented, that if he had been superstitious, he would fear that it was a presentiment: the picture had fallen 'without either the nail that held it or the cord being broken'. At this point Dumas uneasily handed over a letter which had arrived at the same time as he had, and which he had brought up to Villenave's study; it told him that his old friend had died on the night, and at the time, the picture fell. 'I put to myself the question that is so often asked and never answered,' Dumas recalled: 'What are the mysterious bonds which bind the dead to the living?'

It was a question which Koestler reluctantly felt compelled to put to himself, at a time when he was doing his best to follow the Communist Party line and reject such superstitions. Staying with Maria Kloepfer in her home on the Lake of Lugano, he found that she suffered from hallucinations – in particular, of the ghost of an uncle; and poltergeist effects, she said, would follow her encounters with him. Koestler was actually present at one of them. He did not see the ghost, but she did, and her dog reacted with a howl, its hair bristling. Something would soon happen, she warned him. A day or two later,

> while we were sitting at lunch, there was a sudden, loud crash. A large, heavily framed picture which an instant before, had been peacefully hanging on the wall that I was facing, had crashed down on to the sideboard that stood beneath it . . .
>
> 'How on earth did that happen?' I asked, walking over to the battlefield. Maria shrugged, and said nothing. I looked at the back of the picture: the wire was not broken, and the two picture hooks were still in the wall, solid and undamaged. In fact, I was able to hang the picture back in its former place, where it came to rest as firmly and innocently as if it had always stayed there.

When she asked whether the wire was broken, he had to admit it was not; 'but please', he begged her, 'don't ask me to believe in miracles.' Many years were to pass before he could bring himself to accept the possibility that some force – not miraculous, except in the sense it had no place in conventional physics – might have been responsible.

Accounts of pictures falling in strange circumstances have also come in to the Foundation. Sometimes the event seems to herald some distant event: in November 1947 Raymond E. Jones, then in the RAF and subsequently in the Diplomatic Service, was sitting up late in his wife's parents' home,

> awaiting news of the birth of our second child. No one else was still up. At 12.20 am – the exact moment, it emerged, that the child was finally delivered – a large picture fell to the floor with a resounding crash.

Tirzah Loewenstein recalls an even stranger coincidence.

> About fifteen years ago I visited my family in Zimbabwe and then went on to stay with cousins in Cape Town, South Africa. In London I had found copies of a Victorian paper, *The Children's Friend*, and extracted and framed engravings from one of them as gifts for my cousin's children – Charla, Daniel and Joshua Green. A year later, Daniel's picture (of a boy standing before bears at the zoo) fell off the bedroom wall. Because the glass had shattered, he was able to remove the picture and read part of the story on the reverse side: it read, 'Daniel Green said to his brother Joshua'.

The ghost in the machine rarely performs a useful service, but one did, for Mrs Glenys Dean. When Mrs Dean's husband was an assistant governor of Wormwood Scrubs, and she was a teacher, they lived in a house belonging to the prison. At church one Sunday morning she met a man who was awaiting major surgery; his wife, he said, had never been in London before, had poor eyesight and spoke only a little English. Mrs Dean offered to let her have the spare bedroom, showed her where the spare door key was kept, and told her to come and go as she wished.

> Rather than wait at the hospital on the day of the operation, she said that she would come back and make herself at home. I then left for

school, followed by a staff meeting; and at that point I discovered in my handbag not only my own doorkey but also the spare one. I must have absent-mindedly put it into my bag as well.

Very angry with myself, I returned home expecting to find her locked out, but instead she was indoors with good news from the hospital. I asked her how she had got into the house. She said, 'With the key you gave me'. Only when I showed her that I had had both keys all day did she realise that she had opened my front door – Chubb lock and all – with her own front door key.

No doubt Chubbs would say that the odds against this happening are quite steep!

'"Steep" is hardly the word for it, I still get a *frisson* when I think of it,' Mrs Dean concludes – 'though the Chaplain was very rude when we ascribed it to Divine Providence. So perhaps it should come under the heading of "coincidence" after all.'

In 1951 Michael Young – later to be founder of the Consumers' Association and the College of Health, and to be made a life peer – was an even luckier beneficiary of an intervention of a ghost in the machine. He was on a tour which was to take him eastwards round the world. When he reached New Zealand, he was strongly tempted to return to England westwards, by sea, a voyage he had done as a child; but he had his open ticket to Vancouver. He decided, when he reached Auckland air terminal, to book a place on the trans-Pacific flight.

My mother had given me, before I left England, what appeared to be a little ivory elephant – a very small, miniature one that she had got in India when she had been there some months before, and she said this was for luck. I kept it in what seemed to be a safe place inside my washbag, along with my toothbrush and things. I looked at it quite often; sometimes I took it out and stood it on the bedside table.

When I took out my washbag at the terminal I did something which was, perhaps, slightly strange. I looked to see that the elephant was there, where I'd put it. And it wasn't. I looked through all my possessions – very few – and I couldn't see it anywhere. I thought perhaps I'd left it behind somewhere in Sydney. Then I looked more carefully in the bag and in one corner there was just a pocket of white dust which hadn't been there before. And it was where I remembered the elephant had been. It had just disappeared – pulverised.

It couldn't have been crushed, he realised; it had not been in the aircraft hold. 'Anyway, I took it as an omen; as guidance that I should not do what I had been intending to do in the next half hour – that I should not book on that airplane to Canada'. He returned to Australia; and when he reached Sydney, he read in a newspaper that the Vancouver plane had disappeared over the Pacific. There were no survivors.

The 'ghost' also performed a notable service for thriller writer Frederick Forsyth. As a war correspondent in the Nigerian civil war in 1969, he felt uncomfortably that he was being stared at. He could see nothing to account for it, but suddenly there was a movement; a timber post twenty yards away toppled over. As he turned his head sharply to see what had happened,

> I felt the 'whump' of a passing bullet slamming into the doorpost, then the 'whack' of the sound. Jerking my head to the left had stopped it going through my forehead; instead, it went past my ear and buried itself in the door-jamb. I had indeed been stared at – by a Nigerian sniper in the forest fifty yards away.

The timber post, he later discovered, had been eaten away by termites; 'one termite must have given the last nibble that separated the last strand of wood.'

Occasionally these 'physical phenomena' coincidences appear to be sparked off by repressed rage. In 1909, having become interested in psychic phenomena through, among other things, some experiences he found unaccountable, Jung thought he would find out what Freud's views were on the subject. At that time, Freud still clung to materialism: he lectured Jung 'in terms of so shallow a positivism,' Jung recalled in his autobiography, 'that I had difficulty in checking the sharp retort on the tip of my tongue.'

> While Freud was going on in this way, I had a curious sensation. It was as if my diaphragm were made of iron, and were becoming red hot – a glowing vault. And at that moment there was such a loud report in the bookcase, which stood right next to us, that we both started up in alarm, fearing the thing was going to topple over on us.
> I said to Freud, 'There, that is an example of a so-called catalytic exteriorisation phenomenon.' 'Oh, come,' he exclaimed, 'that is

sheer bosh.' 'It is not,' I replied. 'You are mistaken, Herr Professor. And to prove my point I now predict that in a moment there will be another loud report!' Sure enough, no sooner had I said the words than the same detonation went off in the bookcase.

That Jung's memory was not at fault was confirmed by the letter which Freud – clearly shaken, because it had happened on the same evening when he had said Jung was to be his 'Crown Prince' and successor – sent to him, seeking to rationalise the noises by claiming they had continued to occur. In any case, 'for various inner reasons' it seemed to Freud implausible that anything occult had occurred. Later, though he was to remain uneasily ambivalent about psychic phenomena, he was to come round to a modified acceptance of their reality.

Some ten years ago 'Bernard Clapton', in the frame of mind which accompanies the conclusion of a 'highly emotionally charged' relationship, found he was continually having unexpected encounters with the other person, in spite of deliberate attempts on his part to avoid them; 'the "coincidental" qualities of these encounters were such that, at the time, I certainly believed them to be significant.' And after one such occasion, when he had seen her across the road, he 'returned quickly to my nearby flat and on putting the key in the lock it snapped off in my hand.'

In retrospect, Clapton admits, it is only too easy to convince himself that the key was weak, that he turned it with more than usual force.

I am happy with this explanation if I try to recall the event superficially and rationally; but if I delve into my emotions at the time, try to relive the experience in detail, and take an 'honest' look at it, I have to confess the explanation isn't very convincing. My feeling at the moment was extremely strange; I knew that the breaking of the key (which was very symbolic of our relationship) was significant. Of course the key was not defective; it was a perfectly normal key. I would have had to put immense pressure on it to break it; I recall I was actually rather calm.

It happens to be Clapton's profession to teach such problematic subjects. 'I know all the wrinkles in this field – but I can't even now dismiss the experience.'

'On Tuesday 30 July 1985,' 'Mary Wall' recalls (with the help of her diary), at 11 pm I sat down to think about my ex-lover, a hundred miles away. He had treated me very badly, I was bitter and furious and felt that, lest I made myself ill with rage, I should try and let a bit of my anger out. For an hour I thought vengeful thoughts about the 'swine' and imagined all his pictures falling off the walls of his room (adolescent anger frequently has a juvenile side to it). After this hour of concentrated rage, I felt much better.

About a fortnight later I rang him in an attempt to regain contact. He told me that one calm summer night he and a friend who was staying with him had been chatting in his bedroom when suddenly, a tremendous gust of wind had burst open the bedroom door, swept around the room, and blown the pictures off the walls. Shaken, he and his friend had joked about 'ghosts' (he was very sceptical). Stunned, I asked him if he remembered what night it was. July 30th, around midnight, he told me.

'Please believe me,' Mary Wall concludes, 'few people do! It's such a relief to find that such occurrences are being objectively assessed.'

Flammarion, intrigued as he was by the vagaries of wind, would have enjoyed that coincidence.

5

Explanations

Anybody without preconceived theories as to how coincidences come about would be likely, at this stage, to agree that although chance must be responsible for many of them, and others might well have some simple explanation, there is a good case for investigating the whole subject, if for no other reason than that they arouse great interest, sometimes apprehension, and doubtless often misapprehension. This has been the belief of two eminent Harvard University professors of mathematics, Persi Diaconis and Frederick Mosteller (emeritus). Their findings from ten years of research have been appearing in academic journals and were summarised in the *New York Times* Science Times section on 27 February 1990.

Defining a coincidence as 'a surprising concurrence of events conceived as meaningfully related, with no apparent causal connection', they have been applying probability theory to great numbers of accounts (Diaconis has two hundred folders full of them). To those of their academic colleagues who sneer at so undignified a line of research, they point out that coincidences are 'an important source of insight in science and so should not be dismissed out of hand'. A 'cluster' of them may turn out to be meaningful, prompting a new and profitable line of research.

From their investigations, Diaconis and Mosteller have found that coincidences fall into three main categories.

Some have hidden causes and are thus not really coincidences at all. Others arise from psychological factors, like selective memory or sensitivities, that make people think particular events are unusual whether they are or not. But many coincidences are simply chance events that turn out to be far more likely statistically than most people imagine.

Their conclusion is that virtually all coincidences can be explained by some simple rules.

The role of statistics

The most important contribution Diaconis and Mosteller have made
to the study of coincidence lies in the application of their statistical
analysis to those cases where it needs to be applied. Coincidences
which have been hailed as astonishing, they have shown, are not really
surprising, at all. When a New Jersey woman won a lottery twice
within four months, for example, this was widely reported as
astonishing, the odds against it being estimated at 17,000,000,000 to
one. So many lotteries are run in the United States, however, and so
many people buy tickets, that statistically, Diaconis and Mosteller
estimate, the odds are only 30 to one against somebody winning twice
in four months.

The statistical method, though, ceases to carry so much conviction
when it is applied to human interactions – as distinct from actions. In
1979 the *Daily Telegraph* reported that Peter Hill, playing on the
Cherry Lodge golf course near Biggin Hill in Kent, had done a hole in
one; his opponent, Peter Simner, thereupon also did the hole in one.
Probability theory can be applied to an event of this kind, as indeed it is
by bookmakers: according to the paper's columnist Peterborough,
Ladbroke's make the odds against a hole in one 900–1, against a repeat
performance, 800,000 to one. Obviously, though, in the Cherry Hill
case, these figures are not accurate representations of the real odds.
Anybody who has played golf would know that Peter Simner's tee
shot must have been affected by what he had just witnessed.
According to his temperament – and temper – he might have been
amused, annoyed, or exhilarated. Whatever his reaction, it would
have affected his swing. The odds against his doing the hole in one,
therefore, would have depended on imponderables out of a statistician's reach. Although the statistical estimates may be startlingly
accurate over great numbers of people, even of golfers, they cannot be
applied to two, where one is reacting to the other.

The fallacy of applying probability theory in cases where there are
reactions, or interactions, between individuals is increasingly often to
be encountered in party conversation. To illustrate their contention
that many coincidences are predictable chance events, Diaconis and
Mosteller point to the, at first sight curious, fact that there only need to
be twenty-three people in a room for it to be evens that two of them
will share a birthday. Nothing wrong with that: it is the interpretation
which is all too often put upon it which is at fault.

What happens is that two people at a party discover they have the same birthday. 'What a strange coincidence!' they say, and tell other guests. One of them, however, may have picked up a smattering of probability theory and, if there are twenty-three or more people at the party, will point out that there is nothing strange about the coincidence. Properly speaking, in fact, it should not be regarded as a coincidence at all, as it can be traced to a simple cause: the laws of chance.

This increasingly often encountered interpretation of probability theory, that no coincidence is involved in the *discovery* by the two people of the shared birthday, is misleading. Probability theory extends only to providing an estimate of the likelihood that two people at a party will *share* a birthday; it cannot provide an estimate of the likelihood of their meeting, which may depend on the assiduity with which their hostess rushes round introducing strangers to each other.

Nor can it gauge whether, if the two are introduced, their conversation will come round to birthdays – which may depend on whether they both happen to have an interest in horoscopes.

Still less can probability theory assess the likelihood of the discovery of a shared birthday being meaningful, in the sense of appearing to be the product of design. At a party in Dublin the Irish actress Jeananne Crowley met a woman she knew slightly; in conversation they found they had the same birth date; then, that they were actually born on the same day. Their conversation, which without that coincidence might have languished, led on to an introduction to the director who was casting the Granada Television series based on Somerville and Ross's *The Real Charlotte*, and to the appearance of Jeananne in the title role when the programmes were broadcast in Ireland in 1990.

Chance

Diaconis and Mosteller may have had no preconceptions about what coincidences *are* but they make no secret of their presumptions about what they are *not*: 'there are no extraordinary forces outside the realm of science which are acting to produce them.' Diaconis was a founder member of the Committee for Scientific Investigation of Claims of the Paranormal, an organisation whose members are dedicated to demolishing such claims; and he has not changed his disbelief. Nevertheless his acceptance of 'hidden causes' will serve as an escape hatch, in considering the various explanations that have been, and are, on offer. First, and foremost, must be chance.

It is perhaps not a matter for surprise, Plutarch remarked in the introduction to his life of Sertorius, 'if in the lapse of time, which is unlimited, while fortune is continually changing her course, spontaneity should often result in the same incidents.' Two celebrated men, both Atteis, had each been killed by a wild boar; there had been two Scipios, 'by one of which the Carthaginians were first conquered, and by the other, cut up root and branch.' Of the warriors who had been most successful, thanks to a combination of daring and cunning, four had been one-eyed – Philip, father of Alexander the Great; Antigonus, one of Alexander's generals; Hannibal; and Sertorius himself.

Plutarch was mildly warning against too great a reliance on Fate, or other forms of intervention by the gods, in human affairs. A century earlier, Cicero had been even more forthright in *De Divinatione*, putting the case for chance intervening more often than was realised – for example, in what were commonly taken to be divine portents. A door which opened apparently of its own accord could have been blown open by an errant gust of wind, he pointed out; if the statue of a god was seen to perspire, the wind might be responsible for that too, as a wind from the south notoriously left moisture on walls. On balance, however, little attention was to be paid to the role of chance until the seventeenth century when the research of, among others, Pascal laid the foundations of probability theory, which was gradually to elevate chance to the status which led Flammarion to refer to it as the 'little god'.

The process of sanctification began through gamblers' mundane curiosity about how to estimate odds, but by the close of the eighteenth century Laplace, the French astronomer and mathematician, could note with awe how remarkable it was 'that a science which began with a consideration of games of chance should have become the most important object of human knowledge.' And it was Laplace who initiated the process which was eventually to leave 'coincidence' virtually synonymous in people's minds with 'chance'.

'The desire to penetrate into the future, and the ratios of some remarkable events to the predictions of astrologers, diviners and soothsayers, to presentiments and dreams, to the numbers and days reputed lucky or unlucky, have given birth to a multitude of preconceptions, still very widespread,' he commented in his *Philosophical Essay on Probabilities* (1812). Too often, insufficient consideration was given to 'the great number of *non*-coincidences which have made no impression, or which are unknown.'

It was the philosopher John Stuart Mill who effectively beatified chance. It had usually been spoken of as if it were 'in direct antithesis to *law*', he noted in *A System of Logic* (1843). 'Whatever could not happen, because it was contrary to nature's laws, was attributed to chance.' But 'whatever happens is the result of some law; it is an effect of causes, and could have been predicted from a knowledge of the existence of those causes, and from their laws.' It was incorrect to say that any phenomenon was *produced* by chance; nevertheless 'facts casually conjoined are separately the effects of causes, and therefore of laws.'

By this time acquaintance with probability theory was becoming an indicator of intellectual rigour, as demonstrated by Edgar Allan Poe's M. Auguste Dupin – Sherlock Holmes's forerunner – in *The Murders in the Rue Morgue* (1852). The discovery that a consignment of gold had just been delivered to the two women who had been found murdered had led the police to arrest the bank clerk who had brought it, in spite of the fact that the gold had not been stolen. 'Coincidences ten times as remarkable as this,' Dupin asserted, 'happen to all of us every hour of our lives, without attracting even momentary notice. Coincidences, in general, are great stumbling-blocks in the way of that class of thinkers who have been educated to know nothing of the theory of probabilities, that theory to which the most glorious objects of human research are indebted for the most glorious of illustrations.'

The next stage was the canonisation of chance. 'There can be no doubt that, however unlikely an event may be, if we (loosely speaking) vary the circumstances sufficiently, or if, in other words, we keep on trying long enough, we shall meet with such an event at last,' the Cambridge logician John Venn asserted in *The Logic of Chance* (1866). The great interest at that time in spiritualist mediums, table-turning and the beginnings of what came to be known as psychical research were disturbing positivists; they felt compelled to assert that chance could readily account for even the most remarkable and well-authenticated concurrence between, say, a dream or a vision and an actual event. Venn rammed this contention home. If a pair of dice were thrown for long enough, he argued, double sixes would eventually come up a thousand times running.

Now apply this result to the letters of the alphabet. Suppose that one at a time is drawn from a bag which contains them all, and is then replaced. If the letters were written down one after another, as they occurred, it would commonly be expected that they would be found to make mere nonsense, and would never arrange them-selves into the words of any language known to man. No more they would in general, but it is a commonly accepted result of the theory, and one which we may assume the reader to be ready to admit without further discussion, that if the process were to continue long enough, words making sense would appear; nay more, that any book we chose to mention – Milton or Shakespeare for example – would be produced in this way at last. It might take more years than we have space in this volume to obtain such works, but come they would at last.

The assumption that readers would be 'ready to admit without further discussion' so preposterous a notion was, and remains, typical of certain academic cults, particularly, though by no means exclusively, encoun-tered in schools of philosophy. But it was not seriously challenged; and the philosopher William Stanley Jevons concurred. Inevitably, people might sometimes be deceived 'by extraordinary, but fortuitous, coinci-dences,' he warned; but 'there is no run of luck so extreme that it may not happen, and it may happen to us, in our time.' Some people were greatly influenced by coincidences, he feared, even 'regarding them as evidence of fatality; that is, of a system of causation governing human affairs independently of the ordinary laws of nature.' Not so, he insisted; 'they must be attributed to chance'. Small wonder that by the turn of the century Flammarion was mocking chance as 'a minor deity'.

Venn's flight of fancy has remained in common currency ever since, though in an up-dated version; the man drawing letters of the alphabet out of a bag has been replaced by a monkey on a typewriter, churning out *Hamlet* – after, presumably, a period almost as long as the preacher in *Portrait of the Artist as a Young Man* promised his congregation they would have to stay in hell, if they committed a mortal sin: for ever. Whether or not present-day positivists would take Venn's claim literally, its implication that no coincidence can be so strange that it cannot be attributed to chance is accepted; and from that it has been all too easy a step to the contention that chance can be used as a safety net, to account for any coincidence for which no cause can be found.

Yet Mill expressly warned against this assumption. When no cause can be found a coincidence should not on that account be automatic-ally attributed to chance, he insisted: the frequency of its occurrence must be borne in mind.

Not, however, its *absolute* frequency. The question is not whether the coincidence occurs often or seldom, but whether it occurs *more* often than chance will account for; more often than might rationally be expected if the coincidence were casual.

In other words, if John Smith dreams the winner of a horse race the odds against chance being responsible are less than if he dreams two winners – and considerably less than if, as John Godley did, he dreams eight winners (see page 69).

It is this aspect of probability theory which is so often misunderstood. Fundamental to the theory is that each time you spin a coin, assuming that there is no bias (and that it does not, by some perverse fluke, land on its edge and stay there), it is evens whether it will come down heads or tails. If, however, you spin the same coin for long enough, although you will not be surprised to obtain occasional sequences of heads or tails, over large numbers the totals even out. As a result, a bookmaker will confidently give you odds against your obtaining any sequence you would wish to bet on, whether of heads, or tails, or a mixture of the two – say, H-H-T-H-T-T-T-H. The longer the sequence you hope to obtain, the greater the odds he will offer you.

It is not uncommon for people who use the monkey-on-a-type-writer justification for arguing that chance knows no frontiers, to base it on the assumption that the odds against the monkey typing the correct letter of the alphabet remain constant. Far from it: the letters in 'Who's there?', with which Bernardo opens the proceedings outside the walls of Elsinore, form a sequence. The odds against the monkey getting each successive letter increase astronomically.

At this point the argument may be advanced that this is beside the point: that given even more time, *Hamlet* would still be delivered in full. But when? one of the curious by-products of probability theory is that the greater the number of spins of the coin, the greater the likelihood that the sequences will cancel each other out. Given large enough numbers of people the outcome of their individual unpredict-able actions can, as a result, often be accurately predicted – as Laplace found: the ratio of births to the total population of Paris, statistics showed, varied little from year to year, 'and I have heard it said at the Post Office that in ordinary seasons the number of letters thrown aside on account of defective addresses changes little each year; this has likewise been observed in London.'

The way in which an accumulation of chance events can allow remarkably accurate predictions was lent confirmation in a court case in England in 1898. A journal, the *Rocket*, had offered a prize of £1000 to anybody who could predict the exact number of male and female births, together with the number of deaths, in London for the week ending 11 December. John Henry Hall, a Yorkshire butcher, bought 250 copies of the paper, cut out and filled up the coupons as required, and sent them off. In one of them he predicted that there would be 1342 male births; 1213 female births, and 1539 deaths. Checking these figures with the Registrar-General, Hall found to his delight that they were right, and he wrote to the *Rocket* to claim the prize.

According to the report in the *Yorkshire Post*, the proprietor of the *Rocket* stalled, until brought to court. He then claimed that Hall's coupon had not been checked because by accident it had been stuck together with another one. They were unstuck, in court, with the help of a kettle and not surprisingly the figures were found to be illegible. Was it possible, counsel for the *Rocket* then asked the jury, that anyone would be able to guess the exact number of male births, of female births and of deaths in London in one week? The jury decided that it was or, more probably, that the *Rocket*'s excuse of the coupons sticking together was dubious. They found for Hall.

The proprietor of the *Rocket*, however, had taken out what in effect was an ingenious insurance policy. He had earlier been charged, in connection with the competition, with running a lottery. The prosecution had successfully contended that winning the prize involved no skill, which made the competition a lottery, and consequently illegal; he had been fined £20. When the jury in the second trial found in favour of Hall, the *Rocket*'s counsel promptly claimed that he must be allowed to argue the case that, in view of the established illegality of the competition, the £1000 prize should not be awarded.

The following day the point was duly argued, counsel for the *Rocket* parading precedents to illustrate his contention that in such a calculation there could be no element of skill in arriving at the particular results. 'There were – he did not know how many – billions to one against anyone arriving at the accurate figures.' Hall's counsel replied that his client had clearly gone to a lot of trouble to obtain the information on which he could base his estimate. 'He could scarcely inquire at a house,' the judge facetiously interposed, 'when a baby was likely to be born (*Laughter*).' Nevertheless, as the issue was important, 'he was going to give a judgment which would enable the plaintiff to go to the lottery of the Court of Appeal if he wished, and try his luck there (*Laughter*).'

Hall did go to that lottery, as *The Times* reported the following December. The solution of the question did not depend upon mere chance, Lord Justice A. L. Smith decided. 'It depended very largely upon chance, but there was an element of statistical inquiry brought into it.' The other two judges concurred, and the court allowed Hall's appeal. It is unlikely that he benefited financially, however; when Alice Johnson, checking on the story, made inquiries a few days later, she was informed 'the *Rocket* and its late proprietor are both dead'.

This type of mass coincidence has continued to intrigue those who study it. It clearly baffled the celebrated literary lion Logan Pearsall Smith; but he was proud, he claimed in *All Trivia* (1918), to play his humble but necessary role as

> one of the unpraised, unrewarded millions without whom Statistics would be a bankrupt science. It is we who are born, who marry, who die, in constant ratios; who regularly lose so many umbrellas, post just so many unaddressed letters every year. And there are enthusiasts among us, Heroes who, without the least thought of their own convenience, allow omnibuses to run over them, or throw themselves, month by month, in fixed numbers, from the London bridges.

Warren Weaver has since provided some remarkable examples of mass coincidence. Examining the statistics of the New York Department of Health, he found that in the years 1955 to 1959 the average number of people each day who reported being bitten by dogs was 75.3, 73.6, 74.5, 74.5 and 72.4. 'One of the most striking and fundamental things about probability theory,' he commented, 'is that it leads to an understanding of the otherwise strange fact that events which are individually capricious and unpredictable can, when treated en masse, lead to very stable *average* performances.'

As Koestler asked in *The Roots of Coincidence*, however, 'Does it really lead to an *understanding*?' It does not explain *why* the average numbers of people posting letters with defective addresses, or reporting being bitten by dogs, should remain so constant. What it does, though, is to give a warning against chance being invoked to explain any and every sequence of coincidences, up to infinity. Chance evidently does not work in that way; it is self-compensating. The notions of the hand drawing letters out of a bag, the monkey-on-the-typewriter, are logic carried to *reductio ad absurdum*; they are also, in relation to coincidence, misleading.

Sequences of coincidences, in short, have a perfect right to be presented as evidence against chance. If Jack once, and only once, suddenly feels the urge to ring Jill, goes to the telephone, and is just about to pick it up when it rings, and Jill is on the line, the odds against chance are small. But the more often it happens, and for some people it happens very often, chance becomes a progressively less plausible explanation.

Crucial to Diaconis's case, however, is his assumption that 'there are no extraordinary forces outside the realm of science which are acting to produce coincidences'. If such forces exist, some of his case collapses. But he has left his let-out: some coincidences may have 'hidden causes'. It is this possibility, in fact, which he uses to justify his research: the discovery of a hidden cause 'can lead to a new understanding of a phenomenon', and consequently seeming coincidences may be 'an important source of insight in science'. What is the evidence for, and about, possible hidden causes – whether inside or outside science's present frontiers?

Human fallibility

First, though, it is worth examining the 'psychological factors' which Diaconis and Mosteller believe have the responsibility for some of the beliefs about coincidences; in particular, too great a readiness to accept the evidence uncritically.

The evidence may be flawed in a number of ways, among them, obviously, that there may be a straightforward explanation which, for some reason, has not registered, as in the curious case of the code words which Koestler cited in his 'Down and Across' section in *The Challenge of Chance*. Crosswords, he had found from accounts sent to him – and from personal experiences – are 'a favourite playground of library angels'.

Addicts are familiar with what one might call 'the echo phenomenon'; you find a rare word in a crossword which is unfamiliar or unknown to you and in the next few days it keeps cropping up in the newspapers and books; or vice versa: you are preoccupied with an idea and find it the next day reflected in the magic grid.

When he started writing that section, he had been preoccupied with Kammerer's 'clustering effect'.

Sure enough, during the first week of my labours, *The Times* crossword No. 12,427 carried this obliging light: *2 down: 'Close-packed groups of many desirous characters' (8)*. 'Clusters', of course (a hundred vile lusters).

As an inveterate *Times* crossword solver – the months when the newspaper was closed by an industrial dispute were painful to him – Koestler had many other cases he could cite; but the most impressive cluster, he felt, was the one in the *Daily Telegraph* in the weeks leading up to D-Day on 6 June 1944. Among the invasion code names were Overlord for the overall plan; for the naval operations, Neptune; for the artificial harbours, Mulberry; and for the beaches where the Americans were to land, Utah and Omaha.

The first code word appeared in the solution of crossword 5755 in the *Daily Telegraph* of May 3rd: Utah. The second on May 23rd: Omaha. The third on May 31st: Mulberry. The fourth and fifth – the principal code words – *both* appeared on June 2nd, four days before D day: Neptune and Overlord.

MI5 were called in to investigate. The crosswords had been composed by Mr Leonard Sidney Dawe, a schoolmaster who lived in Leatherhead, Surrey. He had been the *Telegraph*'s senior cross-word compiler for more than twenty years. He had not known that the words he used were code words, and had not the foggiest idea how they had come into his head.

The cluster remained unexplained, except on Kammerer's theory – chance could be invoked but only as a desperate last resort – until in 1984 Ronald French, a property manager, wrote to the *Telegraph* to claim that the responsibility had been his. As a boy at Dawe's school in 1944 he had become friendly with members of the American and Canadian forces nearby; he had learned the code words from them. Dawe had the habit of employing his class to make up the crosswords, later contributing the clues himself. French had used the code words without telling Dawe.

French's account was made into a BBC TV programme in the autumn of 1989. Its implication was that the issue could be considered

settled. The programme, however, unsettled it. The decision had
been taken that the original story needed to be reinforced with some
spurious love interest; and it was trivialised in other ways. So doubt
has remained: French's claim that he kept silent because of a promise to
Dawe sounded glib; he was unable to produce satisfactory corroboration; and his claim that he recalled laughing at Koestler's explanation,
telepathy, did not encourage trust in his memory, for Koestler gave no
such explanation.

Another possibility had been suggested to *Sunday Times* columnist
Godfrey Smith by Dawe's nephew, Anthony Ralph. Dawe was
sharing his house at the time with a deputy director of naval
construction who, because of his work on Mulberry, would have been
aware of the code words. There might, Ralph suggested, have been
'some extra-sensory perception between two powerful minds, each
concentrating on its own problems'. More probably, Smith feels, the
words could have been in open use at the time; 'after all, that's what
code names are for. It's the things and places they describe which are
really secret.' A curious element of coincidence remains; according to
French, crosswords were compiled months before they appeared. But
the episode can no longer be ranked among the most inexplicable of
clusters.

Embroidery

Clearing-up operations of this kind can be expected from time to time;
but there is no indication that they could account for more than a tiny
fraction of mysterious coincidences. A much more common source of
confusion is the temptation to embroider an account, consciously or
unconsciously, so that by the time it gets into print it may be far
removed from the original.

The difficulty – indeed, impossibility – of assessing how far an
account can be trusted is illustrated by one of the best known of
coincidences: Mark Twain's dream of his brother's death on the night
his brother died. Although his soul 'was built on the very fabric of
truth', his biographer Paine had to admit that Clemens 'lived
curiously apart from actualities'. He observed what was happening,

but the fact took place, not in the actual world but within his
consciousness, or subconsciousness, a place where facts were likely
to assume new and altogether different relationships from those
they had borne in the physical occurrence. It not infrequently

happened, therefore, when he recounted some accident, even the most recent, that history took on fresh and startling forms. More than once I have known him to relate an occurrence of the day before with a reality of circumstance that carried absolute conviction, when the details themselves were precisely reversed.

In ordinary circumstances this would be enough to rule Clemens' account of his celebrated dream – told, as it was, half a century later – out of contention as evidence to be taken seriously. But in his autobiography, where he related it in detail, he made the point that although he had told the story the evening after seeing his brother's corpse, he had not kept on telling it, because of a warning he had received from the Revd Dr Burton about the dangers of such repetition. A very extraordinary thing had happened to him many years before, Burton claimed, and he had told the story many times – just as Clemens had – 'for it was so wonderful that it always astonished the hearer, and that astonishment gave me a distinct pleasure every time.' But one day it occurred to him to check it with what had actually happened: 'I found that its proportions were now, as nearly as I could make out, one part fact, straight fact, fact pure and undiluted, golden fact, and twenty-four parts embroidery.' He had never told the tale again.

How much of Clemens' tale, Burton had asked, was embroidery?

'Well,' I said, 'I don't know. I don't think any of it is embroidery. I think it is all just as I have stated it, detail by detail.'

'Very well,' he said, 'then it is all right, but I wouldn't tell it any more; because if you keep on, it will begin to collect embroidery, sure. The safest thing is to stop now.'

That was a great many years ago. And today is the first time I have told that dream since Dr Burton scared me into fatal doubts about it. No, I don't believe I can say that. I don't believe that I ever had any doubts whatever concerning the salient points of the dream, for those points are of such a nature that they are *pictures*, and pictures can be remembered, when they are vivid, much better than one can remember remarks and unconcreted facts.

Whether or not Clemens' faith in pictures was justified, Dr Burton's advice remains sound. So does J. S. Mill's: one reason why coincidence stories were so often unreliable, he warned, was that they gratified 'the love of the marvellous,' providing incentives to falsify, 'the most frequent of which is the desire to astonish.'

Yet Mill was careful to make another point.

> There are cases, however, in which the presumption on this ground would be the other way. There are some witnesses who, the more extraordinary an occurrence might appear, would be the more anxious to verify it by the utmost carefulness of observation before they would venture to believe it, and still more before they would assert it to others.

Another, related, danger is that even if the coincidence is accurately reported by the person who experienced it, the truth may be diluted in the telling by other people. As Alan Vaughan has warned in his book, *Patterns of Prophecy* (1973), this can happen all too easily; as it has done in connection with perhaps the best-known of all recent prophecies, Jeane Dixon's, of a forthcoming assassination.

Reading Ruth Montgomery's *A Gift of Prophecy*, Vaughan came across her account of the interview which Jeane Dixon had given in 1956, in which she had forecast that 'a blue-eyed Democratic president elected in 1960 will be assassinated', a prediction which 'appeared in the *Parade* issue of 11 March 1956'. Checking, Vaughan found that there had been no mention of Jeane Dixon in that number of the magazine.

> Could it be that Mrs Dixon did not remember correctly, and Mrs Montgomery had so little research background, that it did not seem important to check it out? The issue of May 13, 1956, is the one that contains Mrs Dixon's prophecy, and it is different in precisely those details that had been formerly so convincing.
>
> The prediction as actually printed reads: 'As for the 1960 election, Mrs Dixon thinks it will be dominated by Labour and won by a Democrat. But he will be assassinated or die in office, "though not necessarily in his first term".'

Conceivably, Jeane Dixon's account to Ruth Montgomery might have been more accurate than the one which appeared in *Parade* (the interviewers did not stick to her words; they explained that they added 'will die in office' to 'will be assassinated', as less blunt). But if Ruth Montgomery was going to cite *Parade* it was rash not to look up the interview. Recently, the story has taken on yet another dimension; some of Jeane Dixon's admirers believe she actually named Kennedy as the assassin's victim.

Some embroidery is inevitable, given the anecdotal basis of coincidences. To carry weight, ideally they should be written down immediately after they are experienced, and the accounts corroborated by witnesses. Alice Johnson was fortunate in that she had both the time and the resources to check accounts, a formidable undertaking; no subsequent investigator has enjoyed the same facilities (Diaconis and Mosteller have been more concerned to assess whether the accounts they have received can be fitted into their statistical framework, than to check them out individually on the Johnson model).

Yet what this amounts to is that tales of coincidences share the disadvantages of all forms of anecdotal evidence. There is no reason to believe that they are less to be trusted that the reminiscences which authors collect and use in biographies of recently deceased men and women; caution needs to be exercised, but lack of corroboration, say, need not be regarded as automatically ruling an account out of court.

Concurrence

For convenience, 'concurrence' will serve in this context to cover those coincidences which can be traced to a common source, sometimes so remote that it is not recognised for a considerable time. Clearly this can be one of the 'hidden causes' Diaconis and Moesteller have in mind, when they insist that the discovery of the cause of a coincidence can be of importance to science. There have been cases, for example, where a doctor, when two patients turn up with identical symptoms, has been alerted to the fact that they may be the rare side-effect of a drug he has prescribed for them. It remains a coincidence that they should have both come to the surgery on the same day. That may be chance, or may itself have some hidden cause; but the discovery of the reason for it shifts it towards concurrence.

The history of science is littered with coincidences for which concurrence may be responsible. An idea or an event may catch the attention of researchers, so that they set to work and produce their findings at around the same time. An example often cited is the rediscovery of Mendel's treatise on inheritance in 1900 by three biologists working independently, one in Berlin, one in Vienna, one in Leyden, thirty-five years after Mendel's paper had been published, and sixteen years after his death; in the meantime, it had been ignored. That the three confirmations of his findings should have appeared almost simultaneously might have been chance; but it seems likely that concurrence played its part, the research having been stimulated by the pressing need to find how Darwinian selection actually worked.

Concurrence, however, can be stretched too far. It does not adequately explain the most remarkable coincidence in scientific history, the outcome of the fever which Alfred Russel Wallace contracted on the island of Celebes in 1858, when – as he was to recall in *My Life* (1908) – the idea came to him of the survival of the fittest. 'In the two hours that elapsed before my ague fit was over, I had thought out almost the whole of the theory; the same evening I sketched the draft of my paper, and in the two succeeding evenings wrote it out in full, and sent it by the next post to Mr Darwin.'

Darwin had been brooding over his theory for years. Sir Charles Lyell had warned him that if he delayed too long before publishing, he might be forestalled. 'Your words have come true with a vengeance,' he wrote sadly. 'I never saw a more striking coincidence; if Wallace had my MS sketch written in 1842, he could not have made a better short abstract.' He even felt that it would be dishonourable to publish his paper. Lyell had to persuade him to allow it to be read to the Linnaean Society at the same time as Wallace's.

Concurrence would be easier to accept as an explanation if there had been a build-up to the discovery. But as the biologist Sir Alister Hardy emphasised, although there had been speculation about evolution, the conception of the survival of the fittest was entirely unexpected. It even, at first, 'fell completely flat' – so flat, in fact, that in his 1859 presidential address, reviewing the Society's proceedings, Thomas Bell actually lamented that 1858 had not been marked 'by any of those striking discoveries which at once revolutionise, so to speak, the department of science on which they bear; it is only at remote intervals that we can reasonably expect any sudden and brilliant innovation.'

Still more remarkable is that the actual wording of the two papers is so similar. If Darwin and Wallace had been working together, the suspicion would inevitably have arisen that Wallace had simply cribbed from Darwin's paper, rewriting it to try to give the impression that it was his own work, but leaving it dangerously close to the original.

'Cumberlandism'

In the closing years of the Victorian era a music hall artiste, Stuart Cumberland, made his name as a professional thought-reader. He would tell volunteers who came up on the stage not merely what they were thinking, but what was going on in their lives; not by telepathy, but by observing their facial expressions and sensing their muscular tensions. These were conscious processes; the notion that the subliminal mind might be capable of performing a similar feat had yet to establish itself. Yet it seems highly probable that the common type of coincidence where two people who live together find themselves answering each other's unspoken questions, humming the same tune, and behaving in other ways as if mentally linked, can sometimes represent a type of unconscious 'Cumberlandism', as thought-reading of the kind he practised came for a while to be described.

The roots may lie deeper than simple thought-reading, as Edmund Wilson, the American literary critic, sought to prove. Although fascinated by ghost stories, he prided himself on his rationalist disbelief; and in the epilogue to *The Shores of Light* (1952), on his friendship with Edna St Vincent Millay, he took pains to explain a coincidence which had disconcerted him. He had come to admire her as a poet while she was still at Vassar, in 1916; when he met her in 1920 he fell in love with her – 'one of those women whose features are not perfect,' he recalled, 'and who in their moments of dimness may not seem even pretty, but who, excited by the blood or the spirit, become almost supernaturally beautiful.' When he asked her to marry him, she did not reject him outright; but while she was in Europe in 1923 she met and married a Dutchman; 'a very sound choice', Wilson admitted. After they settled at Austerlitz, in New York State, he saw her seldom; not at all between 1929 and 1948, and only once thereafter.

> The night of October 20, 1950, I had a long dream about Edna. It began with a kind of revival of the longing I had had for her in the twenties, which was more familiar to me than that in which I had seen her last; but then it turned into a conversation that was taking place in the present . . . The next evening I heard of her death, which had taken place the day before.

Finding 'chance' an unsatisfactory explanation, but determined not to concede the possibility of ESP, he constructed an elaborate alternative to both.

My dream was probably prompted by Sartre's book on Baudelaire, which I had been reading that night in bed and which must have led me to Edna by way of the translation of the *Fleurs du Mal* that she and George Dillon had made, which I had recently re-read and thought better of than at the time of my review of *Conversation at Midnight*. My dream was partly motivated, no doubt, by my wanting, in my sleep, to have somebody to listen to my literary gossip and somebody from old times to talk to but partly, I believe, also, by the impulse to console her in this vicarious way for the neglect that she, too, had been suffering.

Over-elaborated though Wilson's theory was, the possibility is that a dream which links up with an event may have an explanation of this kind, if it can be found. Nevertheless Wilson himself evidently felt that he had not quite covered his tracks. He might also, he admitted,

have had some sort of intuition about what had happened the morning before. I do not mean anything supernatural, but the kind of sympathetic sense of rhythms of another's life that may sometimes persist in absence, as I had, in 1944, the feeling that she needed support, at the time of her nervous breakdown.

Intuition
Of the possible 'hidden causes' of coincidence, one which is often suggested is intuition. But this presents a problem: what *is* intuition? Longing as most of them do for a harder edge to their soft science, academic psychologists have tended to treat the faculty with caution, even with suspicion, as the massive *Oxford Companion to the Mind* has noted; intuition's status has declined over the last century, 'perhaps with the increasing emphasis on formal logic and explicit data' in scientific circles. The Penguin *Dictionary of Psychology* brusquely dismisses intuition as 'a popular rather than a scientific term.'

Popular it has remained, and for many people it provides a possible explanation for the wide range of coincidences; among them the 'library angel' and 'lovers' ally' categories, which leave the impression that an intervener is at work. There is no agreed definition, but the *Oxford Companion*'s will serve: intuition 'is, essentially, arriving at decisions or conclusions without explicit or conscious processes of reasoned thinking.' Everybody has intuitions, from time to time; they can turn out to have been false alarms (or to have raised false expectations); but when they are acted upon, and the action is found to have been justified, the intuition, rather than chance, is often assumed to be responsible. For convenience, intuitions can be regarded as messages from the subliminal mind, pushing their way up into consciousness. The accounts sent in to the Foundation of the coincidences which are the outcome suggest that the subliminal mind has to use a variety of expedients to put the message across.

To take a hypothetical case: suppose you go out for a stroll, forgetting that you have left a kettle on a gas ring. You may simply remember what you have done, and decide to go back home; you may begin to feel uneasy, and decide to return for no reason that you can think of – until you arrive; you may suddenly realise that you have turned around and are walking home, without having consciously decided to; or you may feel what amounts to a compulsion to return, sometimes so powerful that it is as if you are being forcibly driven. The coincidental component is the discovery that if you had not returned, the water in the kettle would have boiled away, and you would have returned to find your house on fire.

In short, it is as if the subliminal mind is aware of the danger, and has used whatever means it has at its disposal to make you conscious of it, too. And in this particular instance, psychologists would probably accept intuition as the explanation. They would maintain, however, that no coincidence is involved (unless it so happens that you arrive home at the very last moment, just in time to prevent catastrophe). Such interventions by the subliminal mind are routine, they would argue, as when it jogs your memory to remind you that you have left something behind which you meant to take with you on the walk.

Most psychologists confine the use of the term intuition, if they use it at all, to cases where the subliminal mind jogs the memory into consciousness. Some people find this inadequate. In her auto-biography *The Infinite Hive* (1964), Rosalind Heywood described how throughout her life she had experienced what she regarded as 'Orders', consisting of 'an inner prompting to action or comment on behalf of other people which seems beyond my normal capacity, or absurd in the light of facts known to me at the time, but turns out to be relevant in the light of other facts learned later on.' To anybody who did not know her, Mrs Heywood could appear to be a conventional upper-middle-class housewife, married to a diplomat, in charge of the local Women's Voluntary Service during the Second World War, a governor of the English Speaking Union. Those who knew her, though, soon found that her 'Orders' were uncannily perceptive, as she would ring up with the solutions to their problems even before they had thought of telling her what the problems were.

As her friends came to know – Koestler among them – her 'Orders' resembled Socrates's in that they came to her at any time, often making her act against her inclinations, and were always justified; but unlike his, usually they prompted her to positive action. The coincidences became almost routine; 'Orders' would tell her, for example, that her husband was going to be coming back from the office on an earlier or later train. 'I could make Orders sound more respectable by calling them hunch or intuition,' she insisted; but they came out of the blue, as if from somebody else, 'and always as a surprise.'

Her implication was that her intuitions were prompted through a sixth sense. This is something which orthodox psychology finds unacceptable, but, to judge from the Foundation's correspondents, intuition is in common use in connection with both types, sensory and extra-sensory, of coincidence. Sometimes the distinction is not easy to make. Having dinner with a friend in 1980, 'Joan Harper' recalls, she expected to stay, as she usually did, until around eleven o'clock.

> I was just about to begin eating when I had the strongest feeling I should return home immediately. This I did and my husband had just had a massive heart attack. I was able to get medical help and he survived.

This has not been the only occasion when Mrs Harper has felt compelled to act out of character. 'I do not understand why,' she comments, 'but when danger threatens my family I do feel some force which I cannot explain.' She is careful to add, 'I am a senior administrator in Social Services, not normally given to flights of fancy.'

It could be argued, in this case, that her subliminal mind had picked up an advance warning of her husband's condition simply because she knew him so well. Some of the accounts of such experiences, though, rule out explanations of this kind. 'Marjorie' has had a number of them (she is epileptic, and used to suffer from 'petit mal' attacks in which she would sometimes have warnings in the form of visions). The most dramatic came at a time when her husband occasionally had to leave home before six in the morning to get to his job.

I was in the habit of getting up to get his breakfast and see him off before I dressed. As I was in my dressing gown, I did not go out into the front garden to see him off, as I should have done had I been dressed. On this occasion, I suddenly felt the compulsion to go down the path and watch the car until it was out of sight, as I knew I should never see it again.

On the M1, my husband drove over a nail, which punctured one of the tyres. The car, out of control, crossed two lanes and rolled down a 13-foot bank, just missing a railway line. Fortunately he suffered only a broken collar-bone, a cut ear and slight concussion, but the car was written off.

Although her epilepsy is completely controlled by drugs, 'Marjorie' comments, 'my "intuition" does not seem to be affected.'

Some migraine sufferers, too, report such experiences as occurring during their headaches. Suffering from one, 'Mary Farquhar' could not get the thought of an acquaintance out of her mind.

I had not seen this person for several months, and had no particular reason to think of her. The thoughts became so strong that I decided to cycle up to her home (some three miles away) despite a throbbing, painful head. When I arrived I found that she had taken an overdose of pills in a suicide attempt. I called the ambulance; her life was saved and I was there to care for her small children.

With most coincidences, 'there is just a startled second of perception, then the incident becomes buried in the mind,' Mary Higgs has found; but occasionally, 'something unforgettable happens'.

My father was killed in a road accident in Ireland in 1973. I lived in England and was busy doing my housework before dashing out to work. A dreadful thought came into my mind. I found myself making a *mental* phone call to my employer saying, 'My father is dead, I cannot go to work.'

For a moment I was shocked at my thinking (I knew my father was in good health). I laughed at my foolishness, and got on with the chores. Two hours later I was told of my father's death. I had to phone my employer and say the words which had come into my mind hours before.

In *Patterns of Prophecy* (1973) Alan Vaughan has related how one morning in Massachusetts Kurt Vonnegut, the author, left his study on an impulse, went to the telephone in the kitchen, and put through a long distance call to the office of his brother-in-law in New Jersey. 'I had never telephoned him before,' Vonnegut told Vaughan, 'had no reason to call him'. A news flash on the radio then announced a railroad accident without giving details. Vonnegut *knew* his brother-in-law had been on the train, though he had never taken it before.

Not long before she died, Lady Diana Cooper recalled in a contribution to Ben Noakes's collection that walking home through London after dinner one evening, she succumbed to a sudden urge to follow a fire engine – something, she claimed, she had never done before. It led to a house on fire in Bruton Street, which turned out to be her father's home, where she was born; and among the onlookers she found her brother.

The outcome does not have to be dramatic for intuitions of the compulsive type to leave the impression that the outcome – the coincidence – has been staged for the benefit of one, or both, of the people eventually brought together. Clio Mitchell illustrates the point. She lives in Paris, and one day when she had to catch a train from the Gare du Nord she set off from her Metro station.

For no reason that I could fathom, and I remember quite distinctly asking myself why I was doing it, I suddenly broke into a run. As a result, I no doubt caught an earlier Metro than I would otherwise have done. I then had to change Metros and go to wait on another platform for one of the very long Metros in Paris that also serve the suburbs. Having chosen quite at random a place at which to stand on the very long platform, I again suddenly found myself making a deliberate movement when the train arrived so that I got in one carriage further to the left, without having any idea why I felt impelled to make this adjustment. At the next station, a good friend got in, whom I had seen shortly before in England but I had no idea whatever that he would be passing through Paris on his way home from Italy on that particular morning. The station is the biggest and busiest in Paris, where I would never have been able to see my friend if he had not actually entered the same carriage. The next stop was the Gare du Nord, which was our shared destination. My meeting with him clearly came as a pleasant surprise for him, as he was somewhat preoccupied and downcast about the prospect of his return home.

Clio Mitchell feels that experiences of this kind are significant only as confirming that 'certain hidden orderings appear to exist in the universe that neither the rational nor the emotional side of my mind can accept as purely arbitrary'. The outcome was pleasant, if hardly meaningful,

but the peculiar way in which I found myself behaving in a curiously impulsive fashion, while being consciously perplexed as to why I was doing it, seems to find a very precise explanation in the encounter, which certainly would not have happened if I had failed to do either of those mysterious actions – the time and place of the incident seemed to be very precise points in an infinity of possibilities – my own vague timetable, the more precise ones of the trains and the enormous length of available platform space.

'Mrs Wilson' had a similar experience in the mid 1960s. During the war, when she was a toddler, her parents had taken in a twelve-year-old evacuee who had subsequently married a local man; they had taken a large house and converted it for Bed and Breakfast purposes.

On this occasion I don't *know* why I decided to *walk* (a fair distance) to a friend's house to deliver a birthday gift for her small son. It was an impulse.

As she reached the crossroads, a car drew up, and the driver asked if she knew of a Bed and Breakfast; he and his companion were on a visit, he explained; he had been stationed in the town during the war. 'Go to Mrs Lewis,' I told him, 'and say that Elaine sent you.'

That's strange, he said. I knew an Elaine when I was here then. She was a very small child and I used to meet the girl who lived with her; we would go for walks.
  I was the Elaine; the girl he remembered was the evacuee, now Mrs Lewis.

'You will see how the two coincidences coincide in such a peculiar fashion', Mrs Wilson comments, 'for not only did the man meet *me*, after so long, but I was sending him to stay with the person who was the link between us.'
  Intuitions, clearly, can be so powerful that they prompt a feeling of

compulsion. In the 1970s Susannah Amoore met the artist Stuart Scott Somerville, who lived in a Suffolk village. Over the next few years she often visited him and his family, never leaving without one of his evocative landscapes, or a still life. When she was appointed managing editor of the *Financial Times*, the work swallowed her up; apart from the odd Christmas card she lost touch with him, and eventually she heard he had died. Two years later she was sitting at home one winter evening, his pictures on her walls.

For some inexplicable reason I suddenly had the compulsion to get up and drive through near-darkness and heavy rain to a favourite art gallery in Barnes, before it shut. As I approached, I could see through the window a beautiful small portrait, propped on a chair, of a little girl in profile, wearing a black velvet dress. I was certain it was by Stuart Somerville, though I had never seen any of his portraits, and his paintings are rarely seen in galleries. It was indeed, an early Stuart Somerville. Only half an hour before, an unknown woman had come into the gallery, carrying the portrait through the rain. Certain even then that I was in some curious way meant to have the painting, and that was the reason I had come, I bore it home with love.

After she moved to the *Economist* in 1989, she was invited for a family lunch in Suffolk by her new colleague Mark Schreiber, the journal's lobby correspondent. On an impulse, she decided to visit Somerville's old home. There was no reply when she knocked, and she was just about to leave when a man trundling a wheelbarrow came along a lane towards the house. She recognised him as Stuart's eldest son, John. They reminisced for a while, and she invited him to lunch to her Richmond home to see her collection.

John was quite overcome to see the pictures filling my walls. But when I pointed to the portrait, told him of the strange force which had taken me to the gallery, and lifted the picture down to show him the name on the back, he went extremely pale, and sat down at once. Shaken, he told me that an elderly woman had written to him, saying her parents had been old friends of the Somervilles, and she remembered sitting when she was a little girl for her portrait. Might it be in Stuart's studio? She would love to trace it. John had vainly looked everywhere, in the studio and in attics, combing through the hundreds of paintings left by his father.

For some people, inexplicable intuitions prove so reliable that they are prepared to obey them even at considerable inconvenience to themselves. Relating some examples, Alan Duthie recalls that he suddenly had the impression that an obscure work he needed was in a second-hand bookshop in Kendal; 'the 90-mile round trip was worth it – the book was there.' At the end of his letter he added 'FCA' because 'it shows that chartered accountants, in whose veins ink, not blood, is said to run, a breed not normally associated with the mystical and spiritual aspects of life, may not be immune from the attention of "odd" forces.'

Understandably, though, intuition's interventions make the greatest impression when they appear to save the person involved from injury, or worse, as in one of the cases Frederic Myers, the psychologist and psychical researcher, included in his *Human Personality* (1903). D. J. Parsons, a doctor practising in Sweet Springs, Missouri, recalled how one evening in 1889 he went after supper to his office with his nephew John Parsons to investigate a case:

> Just as I stepped upon the door sill of the drug store in which my office is situated, some invisible influence stopped me instantly. I was much surprised, felt like I was almost dazed, the influence was so strong, almost like a blow, I felt like I could not make another step. I said to my nephew, 'John, I do not like going into the office now, you go and read Flint and Atkins on the subject.' He went, lighted the lamp, took off his hat, and just as he was reaching for the book the report of a large pistol was heard. The ball entered the window near where he was standing, passed near to and over his head, struck the wall and fell to the floor. Had I been standing where he was, I would have been killed, as I am much taller than he.

In an accompanying statement John Parsons recalled how he and his uncle were going to supper when a man stopped them, and asked for medical aid. 'My uncle requested him to call the next morning; as we walked along he said the case was a bad one, and that we would come back after supper and go to the office and examine the authorities on the subject.' Dr Parsons emphasised that it was not fear that had checked him from entering the office; 'I did not feel that I was in any danger, and could not understand what the strong impression meant.'

Mrs May Badman has often had intuitive experiences, 'knowing when a good or bad thing is going to happen, or a person I know well is going to ring, write or visit'; but one episode sticks in her mind 'because the intuition led to immediate action, and it feels strange to be motivated by something beyond one's will-power, or conscious will.'

> I often used the diesel train to town and for years had the habit of getting into the first carriage, hoping to get the seat beside the driver's compartment. I like to watch the track unfold ahead. One morning I was as usual at the end of the platform, but just as the train came in, I suddenly found myself running down the platform towards the end of the train. When the train stopped I was more than half-way down.
>
> The whole train was packed and I had to stand. When it arrived at St Pancras station, the train crashed into the buffers. In my carriage we were all thrown about but not seriously hurt. I was very shaken, and when I left the carriage and walked the length of the train, the further along I got towards the front the worse the situation of the passengers was, and near the front people were bleeding and crying. Five ambulances were called to take away the injured.

Mrs Badman recalls that as soon as she had got into the compartment, and managed to find a handhold, she forgot running down the platform; it was not until she had gone through the ticket barrier that she remembered.

Some of the saddest accounts sent to the Foundation have come from people who have had such urges, and have been too shy to act on them. Before 'Mrs Thorneycroft's' daughter returned to her university for her second term in 1983, she called on a former teacher who lived a few doors away. A day or two later Mrs Thorneycroft suddenly felt an overwhelming need to go and tell him how much she and her daughter had valued his teaching for the way in which it had broadened her understanding

> I got up from the rug and put on my shoes, walked to the front door, and then told myself that he would find my sudden appearance a bit odd; it was about seven o'clock; I could tell him, I decided, when we next met.
>
> The urge, however, remained very strong; so strong it surprised me. I had actually to restrain myself from visiting him there and then. The next day I heard that later that night the teacher had committed suicide.

For years, Malcolm Selkirk contrived to put various unaccountable happenings in his life down to chance, or to rationalise them in other ways; but after he read *The Unknown Guest* in 1988, 'so many things slotted into place that I began to realise that something more was at work.' Until his retirement, he had been in middle management in the financial world, his job involving him in a great deal of motorway driving and some of the 'happenings' occurred in the course of them.

In the space of five years there were no fewer than three occasions in which I found myself turning off the motorway at a junction, driving back to my previous junction and starting all over again on my journey.

'Why on earth are you doing this,' I asked myself aloud. 'It's stupid!' I could think of no explanation for my erratic behaviour except that 'something' had impelled me to back-track.

Proceeding beyond the junctions where I had first turned off, within a matter of a mile or two, on each occasion, I came upon a traffic accident where the police were just arriving. Comparing times and distances afterwards it seemed likely that, had I not doubled back, I would have been in close proximity to the accident when it happened.

All three incidents took Selkirk completely unawares, unsettling him to the extent that he had to pull up at the next service area to sit for a while and calm down. 'I drove many thousands of miles on motorways (without accident) during that period,' he adds. 'These three occasions stand out in my memory.'

Brought up in the countryside, Mrs J. Martin was scared of traffic in cities, hating to cross busy roads except at controlled crossings.

One day in a busy street I suddenly found myself running across a road almost in front of a truck, which was most uncharacteristic. On reaching the other side I heard a crash – a huge sheet of glass which had fallen off, and smashed on the pavement where I had been standing. I am sure I would have been very badly injured, or even killed, if I had not moved.

Mrs Martin has often pondered her action. 'I just seemed to act on an impulse – I found myself running – and at the same time a part of me was amazed at my own action.'

There is another very common, though more commonplace, type of intuition prompting coincidence; it is as if the 'intervener' provides a correct fact, or gives correctly the outcome of some event, which the percipient could not have known.

In perhaps the most remarkable recorded case, the 'intervener' was also a joker. In 1871 William Morris and some friends, about to set off on a tour of Iceland, bought some stores in London and arranged for their delivery. The following day a message came that the shop had included another customer's parcel in one of the packing cases, instead of the Bologna sausage they had ordered. If the shop wanted to make the exchange, Morris told them, they would have to come round the next day, or the case would be on its way to Iceland and they would eat whatever edible it contained.

Well, they never came; and here was the case, with the hidden and mysterious parcel in its bowels: many were the speculations as to what it was, on the way; and most true it is that I suggested (as the wildest possible idea), fragrant Floriline and hair brushes – now, in went the chisel and off came the lid; there was the side of bacon, there were the tins of preserved meat; there was the Liebig, the soup squares, the cocoa, the preserved carrots and the peas and sage and onions – and there IT was – four (was it) boxes of FRAGRANT FLORILINE, and two dozen bottles of Atkinson Bond Street scents, stowed in little boxes that had hair brushes printed on them.

We looked at each other to see if we were drunk or dreaming and then – to say we laughed – how does that describe the row we made . . .

Heading for Brittany on a ferry in 1989, the author Frank Smyth fell into conversation with a woman standing beside him on deck, watching the sunset. She turned out to be the landlady of a Welsh pub. When she asked him what he did, and he said he was a writer, she pulled a face: 'Oh dear, I have had to leave a writer in charge of the pub. I don't know if I've done the right thing.'

'Jack Howard,' I said. She looked at me with total astonishment.
'How the hell did you know that?' she asked. And I had to admit that I didn't know, nor do I to this day.

Frank Smyth had known Howard ten years before, when they had occasionally met in their local pub; he knew that he was Welsh and a writer. But he had not seen him since, and only rarely had Howard's name come up in the meantime. 'Certainly he's never worked in a pub, as far as I know, and much as he approved of them as an institution I don't imagine he'd enjoy running one any more than I would.'

Spontaneous perception of this type can be even more striking. In 1989 Patrick Stedham lost the note he had made to remind him of the Personal Identification Number to use when obtaining cash from a dispenser. Before the replacement number he requested arrived, he needed cash, and felt it was ridiculous that he could not remember the four-figure number he had so often used.

I sat down and thought, and there came into my mind a picture of the dispenser keyboard (which is how I seek to memorise these numbers) and my finger pressed 'bottom left, up one – press, across to the right – press twice.' However, the resultant number, 4766, did not strike a chord so I gave up. I think it was two mornings later I received notification of the replacement number. As I opened it, I had a strange feeling about what I would find, and sure enough there was my new number, 4766.

Stedham points out that the result came to him 'in the format not of a number, but of a keyboard display'; and, as the numbers are random-generated by computer, and printed through carbon paper onto a slip already sealed in a envelope, 'this number had never been in anyone else's mind.'

Several correspondents have had similar experiences, occasionally profiting from them. 'I can sometimes back a winner not on form, or on tips from owners or trainers, but by looking at the names of the horses in a newspaper,' one of them has found. 'I look at the list and one name seems to stand out, as if in black print.' A characteristic of this kind of intuition is that it can amount to a feeling of total certainty, which is only very rarely proved wrong; but that it is often wrong when the feeling is less strong. And those who are familiar with the experience are agreed that it cannot be induced; even to think about it while perusing a list of runners banishes it.

Some people enjoy spontaneous perception of this kind sporadically throughout their lives. Occasionally it is useful; more often it simply happens. On 5 April 1990 Judy Froshaug's son came in with a letter

from his bank in his hand. Gloomily he said, 'Guess how much?'
Without thought Mrs Froshaug said, '£43.10.' Her family were only
mildly startled when the figure turned out to be exactly right. It had
happened so often before.

Serendipity
Closely aligned with intuition is serendipity: the faculty of making
agreeable or useful discoveries apparently by accident, but in a way
that suggests guidance. Serendipity has obvious claims to be a
coincidence-promoter – if it exists. The editors of neither the
Dictionary of Psychology nor the *Oxford Companion to the Mind* have felt
it deserves an entry.

The reason is obvious: whereas intuition can be grudgingly
accepted so long as it does not imply the existence of 'extraordinary
forces outside the realm of science', towards which most scientists
share Diaconis's aversion, serendipity tends to assume the existence of
a force capable of exerting a 'pull' from outside on the subliminal
mind, taking control of it without the conscious mind realising what is
happening: the process described by George Russell ('A.E.') in 'A
Bibliophile', one of the essays in *The Living Torch* (1937).

Years before, A.E. recalled, he had gone for walks along the Dublin
quays where, as in Paris, booksellers set up their makeshift stands. His
companion had been the poet, Seumas O'Sullivan,

> and I remember how surely the rare book, the first editions,
> brought themselves under his notice. He did not seem to peer about
> or to look up titles. He dropped long delicate fingers, casually as it
> seemed, into a welter of books on a cart, and drew out what was
> rarest. It was attracted to him by some law of affinity like that which
> attracts iron filings to a magnet.

> When A.E. dipped his fingers into a cartload in imitation, nothing
> of any interest emerged. The reason, he speculated, was that he
> preferred whatever edition of a book was most convenient to read;
> whereas O'Sullivan held rare and first editions of books in reverence.

> Books did not recognise in me any lover of their rarity. The expert
> fisherman on our rivers does not know more surely that the fly cast
> will cause the fish to bite than the poet knew the unfailing attraction
> of the magnetism of his fingers. It was most amazing. There would

rise out of that pool of books a first edition of Shelley or Wordsworth, or a rare pamphlet. Or if he drew out a book of sermons, he knew by some instinct that it contained matter of literary interest.

O'Sullivan, A.E. had found, would bring home whatever volume he had found 'to discover what was the affinity between himself and the book, and he would find it.' When he found a first edition of Shelley with the title page and some ten pages missing, 'within a week he had discovered the title page, by itself, and the missing pages elsewhere.' Could it be that there are mysterious laws governing the relationship of books to book-lovers? Or was clairvoyance the explanation, through dreams? 'Either the book is animate and draws the booklover to itself that it may find a refuge for its old years, a shelf where it is honoured, or else we must fall back on the explanation of dream.'

Clairvoyance seemed the more likely explanation, A.E. had to admit; but he could not rule out the notion that there was more to it, as O'Sullivan's experience suggested. The poet had once, from poverty, been compelled to sell some of the precious books; after that 'books no longer came to his fingers with the trustful confidence of children to a kind guardian.' He could still *find* rare books, 'but it was not by any transcendental process like that which enabled him in those days of innocence before his fall almost unconsciously to pick up master-pieces.' Eventually, though, with poverty behind him, he recovered his former powers.

Serendipity features in many of the accounts the Foundation has received. On becoming engaged to be married, Peter Richardson determined that his fiancée would have 'a Very Special Ring; no High Street kitsch for my Anne'; but his intention had been frustrated until, on the day before the wedding, he was with her on a protracted and fruitless shopping expedition in Birmingham when she suddenly, and for no apparent reason, crossed a street, went down a dingy lane, and entered 'the grimiest, filthiest shop, whose windows were so opaque that all I could see were two cards of air-pistol pellets and three or four packets of foreign stamps.' He did not bother to go in with her, but eventually curiosity got the better of him.

Miles down a long, empty counter, there was Anne facing the shopkeeper, who sported a jeweller's glass and was inspecting the inside of a gold ring. 'We're trying to find how old it is,' she said. 'I like the look of it and it fits all right.'

I asked if I could have a look. When I saw what was engraved inside that ring, it was all I could do not to seize Anne and dance along the shop for joy. I just daren't say a word to Anne except, very quietly, 'This is it', lest she and I made an exhibition of ourselves. Instead I quietly paid the shopkeeper, pocketed the ring and led Anne to the first café we could find. Inside that ring was what I assume was purely a pattern number: 'A 23 P' – 'A' for Anne, '23' for the 23rd October (our wedding day); 'P' for me. Anne is wearing it to this day.

In 1981 Guy Lyon Playfair – author of, among other books, *If This be Magic*, a survey of the evidence for the mind's powers in healing – had a striking example of serendipity, when he was researching events at Fatima, in Portugal, in 1917, where tens of thousands of people believed they had seen the sun burst through the clouds and go round in zigzag circles: 'the most colossal miracle in history', a Jesuit had called it. After consulting the relevant papers in the British Library's newspaper repository in Colindale, Playfair was in the canteen having a sandwich and looking up at the clouds racing through the sky when suddenly they parted, and the sun came out through at least three cloud layers, its rays causing bright spots on their edges

> The lower cloud layer was moving faster than the upper ones, and for one or two seconds bright spots moved from one edge of the gap above to the other, giving a striking impression of a zigzag motion of the sun – a feature common to many of the eyewitness accounts from Fatima. Seen through moving clouds, I found, it is indeed the sun and not the clouds that appears to move, as it appears after each occultation. The whole sighting took place slap in the middle of my vision and the timing was exactly right. A few minutes earlier, and my attention might have been on my food and drink. A minute later, and I would have been on my way home.

It is ironical, Playfair thinks, that what could be regarded as a debunking of the Fatima 'miracle', and in itself was an entirely natural phenomenon, 'gave the impression that it took place when and where it did solely for my benefit. It taught me that if one applies the mind to a specific problem with enough determination, the solution is likely to appear, sometimes in the least expected ways.'

Most such experiences, though, are less dramatic; what has interested the Foundation's correspondents is the way in which, say, information which they are looking for appears quietly to be fed to them, from time to time, as if the 'intervener' is keeping an eye on them, helping them along. Tony Garner had a succession of such interventions after he became interested in an account of a polar expedition; periodically prompting him, until he eventually met the scientists involved.

This took from March 1987 to April 1988, and it appeared at times that I was receiving help from someone, or something. I felt like a ship in an ice field, in that when I seemed to have reached a dead end, a new lead would open up. I discussed this with a friend who suggested that it was due to the phenomenon of Serendipity.

I can see that what I have written does not seem very remarkable. I am a retired telephone engineer, not given to extrovert behaviour; yet such was the momentum of the search that I was able to persuade people to help. And in the end it led to my establishing a friendly relationship with the explorers.

Destiny

The simplest 'hidden cause' of coincidences is that they are pre-destined. 'Everything is governed by immutable laws,' Voltaire claimed in his *Philosophical Dictionary*. We are all 'toys in the hands of destiny.'

Support is lent to this assumption by a few remarkable instances of prophecy, the most striking being in Nostradamus's *Centuries* (1555). Most of them, admittedly, are vague, even opaque, but some have proved to be uncannily accurate: one quatrain, in particular. In James Laver's translation, it runs:

'By night will come into Varennes through the forest (of Reines) two married persons, by a circuitous route, Herne, the white stone, and the monk in grey, the Elected Capet; and the result will be tempest, fire, blood and slice.

In 1792 Louis Capet, the first king of France to be sanctioned by a vote of the Assembly, left Paris dressed in grey, with a wife dressed in white, by a circuitous route which took them to Varennes, where they were stopped; the outcome was the Terror, and the death of king and queen under the guillotine's blade.

Although there are obscurities – 'Herne', for one – this and other prophecies which came close to what was eventually to happen convinced Laver that his initial assumption that Nostradamus was a charlatan could not be sustained. 'Complete scepticism is as unwarrantable as complete credulity,' he concluded, 'and while I feel obliged to reject much that others have found in Nostradamus, I find myself quite unable to explain him away.'

Schopenhauer became convinced of the reality of predestination through a coincidence which occurred one morning when he was writing, with great care, an important business letter.

When I reached the end of the third page I took the ink-well, instead of the sand-box, and poured it over the paper; the ink ran off the desk to the floor. The servant came in at my ring, brought a pail of water, and began to wash the floor to get off the spots. While she was doing this she said: 'I dreamed last night that I took some ink spots off here by rubbing the boards.'

Sceptical, Schopenhauer taxed her with inventing the dream. She had already told it, she replied, to his other servant – who happened to come in to the room at the time, enabling him to ask whether she had heard of the dream. 'Oh, yes,' she told him; 'the girl had dreamed that she washed an ink spot off the floor here.'

There was no way by which the servants could have known what was going to happen, Schopenhauer decided; it had been an involuntary action on his part, a mistake. Nevertheless it must have been 'so inevitably determined that its effect existed, several hours in advance, as a dream in the consciousness of another.' It was the clearest possible demonstration, he felt, of his belief in 'the rigorous necessity of what happens, even of what is most accidental'.

If Schopenhauer was right, research into coincidence would become a waste of effort for the opposite reason to the one sceptics usually give – chance would be entirely excluded, as would all other possible causes, whether real, or undiscovered, or occult. Curiously, though, he had missed the obvious fallacy; if the girl had happened to tell him of her dream, he could have taken precautions to prevent it from coming true.

Believers in predestination now appear to be outnumbered by those who, dismissing it, use it to ridicule the case for precognition. If a dreamer really is 'seeing the future', they argue, the implication must be that the future is preordained. But there are many accounts, and not just of dreams, where perceptions of the future have led people to take some action they would not otherwise have taken, such as avoiding a predicted involvement in a disaster. The disaster duly occurs, but the dreamer escapes. It is, of course, open to a believer in predestination to claim that the dream warning, the decision to heed it, and the disaster were all predestined; but this stretches plausibility even further than the claim that all coincidences between an account of a dream and a later event, however close, can only be the outcome of chance.

In *A Vision* (1925), Yeats came close to providing predestination with an acceptable face, but the language was tortuous, and most people would share A.E.'s critical assessment. He had followed Yeats' mind, he claimed, 'I think with understanding, since I was a boy'; but he could follow it no longer – not, at least, in the direction *A Vision* had taken.

> I allow myself to drift apart because I feel to follow in the wake of Yeats' mind is to surrender oneself to the idea of Fate, and to part from the idea of Free Will. I know how much our life is fated, once life animates the original cell, the fountain from which the body is jetted, and how much bodily conditions affect or even determine our thought; but I still believe in Free Will, and that, to use the language of the astrologers, it is always possible for a man to rise above his stars.

The extent to which people accept A.E.'s version is hard to estimate; no two people have the same idea of the part it plays in their lives. Different terms, too, are used to describe it; not only the big three, Fate, Destiny and Providence, but also words like 'guidance', or the vague concepts used by people who do not care to commit themselves to a superstition.

When, in the course of a conversation with André Malraux, Koestler brought up the subject, Malraux replied in a dry, flat voice, 'Coincidence is the language of destiny'. Certainly throughout history and myth the two are powerfully linked, as they were in the most familiar case of all: the coincidence in myth by which Oedipus, warned by the pythoness at the Delphi oracle that he would kill his father and marry his mother, was led inexorably to the meeting with a stranger, the quarrel, and the death of the stranger – his father; and then to marriage to his mother.

In France, '*destin*', and in England, 'Fate' (with a capital F) are usually attached to myths of that kind; sometimes also to similarly doom-laden stories today where in retrospect the course of events leading to tragedy makes it appear inexorable.

'Destiny', on the other hand, usually does not command a capital 'D'. It commonly conveys a vague sense that something may be operating, from time to time, to nudge people in directions they need to take – and to make them uncomfortable if they fail to take them, as Gissing illustrated in *The Crown of Life* (1899).

On a visit to Liverpool, the book's central character, Piers Otway, had chosen without thinking the hotel where he proposed to stay. On arrival, the man he had come to meet recommended a different hotel, and Piers told the cabman to take him to it. 'But no sooner had the cab started than he felt an unaccountable misgiving, an uneasiness as to this change of purpose'; a feeling which became so strong that he told the cabman to take him to the hotel he had originally decided upon. 'A downright piece of superstition,' he said to himself, with a nervous laugh. He could not remember ever having behaved so capriciously.

At the hotel that evening he defended the Russians from a critic. In the room, without his knowing it, there was a young Russian, who came over after the conversation ended; 'they got along together, admirably'. Back in his room, there came into Piers' mind the inexplicable impulse which had brought him to the hotel. 'It helped a superstitious tendency of Otway's mind, the disposition he had, in spite of obstacle and misfortune, to believe that destiny was his friend'; and so it proved – as the book went on to show.

Novelists in fact provide an invaluable guide to their contemporaries' attitudes to coincidence, through the ways in which they exploit it in their books. Dickens often used improbable coincidences to lubricate his narrative, as in *Great Expectations*; whatever his own beliefs might have been, he did not hesitate to leave the impression that through them, destiny played a large part in Pip's life. E. M. Forster used coincidences even more directly. In *A Room with a View* they keep on bringing George and Lucy back together, until George bursts out, to Mr Beebe, 'It is Fate. Everything is Fate. We are flung together by Fate, drawn apart by Fate' – shocking Mr Beebe, who had once planned to write a book about coincidences, apparently with the intention of showing they did *not* support a belief in Fate. In his autobiography, H. E. Bates went a step further. Shaken by the coincidence of finding scenes from the novel he had written coming into his life in reality, and in awesome detail, a couple of years later, he recalled Oscar Wilde's remark that life imitates art.

Is it perhaps not also possible that imagination creates life, as it were, by some process of magical foresight, before life itself does? The temptation to say that all human life exists as in some of my stories, in some strange way, preordained? I wish I knew.

Novelists also reveal how the distinctions between the terms in use to describe what is preordained have become blurred. 'Providence' is now more rarely encountered except in the form of 'providential', and that can often be almost synonymous with 'lucky', but in *The Good Soldier* Ford Madox Ford, referring to 'one of those sinister and merciless proceedings on the part of a cruel providence that we call a coincidence', seemed to put it on a par with Fate. In 'The Purple Pileus', too, H. G. Wells described how when the henpecked husband Mr Coombes, leaving his home in a state of unendurable frustration, found that the path he took 'was planted with evil-smelling fungi', tempting him to commit suicide, he called it 'destiny'. Still, as Coombes' decision to eat some only led him to return home in so effectively belligerent a condition that his wife was cowed into submission, perhaps Wells was using the term in its usual sense.

One thing is obvious, from the Foundation's correspondence, as well as from fiction: a belief in destiny (even if the actual term is avoided) as a positive force in people's lives is widespread. It is not thought of simply as implying that life is preordained. On the contrary, it can allow and encourage interventions, often in the form of coincidences, to rouse people to introspection or to action, or to sound a warning. 'The element running through entire nature, which we popularly call Fate, is known to us as a limitation,' Emerson noted. But 'if we must accept Fate, we are not less compelled to affirm liberty, the significance of the individual, the grandeur of duty, the power of character.'

'The free man believes in Destiny,' as Martin Buber felicitously put it, 'and believes that it stands in need of him.'

Koestler had several intimations of its existence, and one in particular was to prove decisive in altering his life: a quick succession of 'grotesque events' one night in December 1931, the recollection of them prompting him to comment, in *Arrow in the Blue* (1952) that in his experience, 'the "language of destiny" is often couched in vulgar slang.'

He had established himself as the leading science correspondent in Germany. On this particular night he had lost the equivalent of several months' salary at a poker session and, going on to another party, he had got very drunk. Emerging at two in the morning, he found that because he had forgotten to take de-icing precautions the engine block of his car, which he had brought back from the garage only the day before, had burst. A girl who got on his nerves took him to her flat, and he woke up the next morning 'with a super-hangover mixed with self-reproach, anxiety and guilt, next to a person whom I disliked, financially broke and with a bust-up car.'

I have always held a perhaps superstitious, but deep belief in the significance of events which come in series. When major and minor calamities crowd together in a short span of time, they seem to express a symbolic warning, as if some mute power were tugging at your sleeve. It is then up to you to decipher the meaning of the inchoate message. If you ignore it, nothing at all will probably happen; but you may have missed a chance to remake your life, have passed a potential turning point without noticing it. It is not an altogether naive superstition if one concedes that such series are often produced by unconscious arrangement.

The series of misadventures that night 'looked as if they had been arranged by a crude jester; but the face of a clown, bending close against your own, can be very frightening.' By the time he got back to his flat he had decided that the life he was leading, 'climbing the worm-eaten ladder of success', was destructive; he joined the Communist Party, and his career took on its drastically altered form.

Koestler was not then using the term 'series' in Kammerer's sense; his experience, in fact, could have come closer to Jungian synchronicity. At the time, though, he had not begun to investigate coincidence; he was simply speculating whether the sequence of events, linked as they were to their outcome, provided evidence for destiny, in the loose sense of some unexplained force manipulating events to change people's lives. His experience impressed him because it was squeezed into twelve hours, but it appears to be more common for the sense of destiny to come to people through a drawn-out sequence of events, often trivial in themselves, the element of coincidence being provided by the feeling, in retrospect, that a guiding hand has been at work.

One of the most remarkable series of coincidences pointing to such guidance has been experienced by Ann Victoria Roberts, the author of *Louisa Elliot*. As a child, she was given a diary kept by Liam Elliot in the trenches during the First World War until he was killed in 1917. She was deeply moved by it and eventually, married and with a family, she felt compelled to write a novel around it. A fortunate meeting in a library precipitated a succession of 'library angel' episodes and other coincidences, pushing her into writing a book on a much more ambitious scale than she had originally planned. The coincidences, usually trivial in themselves, were cumulatively significant for her; 'All the time I was working on the book,' she recalls, 'I felt quite strongly that I was being nudged by some mysterious power' – and it was not to lose its hold on her during the six years before the book was finished. Twenty years earlier she had written a novel which had failed to find a publisher. Not merely did *Louisa Elliot* become a best-seller: on the strength of her synopsis for a sequel, based more specifically on the life of the soldier himself, a publisher in the United States secured the rights, after a four-day auction, for $900,000. She surmises:

Perhaps we do have guardian angels, after all, who love us and guide us and try and keep us on the right track – the track that is right for us, I mean. I do know this – that once I'd begun to suspect that other hands were at work in my life, I stopped questioning those strange impulses and just went along with it all.

The process may be less dramatic, yet leave the same impression. On 26 April 1988 Harriet Llewellyn came home from work 'and announced out of the blue that I felt we had to live in France'. Her husband agreed, though it meant totally changing their lives; but he had to finish his degree as a mature student, so they decided to postpone departure for fifteen months. That autumn, however,

he arranged an exchange visit to a university in France. In France he found 'our house'. I was unenthusiastic. While agreeing it felt right, it was much too expensive, and he had found it nine months too early. With very little persuasion, the vendor drastically dropped the price and agreed to defer payment for nine months. It felt to us both as if unseen hands were pushing us. We did move, in July 1989, and have found a perfect happiness – a rightness – *a coming home*. It is better than our wildest dreams.

In November 1936, Tom Girtin recalls, Monica Don paid one of her infrequent visits to London; and while she was there her oldest friend rang to say that she and her husband had a terrible evening ahead of them: an amateur performance of *Beggar on Horseback* at the Rudolf Steiner Hall; would she go with them to lend moral support? She allowed herself to be persuaded.

On opening her programme she read

Butler . . . . . . Tom Girtin

'Tom Girtin! That must be the little boy I met at Epsom!' It was indeed. Nineteen years earlier, when she was 16 and I was 3, she and her mother had paid just one visit to my parents' house. 'He was a little boy in a round grey felt hat and gaiters!' she remembered.

We all went on to the Café Royal after the show; I saw her home to Belsize Park – and from then on there was never another woman in my life. We had 44 very happy years together – of which 36 were married.

'If ever a union was meant,' Tom Girtin believes; 'and brought about by a series of pure coincidences – ours, I believe, was that one.'

In 1958, when he was 16, John Highley was a soloist in a brass band which won a national competition. If for some reason a band needs a substitute, the rule is that they must take somebody from the band playing immediately before them; he was called for as a substitute by a National Coal Board Colliery Band, which came second. The secretary thereupon asked him to join them, saying he could be found an office job at the colliery. He declined, explaining that he wanted to stay on at school to get his 'A' levels, and then go on to university. By 1966 Highley had obtained a degree in chemical engineering and was working as a research assistant at Bradford University.

I travelled to work by bus, and the journey involved a change at the town centre, where I bought the *Guardian* every morning. One morning I overslept and missed my first bus (this happened occasionally); and when I went to buy my paper, I found they had run out of *Guardians* (this was the first time in two years). I bought a *Telegraph* instead, and decided to look through the job advertisements. In the small ads there was a description of a job which was concerned with the specialist area of engineering on which I was working. I exactly fitted the qualifications and experience required

The coincidence of being led to the advertisement was so strong that I immediately knew I would be appointed. I applied and within two weeks had an interview and was given the job. It was at the Research Establishment of the National Coal Board. The job was advertised only on that day.

Two years ago, Highley left the Research Establishment to become a tutor at the NCB's management training college – a position which he could also have arrived at if he had joined the NCB at 16. 'I feel that I was destined to work for the NCB, and to come to this point in my career.'

Sometimes it is as if destiny is determined to get its way, in spite of the indifference of the person involved.

Having had two marriages which had foundered, and with three teenage children, Valerie Press decided, 'no more marriage for me!' At a surprise ruby wedding party she gave for her parents, old photograph albums came out which her children had never seen, with some pictures of Valerie and her first boy friend, David, with whom she had 'gone steady' between the ages of 15 and 20.

I hadn't seen him for twenty years; nor did I know anything of his whereabouts. My eldest daughter said, 'I know him – I've seen him. He has a shop that sells clothes.' She was vague and I wasn't interested in pursuing the matter. That week I had to go shopping and my daughter asked me to return a skirt she had bought. I went to the shop and collided with David outside – his shop was next door (I didn't know). Four months later David proposed.

The day on which Mrs Press wrote this account was their wedding anniversary; 'We have spent ten loving years together.'

Sometimes people who have come to think of themselves as coincidence-prone, but otherwise have not taken the subject seriously, are eventually shaken by some explosive event – as Harriet Stanford was. Her husband, a teacher, used to drive to a job he had on certain evenings. One afternoon, before he left, a fearful foreboding overwhelmed her; she even felt she heard glass shattering in her subconscious: 'Worse, my tiny daughter kept saying, "What is death?" over and over again.' After he had left, when it was too late, she felt a strong urge to warn him; and later that evening, when she became sure something dreadful had happened, she became upset that she had not heeded the afternoon's frightening warning. At midnight a policeman arrived to tell her that her husband had been in a ghastly crash, and had to be cut out of his car; he was unlikely to survive ('by some miracle he did, but with permanent injuries'). 'This served as the first real warning to me that one must heed these things,' she comments. Now, she accepts Fate.

'But not,' she adds, 'in the usual sense of Fate – I do not know what that is.' Evidently many people feel the same: that it leaves too negative an impression. They feel more at ease with the idea of a guide, or protector, sometimes offering a lifetime's assistance – occasionally with coincidences providing it, as they often did for Sir Winston Churchill; starting with the one which enabled him to take part in the cavalry charge which routed the Dervishes at Omdurman.

Serving with the Indian army at the time, Churchill had come to the conclusion that it offered insufficient scope for his ambition; he must wangle his way to Egypt. Already, though, he had made himself unpopular by openly criticising his superior officers in despatches to the newspapers. Kitchener did not want to have him; and the Adjutant-General would not listen to the pleas from the influential men and women Churchill had enlisted in his support.

'The way seemed firmly barred,' his biographer Lord Birkenhead recalled, 'but at this black moment Winston had one of those extraordinary strokes of luck that make one think that some protective Providence was certainly watching over him.' Lord Salisbury, the prime minister, happened to read and enjoy Churchill's account of the campaign he had fought in on the North-West Frontier. Finding Winston was on leave, he invited him to lunch, and Winston seized the opportunity of the lunch to ask Lord Cromer, effectively the British governor in Egypt, to intervene to override Kitchener. A few days later he heard that 'his intrigues in high places had brilliantly succeeded, and the wishes of the mighty Kitchener had been ignored.'

Two years later Churchill was in South Africa, working for the *Morning Post*, when he was invited to join an expedition against the Boers in an armoured train. He did not want to go but, as he told his fellow war correspondent J. B. Atkins of the *Manchester Guardian*, 'I have a feeling, a sort of intuition, that if I go something will come of it.' The train was ambushed by the Boers; Churchill, after displaying great coolness under intense fire while he tried to free the engine, was taken prisoner. But the episode which most impressed him was the coincidence which facilitated his escape from captivity, and the way in which it came about.

Plodding along the railway line towards Mozambique, almost exhausted, he saw lights in the distance which he took to be from a Kaffir kraal. Should he approach? Or would the Kaffirs hand him over to the Boers? 'Suddenly, without the slightest reason, all my doubts disappeared,' he recalled in *My Early Life*. It was not by any process of logic; 'I had sometimes in former years held a Planchette pencil and written while others had touched my wrist or hand. I acted in exactly the same unconscious or subconscious manner now.' It was not a Kaffir kraal, he found; it was a mining community. But he felt he had to take a chance, and he knocked at the door of one of the houses. Suspicious character though he must have appeared – the owner took care to cover him with a revolver – he was allowed in, and confessed his identity. 'Thank God you have come here,' his host told him. 'It is the only house for twenty miles where you would not have been handed over.' Churchill had happened on one of the few Britons whom the Boers had allowed to stay on, who was able to smuggle him out to Mozambique.

In the First World War, Birkenhead felt, Churchill could reasonably, with Macbeth, have boasted 'I bear a charmed life' – but with more justification; he could have lived the relatively plush existence of a staff officer, but he insisted on remaining in the trenches. On one occasion his dugout was wrecked by a shell just after he had left. On another, after he had been given command of a battalion, a shell landed in a room next to the one in which he was having lunch with some fellow officers, covering them with debris but leaving them unharmed.

Once during the Second World War, too, a coincidence saved him. According to his wife Clementine, he always automatically entered the nearside door of his car. But on one occasion during the Blitz he paused, then walked round deliberately and let himself in the other side. On his way back to Downing Street a bomb exploded, lifting the car up on his side so that it almost overturned, as it would unquestionably have done had his weight been on the other side. Why, she asked him, had he changed his mind? At first he said he did not know. Then, 'Of course I know. Something said to me "Stop!" before I reached the car door held open for me. It then appeared to me that I was told I was meant to open the door on the other side, and get in and sit there.'

Small wonder, then, that Churchill came to accept the existence of a form of destiny. 'I sometimes have a feeling – in fact I have it very strongly – a feeling of interference,' he told an audience of miners in 1943. 'I want to stress it. I have a feeling that some guiding hand has interfered.'

In Churchill's case, the guiding hand appears usually to have been a protector, keeping him, or rescuing him, from scrapes. For Ardus Salam, Professor of Theoretical Physics at Imperial College, London, winner of a Nobel Prize for Physics in 1979, coincidences have been the other kind – promoters.

Initially he had no intention of becoming a scientist. He meant to join the Indian Civil Service, and to make sure of a place he concentrated on his best subject, mathematics, but because of the war the examinations were not being held. Scholarships had just been made available from a Punjab welfare fund, however, to enable the sons of families with small peasant holdings to go on from Lahore University to Cambridge. He was the only student to qualify, that year – and by the following year partition had come in, and the scholarships had disappeared. 'The only purpose of that fund and those scholarships,' he told Professor Lewis Wolpert in a BBC radio interview, 'seemed to be to get me to Cambridge.' There, he became hooked on research in nuclear physics.

'Did you really think that Fate was playing a hand?' Wolpert asked him. 'After all, each of these events was very much a matter of chance.' Salam did not commit himself; but his father, he recalled, 'always said that this was a result of his prayers.' The whole sequence, however – 'my getting a scholarship at the right time, my getting to Cambridge at all at the right time, and then being interested in science' – was, his father thought, 'very much a part of something deeper.'

In a letter to the novelist Francis Stuart, Lord Glenavy – father of Patrick Campbell, familiar to television viewers for the remarkable way in which he mysteriously managed to turn his stammer into an asset – wrote during his last illness of the extraordinarily good fortune which he had throughout his life, 'unsupported by any aims or ambitions on my part'. A civil servant, Glenavy had become Governor of the Bank of Ireland by a succession of (as he thought of them) lucky breaks. 'It has left me with the superstition that there was some function of significance which I was being facilitated to discharge, but of which I have never been able to conceive.'

For the Independent Television News correspondent Michael Nicholson, lucky breaks have an uncanny way of turning up, to bring him to the right place at the right time. 'It can happen again and again,

there's got to be a reason for it,' he told Ena Kendall in an interview for
the *Observer* series 'A Room of My Own'; 'someone is looking after
you.'

A few people claim that they have actually begun to learn from
coincidence what destiny has in store. In 1977 Dr Steve Wright, a
postgraduate student at Lancaster University, was engaged in research
in the controversial area of the development of new police tech-
nologies for use in social and political control. His wife grew worried,
and one night they had quite a heated row about it.

> I said to Christine that she didn't understand the nature of my work
> and that one day it would come walking through that door – a
> strange thing to say.
>
> Early the next morning, two car loads of Special Branch officers
> arrived, demanding access to all my university research. Both my
> wife and I were frightened out of our wits. Yet because of the
> argument the night before there was a bizarre sense of 'I told you so'
> and a grim determination not to be flustered.

The officers took Wright to the University, the first time a British
university had suffered such a raid (an action later roundly condemned
in the press and in parliament). As his research in this area has
continued, from time to time it has put him again at risk.

> The 'warning phenomena' have occurred on several occasions and a
> pattern has emerged. There is usually a cluster of noticeable
> coincidences which alerts me to be more aware and careful of
> undercurrents. Sometimes it's as if an unusual turn of phrase pops
> out, in ordinary conversation, and – for want of a better term –
> 'reverberates'.

There is a sense, he admits, in which this does not permit him 'to
change the structure of what is about to happen; but the giving of the
warning can potentially change the outcome.'

The stars

Every day, millions of people read their horoscopes in the newspapers
and magazines. There is no way of estimating how much influence
they exert; people who insist they read the 'What The Stars Foretell'
columns for amusement rather than for instruction may in fact be

taking the predictions seriously from time to time, particularly when they happen to seem particularly pertinent. But until very recently astrology was not taken seriously even by psychical researchers, for whom the whole subject was virtually taboo. Manifestly, the assumption was that belief in the power of planetary positioning at the time of birth to influence lives was untenable; it would be demeaning to investigate so palpable a superstition.

Occasionally campaigns would be waged against astrology, on the ground that its practitioners were earning their fat incomes by false pretences; and in 1975 it was formally denounced by 192 leading scientists, including nineteen Nobel prizewinners. It could only contribute to 'the growth of irrationalism and obscurantism,' their manifesto claimed. 'We believe that the time has come to challenge directly and forcefully the pretentious claims of astrological charlatans.'

This caused some surprise: why crush a butterfly upon a wheel? A BBC producer asked some of the Nobel laureates to come on a programme to explain the need for the manifesto: the gist of their replies was that they did not know enough about the subject to discuss it.

That so many of them should have signed without giving a thought was, on the basis of current scientific dogmas, predictable; why, though, had the issue been brought up at that time? Such reactions have usually occurred when a dogma is threatened; and this one had in fact come under threat in the early 1970s, as the news spread that research conducted by Michel Gauquelin and his wife Françoise was showing that astrology is not the pseudoscience scientists had taken for granted it must be. Astronomers were particularly concerned; Bart J. Bok, Professor Emeritus of Astronomy at Harvard, had taken the initiative in the denunciation and many of the signatories held academic posts in astronomy and astrophysics.

The principle upon which Gauquelin worked was so simple that it remains strange nobody had thought of it before (though if anybody had, he might well have been daunted by the labour involved). In France, birth certificates give the time as well as the date and place of birth. It should be possible, Gauquelin reasoned, to check whether planetary positions at birth have an influence on later life by finding whether there was any manifest coincidence between what, in effect, were the predictions at birth and the outcome in life. This had often been done with individuals, but with inconclusive results. A sample large enough to enable a statistical analysis to be made was required, he decided.

The procedure he eventually followed, described in *The Truth about Astrology* (1983), was to concentrate on single professional groups. By a stroke of good fortune there was a directory available which gave the place and date of birth of every member of the Medical Academy from 1820 to 1939. Laboriously, he worked out the positions of the planets at the hour of birth of each of the doctors listed.

Suddenly, I was presented with an extraordinary fact. My doctors were not born under the same skies as the common run of humanity. They had chosen to come into the world much more often during roughly the two hours following the rise and culmination of two planets, Mars and Saturn. Moreover, they tended to 'avoid' being born following the rise and culmination of the planet Jupiter.

Were all doctors susceptible to this effect? Gauquelin compiled a list of doctors who were not members of the Academy, to provide a control group, and went through the same procedure. The pattern that emerged was no different from the normal one for the public as a whole; 'it was only outstanding doctors who "chose" to come into the world under Mars and Saturn.'

The findings, Gauquelin was careful to stress, did not suggest that being born under 'Mars rising' could be held responsible for achieving distinction in the medical profession. They merely showed that on balance, those doctors who were born under 'Mars rising' were significantly more likely, in statistical terms, to achieve it than doctors who were not. Here, in fact, was an extraordinary 'hidden coincidence' of the kind Diaconis had noted as important for science; comparable in its psychological implications to the recognition of the relationship between the moon and the tides, especially if similar results came from research into members of other professions.

They did.

The planet Mars, when positioned at birth in the sectors following its rise and culmination, favoured the success of sports champions and exceptional military leaders; Jupiter, in the same sectors, featured most frequently at the birth of actors and politicians. Where scientists were concerned – that is, members of the *Académie des Sciences Française* – it was Saturn which was dominant; on the other hand, artists – painters and musicians – presented an entirely opposite picture, since they 'avoided' being born when that planet occupied the key sectors of rise and culmination.

The possibility remained that Gauquelin was a fraud or a fantasist, and was either rigging the statistics or putting a false interpretation on them. This could be settled with the help of trials by other researchers; better still, by scientists in other countries, in case France should turn out to be an exception.

There followed some of the most regrettable episodes in the history of science. A committee was set up in Belgium, a majority of whose members felt confident that they could demolish Gauquelin's findings. When to their discomfiture they found that his findings were confirmed, they simply declined to publish their results.

An even more deplorable course was taken by the Committee for the Scientific Investigation of Claims of the Paranormal, set up in the United States following the publicity given to the manifesto against astrology. Its members pledged themselves to fight occultism, and 'CSICOP' set up an inquiry into Gauquelin's findings, repeating Gauquelin's work with sportsmen. To their embarrassment, the investigators found that the 'Mars effect', as it was coming to be known – the percentage difference, in this group, between outstanding sportsmen and run-of-the-mill sportsmen – was slightly greater than Gauquelin had found. Unable to contradict his figures, they pretended that their results had not confirmed them. Five years passed before the members of the investigating committee were compelled to admit their 'error'.

Wherever Gauquelin's research method has been used – be it with athletes, military leaders, scientists, physicians, politicians, actors, writers – the outcome has confirmed his results. The difference is small: the 'Mars effect' means that the proportion of, say, great athletes born under 'Mars rising' and the rest is only 6 per cent. It has been the consistency of the effect which is so convincing.

Could the method be adapted to discover more about the relationship of individuals, as distinct from groups, to planetary influences at birth? Might there be some similar link between, say, the dispositions of people thought of as 'saturnine' or 'jovial' and the planets' positions at their births? Subjective judgement would have to be used, Gauquelin realised; the results of the research could not be presented with the same confidence. Still, he thought it worth studying the biographies of the famous to find and list the terms which were used about them. The notion has proved fruitful; Gauquelin has been able to type-cast 'élite' figures reasonably objectively, giving them similar-sounding characteristics to those familiar from traditional astrology – individuals born under 'Mars rising' tend to be 'brave, dynamic, reckless'; under Venus rising, 'affable, attractive, charming'. Again, it is only a small proportion of the sample who display the characteristics; but it, too, is statistically significant.

Orthodox scientists who took the trouble to study Gauquelin's results had one consolation; traditional astrology received little support. There was nothing to show that Scorpios actually display Scorpio characteristics. Gauquelin, in fact, has understandably tried to distance himself from astrology as it is generally practised. He admits, though, that future research may provide evidence to account for the many remarkable predictions with which traditional astrology has been credited – and still is being credited, as in a case Ivor Grattan-Guinness recalled in his 1983 article on the relationship between coincidences and psychical phenomena.

Ten years before, an astrologer friend had sent him a set of predictions for 1974, 'by far the strongest being that early June would be very favourable for publications'. Without hesitation, Grattan-Guinness discounted this, for the work he was engaged upon would not be ready by then. Consequently he did not look at the predictions again until the following autumn. He was then reminded of what had happened that summer.

Early in June, after some lengthy negotiations, I was invited by the publisher to join the editorial board of a journal. We had a long meeting discussing the journal's future; and it was clear that we would have to have a meeting with the acting editor. The publisher phoned him up there and then, in my presence – and interrupted him typing out a letter of retirement in which he proposed me as his successor.

The acting editor had known of Grattan-Guinness's recruitment to the board of the journal, *Annals of Science*, but he had not been aware that the meeting was taking place.

It would be easy to fill a book with such accounts of astrological predictions which have come true; one will have to suffice – the 'joker' intervening. While Philip Scull and his wife were staying at a seaside hotel with another couple, entertainment was provided one evening by a man who cast horoscopes.

> My wife went for one for each of the four of us, all different. She brought them back unopened and we started to read out of curiosity. I got a shock; mine started with a description that was quite amazingly accurate. When I remarked that perhaps there was something in this rubbish after all, the other girl said that hers, too, had come very close. My wife fell about laughing, and we wrenched from her the confession that she had switched the two.

For years, Scull has been telling the story as a joke against astrology; 'no one has ever, nor I until this moment,' he remarks in his account to the Foundation, 'observed that there was a remarkable coincidence in it as well.'

That Gauquelin's results, if confirmed, would be important for the study of coincidence was noted by the psychologist John Beloff in an article in 1977. Discussing the hypothesis of synchronicity as 'an acausal connecting principle', he pointed out that despite what critics had alleged, it was not devoid of meaning.

> If, for example, we were once again forced to take seriously certain astrological ideas – and this is beginning to look increasingly imminent – we may have to settle for a universe which exhibited meaningful and yet acausal connections. In any case, there could be no a priori reason why the world should not be so constituted that coincidences occur to a greater extent than they should do, given the accepted laws of probability, however fantastic this may seem.

In *The Message of Astrology* (1990) Peter Roberts, Professor of Systems Science at the City University, London, goes into these implications. Although Gauquelin's work does not confirm traditional astrology, 'it bears a striking resemblance to its forebear,' he points out; the similarities are more striking than the differences. What has happened, he surmises, is that astrology began through subliminal perception – hunch – about the role of the planets; but that it was later twisted out of its original form when it was taken over by professionals, in much the same way as Christianity was by the priesthood.

The basic assumption, however, remains unchanged: that the time of birth exercises a measure of influence over the life that follows – if Gauquelin's theory is accepted – by pushing, or pulling, gifted individuals into their group's élite. That only a small proportion are able to exploit the advantage which their birth time has given them can be accounted for by the fact that society will inevitably deny many of them the opportunity; poverty alone severely restricts entry into the professions. In any case, Fate's powers to intervene may themselves be limited. 'Fate, for whose wisdom I entertain all imaginable reverence, often finds in Chance, by which it works, an instrument not over-manageable', a 'stranger' (one of Goethe's devices to allow him to preach) told Wilhelm Meister in the novel of that name. 'At least the latter very seldom seems to execute precisely and accurately what the former has determined.'

If the hypothesis that the time of birth selects certain people for eventual entry into an élite is correct, quite how does Fate work for them, through chance? They must enjoy 'a more generous slice of luck', Roberts argues. 'Being at the right place and at the right time and being noticed by the right people certainly counts if you are in aspiring politician.' Or, for that matter, an aspiring footballer. The coincidence of being in the right place at the right time may occur no more often in his career than in the careers of other footballers; if the accident of his birth time is to be held responsible for his elevation to the élite, the presumption must be that he will happen to be on his best form when the talent-spotter happens to be present.

But is birth time an accident? Gauquelin has found that people whose births were induced for clinical reasons, or to suit the obstetricians' convenience, do not comply with the pattern of natural births. Could a design be formed while the infant is still in the womb; so that destiny 'chooses' the 'right' time to be born? This could also help to explain, Roberts surmises, why non-identical twins may have such different characteristics; 'because of the special constraint of their occupying the same womb, one or both of the twins is necessarily born at the "wrong" time.'

Numerology
'At its popular level,' the author Richard Cavendish has explained,

> numerology is an entertaining and comparatively simple method of analysing character and predicting the future, in broad and vague terms at least. At a deeper level it is claimed to be one of the major

keys to an understanding of the true nature of the universe and it plays an important part in magic and occultism. Like other systems of divination, it finds order and regularity behind the bewildering multiplicity of phenomena and the confusing muddle of events and influences that confront us in the world outside us and in ourselves

In its simplest form, the letters of the alphabet are given numbers from one to nine – A=1, I=9; J=1, R=9; S=1, Z=8. You can add up the total of the letters in your name; if they come to, say, 67, you add 6 to 7 to make 13; then 1 to 3 to make 4, the number which supposedly indicates your character and your future, according to an ancient formula. Four being an unlucky number numerologically, an alternative method was developed to escape it, using the date of birth, rather than the name, adding up the digits and reducing them to a single figure, which might hold out more promise. This, in turn, launched a new pastime, the manufacturing of bizarre historical coincidences, which became very popular in the nineteenth century, much to the indignation of the hard-line positivist William Stanley Jevons, who in his *Principles of Science* (1874) cited a typical example.

If to 1794, the number of the year in which Robespierre fell, we add the sum of its digits, the result is 1815 the year in which Napoleon fell; the repetition of this process gives 1830, the year in which Charles the Tenth abdicated. Again, the French Chamber of Deputies in 1830 consisted of 402 members, of whom 221 formed the party called 'La queue de Robespierre', while the remainder, 181 in number, were named 'Les honnêtes gens'. If we give to each letter a numerical value corresponding to its place in the alphabet, it will be found that the sum of the values of the letters in each name exactly indicates the number of the party.

Jevons was scathing about the occult interpretation that the numerologists of his time tended to put upon such calculations: 'In historical and social matters, coincidences are frequently pointed out which are due to chance, although there is always a strong popular tendency to regard them as the work of design, or as having some hidden meaning.'

In her 1899 article, Alice Johnson shared his scepticism. 'Much time and ingenuity had been expended', she noted, on such discoveries, and she gave examples, among them one concerning Louis Philippe, who became king of France in 1830 and abdicated eighteen years later:

Accession:	1830		1830		1830
Date	1	Date	1	Date	1
of	7	of	7	of	8
Birth	7	Wife's	8	Marriage	0
	3	Birth	2		9
	1848		1848		1848

'A little consideration will show that the particular dates involved are specially favourable ones for the occurrence of these coincidences,' she pointed out: the first two digits had to add up to eight or nine, and this meant it would require no great ingenuity to provide what might seem to be remarkable examples. 'If any argument is needed to show the utter irrationality of attaching any significance to coincidences such as these', it lay in the fact that for anybody who happened to be born in 1800, the digits could not possibly add up in the same way to be tied in with major events in later life.

Historical titbits of this kind still arouse curiosity. There are indications in the Foundation's correspondence of interest in the way in which certain numbers come in clusters, as they did for Kammerer (see page 4); or, more commonly, keep on recurring until the people who notice them begin to feel that destiny has linked the number to their lives. A few accounts list such sequences in detail. What is impossible to assess is whether some other number, if it had happened to emerge in a sequence, and been noticed, might have made a similar impression. Occasionally it is clear that these latter-day numerologists are hooked on their own number, even to the point of creating it out of combinations of other numbers. It is all too easy to find the evidence you want in such cases, as, in the 1930s, those who hoped to prove that Sir Francis Bacon wrote the plays of Shakespeare were often able to find superficially impressive-sounding evidence from the plays, in code, to sustain their belief.

Jung had his own version of numerology. Numbers, he thought, clearly showed 'that there is something beyond the borderline, beyond the frontiers of knowledge'. This side of the border, they are simply quantities; but 'on the other side they are autonomous psychic entities, capable of making qualitative statements which manifest themselves in a priori patterns of order.' This would suggest at least the possibility that they can be responsible for coincidences. But

according to Hildi Hawkins in an article on the numerologists' creed,
they claim there is no such thing as coincidence. 'They believe the
Universe is like a vast harp with countless strings, each vibrating at a
certain rate, characterised by a number. Number, they believe, is at
the root of all things' – expressing itself through predestination.

Prayer

In *Dimensions of Prayer* (1968) Douglas Steere recalled that he had once
asked William Temple, Archbishop of Canterbury, whether the
occasions they had been discussing, in which prayer seemed to have
caused individuals to change their ways, were merely coincidences?
All that Temple, who himself practised intercessionary prayer, would
say on the point was, 'When I pray, coincidences happen; when I do
not, they don't.'

Temple was evidently aware of the theological issues involved in
replying to the question. Christians must assume that God has the
power to intervene directly and miraculously in worldly affairs, when
such intervention is desirable. But the Anglican Church's teaching has
tended to be that God, satisfied with his handiwork and his laws of
nature, does not intervene, certainly not through miracles, which are
thought to be a Papist superstition. Yet uncertainty remains. Prayers
for the sick, and even for rain in times of drought, are sent up as if in
hope of a direct response. Temple was framing his reply so that it
would not commit him to the claim that he expected God to arrange
coincidences for his personal benefit, but left open the possibility that
prayer may trigger them, through some form of divine energy latent
in the community.

That many Christians (and even lapsed Christians, in emergencies)
do hope their prayers will be answered, whether directly or indirectly,
can be gauged from the files of the Religious Experience Research
Unit, founded in 1969 by Sir Alister Hardy and carried on after his
death as the Alister Hardy Research Centre at Manchester College,
Oxford, with an American branch in Princeton, New Jersey. It
seemed sensible to us at the Koestler Foundation not to duplicate the
Centre's work, which has brought in several thousand case histories
from individuals all over the world, many of them with echoes of
Temple's comment. However, a couple of examples will show the
kind of tales that we receive.

In 1989 a *Spectator* reader sent us a clipping from the *Newcastle-upon-
Tyne Journal*; a letter from a correspondent, Jim Ross, describing the

experience of one of the *Journal*'s readers, who had been looking for some brass washers to re-hang his church's title board. Failing to find any in Berwick or Alnwick, he tried Newcastle,

> where he still couldn't find any for sale. Then, in Clayton Street, under a street lamp, he found something glinting. It turned out to be a brass washer, and just the size he needed. Looking around he discovered another three. Exactly the amount he wanted.

'I am sure there are many instances where miracles happen,' Jim Ross concludes, 'only we don't accept them as miracles.'

Catholics need have fewer reservations. The *Observer* questionnaire reminded Robert Laversuch of an occasion when he was teaching at a school in Birmingham, and he heard from his headmaster that things were getting desperate because there had been no replies to repeated advertisements for a school matron. Laversuch said he would 'ask St Joseph', an offer which was 'received by both the Head and the rest of the staff in stony silence.' But the next day happened to be St Joseph's Day; Laversuch went to Mass at the Birmingham Oratory to ask God, through Joseph's intercession, to help. That afternoon, walking through Birmingham, he met a woman he had known four years earlier when she was assistant matron at a Weybridge school run by the Josephite Fathers. She told him she was looking for a job; he told her of the vacancy at his school; she applied, and was appointed. 'Incidentally, she had a brother named Joseph. I am quite sure that the whole thing was an answer to prayer.'

It is clear that coincidences not prayed for are occasionally taken to come from some divine source.

Soon after 'Jane Marsh' married, her husband's great-aunt Betty, christened Elizabeth, developed senile dementia. When they visited her she insisted that they had a baby called 'Betty'; she used to say she had 'heard it on the radio'. They had no plans at the time to start a family; but they agreed that if ever they had a baby girl they would call her Elizabeth.

> Years later, after numerous tests, we were told that we could not have children. We decided to adopt a baby girl which we knew we would call Elizabeth. When the details came from the adoption society the name which had been given to her by her natural mother was none other than 'Betty'.

We knew at once she was meant to be ours.

The coincidence did not stop there. Three years later when we were trying to agree on a name for the baby son we were soon to adopt to complete our family, with Elizabeth's help we decided on Frederick. When we collected him we were told that the name given to him by his mother was 'Fred'.

'Our children are grown up now,' Mrs Marsh comments, 'but we have always believed that some divine hand had chosen them for us.'

In a few cases, life-saving coincidences are attributed by correspondents to divine intervention; but in our sample agnosticism is prevalent, even among those who would like to become believers. In 1976 'John Carr', deeply depressed because his first serious homosexual affair was ending, decided to die. He had lost a great deal of weight, as his lover liked him thin; his method, he decided, would be starvation – 'I know it sounds silly,' he comments, but probably because he was eating so little anyway, it seemed perfectly logical. One day when he had eaten nothing at all the doorbell rang; a woman he knew only slightly handed him a cake which 'she thought he might like.' It was to prove a turning point; he stopped starving himself and 'health and spirits began to return.'

She had been the caterer at a cricket match he had been to the summer before, and he had been appreciative. But why did she happen to bring the cake round when she did? Later, getting to know her, he inquired; she told him she had no idea. 'She had *suddenly* conceived the idea of making and delivering a cake to me.' As a result, John Carr has 'frequently tried to believe in a good and loving God, because I am sure that this smacks of a *Deus ex* . . . but I have not been able to make the leap of Faith.'

Agnosticism appears to have put down deep enough roots to remain unshaken even when there are intimations of divine wrath. Jove's reaction to insubordination was a thunderbolt; one such 'God is not mocked' coincidence has been sent to us, but Trevor Danson, who was at the receiving end, was more intrigued than alarmed. With two flat-mates he had been moving furniture, carpets and so on down the road to a new flat. Although they had been interrupted by thunder storms, the carpets were laid, the furniture in place; tired and irritable, they were just about to make the last journey with a trunk when they heard the rumble of another approaching storm.

My frayed temper finally tore completely apart and I bellowed (with deeply-held sincerity), 'Oh to *Hell* with you, God!', shaking my fist vehemently at the heavens, whence came an instant response: a violent lightning stroke, far too close for comfort; a deafening crack, and a sudden downpour, as if a giant tap had been turned on. The road outside, on a gentle slope, soon became a river in spate.

When the rain stopped and the torrent no longer hid the street, we arrived back at the basement flat carrying the trunk to find a foot or two of water flowing steadily from front door to back.

The storm inundated Hampstead with nine inches of water; 'the drains had "backed up" through the toilets of the basement flats,' all of which were flooded, and it took several days' further work to make the basement habitable again.

He and his flat-mates – all lapsed Christians – were understandably fascinated. None was in any doubt that the storm and the blasphemy were in some way connected; to Trevor Danson, 'the coincidence was in some way "meaningful", in spite of the fact that everyone was at pains to dissuade me from any excessive guilt feelings by pointing out that, if I had *not* shouted at the sky, the flood would still have occurred.' Nevertheless he admits to 'abiding scepticism'.

With even committed Christians coming to accept the idea of God as an abstraction, it is not surprising that direct divine intervention is less often suggested than it used to be as an explanation for particularly fortunate coincidences. As Geoffrey Ashe found, a proliferation of them made it easier for him to believe in intervention of some kind, rather than put them all down to chance; but, as he put it in *Miracles* (1970), 'the question "intervention by whom, or what?" raises perplexing issues.' He could not believe that God is responsible; they appeared to him to be the work of less exalted beings.

I see them as more like the tutelary spirits of pagan lore, or the guardian angels of traditional Christianity. Many have special links with particular individuals or places. Where one of them has an interest in a person, he (or she, or it) may be so close to the person as to be virtually a higher self.

This is a fair reflection of a very prevalent uncertainty. Guardian angels are quite commonly awarded the credit for interventions, but often simply as a convenient label; it does not appear that many people in this sample still believe in their existence as spirits.

Most of the evidence for the apparent interventions by deceased men and women in the affairs of the living has been provided by mediums; but it is clear that some people accept them – as in the account sent by John Stent – as a possible explanation for certain coincidences which have occurred in their lives.

> In 1965 I was listening to the radio in my flat in Croydon. The music being played was not known to me but I almost immediately had a very vivid picture in my mind of Aranjuez, a village near Madrid where one of the old royal palaces was situated and which my wife and I used to visit as often as we could at weekends. The music finished and the announcer said, 'That was the Concierto di Aranjuez by Rodrigo.' I tried to buy the record without success but finally was able to borrow a copy from the Croydon Library, very scratched and worn. I didn't feel like taping it.
>
> I then went to work and live in Holland. One Saturday I was doing my weekend shopping in den Haag, either in the Bijenkorf or Vroom & Dressman. Suddenly the guitar solo from the Aranjuez Concierto came through my brain and I wandered along the floor I was on and came to a section which I never knew existed – the record section. I gravitated to a counter and the very first record I saw displayed was – Concierto di Aranjuez. Of course I bought it. Who or what guided me to the very record I had been trying to buy for all those years? Was it my first wife, who had died suddenly in London just before I went to live in den Haag?

In some cases, the appearance of a dead friend in a dream can have a profound impact, particularly when it is related to waking events, as one was for the novelist Susan Hill. In *People*, she described her friendship with her fellow novelist J. G. Farrell. When he was drowned in an accident while he was fishing in Ireland, she was abroad; looking at a newspaper on her return,

> I noted that the other J. Farrell, author of *Studs Lonigan*, had just died. Oh look, I said lightly, the other J. Farrell is dead. A silence fell, and then one of the children said that ours had just died too.

For weeks, she was so stunned by the news and the circumstance in which she heard it that she did not shed a tear. Then one night she dreamed she was at an oddly frightening party, where many of the people were sinister, as if half changed into animals. She was in a state of panic until she saw Farrell.

> I walked towards him, overcome with relief, reaching out my hand, and just as he was about to take it I remembered he was dead, and he began to fade and recede from sight. He was untouchable. But he was smiling, quizzically, and was so much himself, so vividly himself, unlike all the other people there: he shook his head slightly, and continued to smile, as I began to cry, and he said, very distinctly 'It's all right, you know, it's quite all right.' And then I woke, weeping. But it was a good dream: I felt that I had truly seen him.

That morning she received a letter from Farrell's mother; then, hoovering the carpet under the dressing table – 'which I rarely do' – she found the lost last postcard he had sent to her, from Ireland. 'I don't think I believe in a spirit world or an afterlife,' she comments, 'but I do believe in the truth of some dreams.'

Even sceptics can be impressed, in spite of themselves, when coincidences appear to be a dead man's handiwork – as Koestler noted when the 'shower' of them descended on him while he was writing Kammerer's biography; 'it was as if Kammerer's amiable ghost were beckoning with a malicious grin: "I told you so".'

'I have always been sceptical of unworldly coincidences,' Michael Holroyd claims,

> so when a friend of mine, the novelist William Gerhardie, died in the summer of 1977, having said that if there was another life he would pull the leg of his disbelieving fellow novelist Olivia Manning – who fell and broke her leg at the scattering of Gerhardie's ashes in Regent's Park – I dismissed this as a joke in rather painful taste.

Later, after collaborating with Robert Skidelsky in editing Gerhardie's posthumous *God's Fifth Column*, Holroyd received a copy from the publisher, and turned to the end where Gerhardie described the feelings aroused in him by the concluding bars of the Andante in Mozart's Sinfonia Concertante for violin and viola – which the book had used as its motif, representing the influence of the imagination versus the will. 'As I read it, these very bars of music were played on the radio exactly as he described them,' Holroyd recalls. 'The emotional force of that coincidence, as if William were signalling his approval of our work, has seriously dented my scepticism.'

The shade of James Joyce presided over a coincidence to celebrate the fiftieth anniversary of Bloomsday, in *Ulysses*. In *Dead as Doornails* Anthony Cronin has recalled how in 1954, the poet Patrick Kavanagh, Brian O'Nolan (better known by his pseudonyms, Flann O'Brien and Myles na gCopaleen), Con Leventhal (Registrar of Trinity College, Dublin) and others took horsedrawn cabs to follow Joyce's itinerary through Dublin, with frequent pauses for refreshment. Kavanagh and Leventhal were keen students of form, and as it happened to be Ascot Week – as it had been in *Ulysses* – they stopped at one point to lay bets on the outcome of the Gold Cup, and to listen to the broadcast of the race. The favourite was a stayer, and its owner Marcel Boussac had taken the precaution of entering a pacemaker from his stable. But the pacemaker, Elpenor, outstayed the entire field, winning at 50–1, record odds against a Gold Cup winner.

> Now, Elpenor is a character in the *Odyssey*. He is a companion of Ulysses who falls off a height during some fighting, as some of our party had so nearly done, cracks his skull and dies. Although Ulysses remarks that it didn't matter 'since he wasn't much of a fighting man nor ever very strong in the head', he nevertheless goes down into the underworld after him to see what he can do. This descent is paralleled in the book by the scene in Glasnevin cemetery, for in Joyce's *Ulysses* Elpenor is represented by the deceased Paddy Dignam; and it was the route of Paddy Dignam's funeral that we were following; indeed the whole idea of a commemoration which would involve horse-cabs grew out of the Dignam funeral sequence.

The joke was on the two experts – particularly Leventhal, a man of considerable erudition and a friend of Joyce – for their failure to make the connection; all the more so in that 'Joyce always believed his book to have strange prophetic powers of which he himself only became aware after the event.'

Memory must have played a trick on Cronin: Elpenor won the Ascot Gold Cup on 17 June – the day after Bloomsday. But the coincidence remains striking; and Con Leventhal's failure to make the connection remained, for him, a source of amused irritation.

Luck

In *God and the New Physics* (1983) Paul Davies, Professor of Theoretical Physics at the University of Newcastle, criticised those who 'choose to read divine significance into improbable coincidences' as 'simply giving a theistic interpretation of straightforward, if unusual, natural events.' The survivor of a plane crash may feel he has been saved by a miracle; but what of those passengers who were killed?

> Nobody suggests that surviving a plane crash must entail suspension of the laws of physics. Such events are merely remarkable coincidences within the normal operation of physical processes. The proverbial parachutist with a malfunctioning parachute who lands in a haystack is simply lucky to have fallen where he did. No direct divine intervention seems to have been involved.

Davies is cautious enough to say only that no divine intervention *seems* to be involved. Leaving aside 'divine', may intervention of some as yet unexplained kind be responsible? Certainly the parachutist has been lucky; is it possible that luck is not just a chance affair?

Take the case of Flight Sergeant Nicholas Alkemade, tail-gunner in a Lancaster bomber on a mission over Germany in 1944. His aircraft was crippled by a German night fighter, and his captain instructed the crew to bale out. Turning to get his parachute, Alkemade found it in flames; confronted with the option of burning to death or jumping into space from 20,000 feet, he chose to jump. Three hours later he recovered consciousness, realising to his astonishment he was alive. Trees had broken his fall, and snow on the ground had saved him. It was difficult to persuade his German captors that his account was true. They thought he must be a spy, but when the crashed bomber was found, his story was matched up with the wreckage. They had to accept it, and he was given an affidavit signed and witnessed to that effect.

If this had been Alkemade's only lucky escape it could easily have been attributed to chance. But it was not. In his subsequent peacetime career he continued to lead, as a magazine article inevitably described it, 'a charmed life', three times surviving what could have been expected to be fatal accidents. A few RAF pilots had even more astonishing records of narrow escapes, notably D. H. 'Nobby' Clarke, leaving them and their friends with the impression that 'lucky' is an ambiguous term. (In Clarke's view, a great deal could be learned from studying people such as Alkemade: 'isolated "survivals" can be attributed to luck, but continuous "luck" for one person is a mathematically unsound premise.')

Emerson would have agreed. 'Some people are made up of rhyme, coincidence, omen, periodicity and presage,' he thought. 'They meet the person they seek; what their companion prepares to say to them, they first say to him; and a hundred signs apprise them of what is about to befall.' And Sir Alister Hardy, discussing the results of card-guessing trials for ESP in his contribution to *The Challenge of Chance*, admitted he was sometimes tempted 'with an awful thought', one he hardly cared to admit. He did not doubt that above-chance results had been obtained in thousands of experiments all over the world, but

Is it possible that what all these experiments with cards are really demonstrating is a measurement of what we *in our ignorance* more usually call luck; that some people *are*, in fact, at any rate at times, much luckier, whatever that may mean, at card-guessing than others? This indeed is a shocking thing for a scientist to say, but I say it because I want to make the point that this should in fact be *no more shocking* to the scientific position of today than the fact now statistically established by significance tests that there are a number of people who are able to guess correctly, more often than can be accounted for by the present theory of probability, which cards are which in a pack they haven't seen. The idea of luck and that of clairvoyance are *equally shocking* to our present scientific view of the universe.

Hardy felt he had been left with an uncomfortable choice. 'Is there something about probability which we do not understand, as suggested by Spencer Brown? Or can it be that there is something about card-guessing trials and experiments with dice' (most of the experimental work on psychokinesis at that time had been done with dice) 'which is just as queer as what we call luck, but which scientific law has not yet got hold of? – in other words, psi?'

Psi
Sending 'a bundle of rusty old manuscripts' to the editor of *Harper's*, Mark Twain (Samuel Clemens) claimed it would prove to him that

I had once made a great discovery: the discovery that certain sorts of things which, from the beginning of the world, had always been regarded merely as 'curious coincidences' – that is to say, accidents – were no more accidental than is the sending and receiving of a telegram an accident. I made the discovery sixteen or seventeen years ago, and gave it a name 'Mental Telegraphy'. It is the same thing around the outer edges of which the Psychical Society of England began to grope (and play with) four or five years ago, and which they name 'Telepathy'.

The manuscripts dated from 1878. They had been intended for use in *A Tramp Abroad*, but Clemens feared that they would be taken to be a joke, 'whereas I was in earnest'. Later he had tried them on the *North American Review*; the editor had demurred. 'See how the world has moved since then,' Clemens commented; what had been too much for a serious magazine had become a commonplace. The Society had managed to do

what I could never have done – they have convinced the world that mental telegraphy is not a jest, but a fact, and that it is a thing not rare, but exceedingly common. They have done our age a service – and a very great service, I think.

As things have turned out, the Society for Psychical Research has not convinced the world; in the eyes of orthodox scientists telepathy remains as unacceptable as ever. Yet in a sense, Clemens has been proved right. Most of us accept extra-sensory perception. The reason is obvious; too many people have had, or come to know about, coincidences of a kind for which chance seems a comically unlikely explanation; they no longer bother to heed orthodoxy's commands.

Koestler provided a typical example in the second volume of his autobiography. While he was under sentence of death in a Seville gaol during the Spanish Civil War, he suddenly remembered, and got great spiritual comfort from, a passage in Thomas Mann's *Buddenbrooks*. Knowing he is about to die, Consul Thomas Buddenbrook falls under the spell of Schopenhauer's essay 'On Death', 'which for years has stood unread in his library, and in which he finds explained that death is nothing final'; he feels 'a profound intoxication, a strange, sweet, vague allurement'. The day after he was released Koestler wrote to thank Mann, explaining what had happened. In reply, Mann wrote to say that on the day Koestler's letter had arrived, he had felt a sudden impulse to re-read the essay 'On Death', after nearly forty years; he went indoors to his library to fetch it, and at that moment the postman brought Koestler's letter.

In *The Challenge of Chance* Koestler, excusing himself for quoting the story again, recalled that it had been 'instrumental in changing my attitude to ESP'. His only regret was that in the course of his flight from France in 1940 he lost most of his possessions, including Mann's letter; he had no proof that the incident had occurred. Mann's diaries, however, published after Koestler's death, confirmed it.

The problem, though, as Koestler put it, is that methodology is lacking which would enable ESP to be distinguished from chance with confidence; for the present, coincidence has to serve for both. Yet this is no reason for abandoning the attempt to make the distinction. Alice Johnson was right to assert (as Diaconis was to do, a century later) that such research 'may lead to the discovery of a cause hitherto unknown, or at least unrecognised by science'. The question, she thought, was:

> Are those coincidences which form the main material for our study
> – the apparitions seen at the time of death or of some crisis in the life
> of the person represented, the cases of detailed foreknowledge of
> events, the mass of correct information to be found among the
> utterances of at least one trance medium, the precise resemblance
> between the thoughts of two persons in successful experiments in
> thought-transference, the movements of the divining rod over
> concealed underground water – are all these coincidences to be put
> down to chance, or is there something more in them?

It would be outside this book's scope to attempt a survey of the evidence for ESP – let alone for psi, embracing as it does a wider range of anomalous phenomena. Of the particular coincidences to which Alice Johnson referred, however, one type clearly arouses great interest today: the case of 'detailed foreknowledge of events', particularly in the spontaneous form in which they are commonly reported, 'dreaming the future'.

Precognition
Reports of dreams which 'came true' have always been disturbing to positivists. They could not deny that such dreams actually occur; rationalisations have had to be searched for to explain them away.

'There can be no doubt that many circumstances occurring in our dreams have been actually verified,' McNish conceded in *The Philosophy of Sleep* (1830), 'but this must be regarded as altogether the effect of chance; for one dream which turns out to be true, at least a thousand are false.' At the end of the century, Herbert Spencer was taking a similar line. Because of 'repeated experiences of coincidences' he had reached a point where 'simple induction would, I think, almost have led me to believe in supernatural agency, were it not that with me, the conviction of natural agency is so strong that it is impossible to think away from it.' The natural agency he fell back on was chance. 'A dreams he meets B, does not do so and thinks nothing about it,' he wrote in 1894 to Andrew Lang, whom he suspected of being too ready to accept second sight. 'But after a million cases have occurred A does meet some B; thinks it supernatural and tells about it.' And in his autobiography ten years later, recalling what he sarcastically described as a 'remarkable' coincidence – in his youth he had twice taken a job as a sub-editor, in 1844 and again in 1848; on both occasions his editor was a Scot, called James Wilson – Spencer went on to proclaim, 'Here comes the lesson'. Millions of people in Great Britain dream every night, and in the space of a year there are probably at least a hundred millions of dreams vivid enough to be recalled on awakening. 'May we not say that the alleged fulfilments are not more common than, in conformity with the law of probability, we may expect them to be?'

Spencer's argument has often been echoed in connection with dream winners. 'Some years ago, the night before the Grand National, I had a dream in which I could clearly identify the winner,' Professor Hans Eysenck has recalled. 'The following day I kept an eye on that particular horse, as I was very interested to see the outcome of the race. She fell at the first hurdle.' Reports of dream winners are frequent; not so, reports of dream losers. If they could all be collected, would they perhaps reveal that dream winners can satisfactorily be accounted for by chance?

John Godley's dream sequence (see page 69) would alone make this implausible; but in any case, whether or not a dream of a horse race foreshadows the future may also depend on details. One of Godley's winners, for example, he recognised in his dream from the face of the jockey, Edgar Britt, and the colours – 'terracotta and scarlet chevrons, the Gaekwar of Baroda's'. He did not hear the horse's name but in *The Times* the next morning he found that the Gaekwar of Baroda had only a single runner that day, and Edgar Britt was the jockey. It was his 'double', that day, which he reported to the *Daily Mirror*, launching him into journalism.

This was an aspect of precognition which Christopher Evans failed to deal with in *Landscapes of the Night*, posthumously published in 1983. Evans had been the most effective critic of psychical research in Britain; he claimed to have kept an open mind, but there was no trace of it in the book. Although unable to avoid discussing the evidence from Dunne's *Experiment with Time*, he brushed it aside by claiming that he had been impressed by it when he read it as a teenager, but when he read it again he found 'only one or two of his "precognitive" dreams to be even remotely interesting, and most of them to be thin to the point of insubstantiality.'

Many of the dreams are, indeed, of little intrinsic interest, but from Dunne's point of view of demonstrating that, in them, he was seeing what he would see in reality within the next few days, the trivial details remain just as impressive as evidence as the moments of drama.

This, at least, was Kipling's impression, as he related in his autobiography.

> I dreamt that I stood, in my best clothes, which I do not wear as a rule, one in a line of similarly habited men, in some vast hall, floored with rough-jointed stone slabs. Opposite me, the width of the hall, was another line of persons and the impression of a crowd behind them. On my left some ceremony was taking place that I wanted to see, but could not unless I stepped out of my line because the fat stomach of my neighbour on my left barred my vision. At the ceremony's close, both lines of spectators broke up and moved forward and met, and the great space filled with people. Then a man came up behind me, slipped his hand beneath my arm, and said: 'I want a word with you.' I forget the rest: but it had been a perfectly clear dream, and it stuck in my memory.

Kipling was a member of the War Graves Commission, and a few weeks later he had to attend a ceremony with his fellow members at Westminster Abbey.

> We Commissioners lined up, facing, across the width of the Abbey Nave, more members of the Ministry and a big body of the public behind them, all in black clothes. I could see nothing of the ceremony because the stomach of the man on my left barred my

vision. Then, my eye was caught by the cracks of the stone flooring, and I said to myself: 'But here is where I have been!' We broke up, both lines flowed forward and met, and the Nave filled with a crowd, through which a man came up and slipped his hand upon my arm saying: 'I want a word with you, please.' It was about some utterly trivial matter that I have forgotten.

So shaken was Kipling by the experience that he did not tell anybody about it at the time; excusing himself in retrospect by claiming that he feared it might put ideas into the heads of the 'weaker brethren – and their sisters', who might be tempted to explore the slippery occult road 'down to Endor' (as his own sister, who practised automatic writing, had done).

Christopher Hollis, a prolific writer of books and articles on current affairs, and a Conservative member of parliament, was impressed (but not alarmed) by a similar experience.

In my dream there appeared to me a man who had been at school with me, though older than I, a quarter of a century before, but whom I had hardly seen since and whose career I had not followed. He came up to me and said, 'I don't think you know my wife, do you?' When I awoke the next morning, I remember thinking it strange that this man, who had been so little in my life, should have appeared in my dream at all. But then I got up, went about the occasions of the day and thought no more of it. That evening I went to a cocktail party. A staircase ran up from the hall to the room where the party was being given. I was standing at the foot of the staircase, waiting to ascend, when the front door opened. In came the visitor of my dream, came up to me and said, 'I don't think you know my wife, do you?'

There was more than chance in that dream, Hollis felt; he had 'genuinely experienced in it "a little piece of the future".' Dunne, he had concluded, was right.

Further to back up the contention that chance, rather than precognition, was responsible for dreams foreshadowing the future, Christopher Evans updated Spencer. He did not dispute that there were well-attested reports of airline passengers who, having dreamed the night before they were due to fly that their plane would crash, had cancelled their reservations and thereby escaped death when the plane *did* crash. What was required, Evans insisted, was an estimate of the frequency of such dreams where 'the person cancels his flight reservation and then feels a big chump when the plane steadfastly refused to crash.'

To dream of a crash the night before going on a flight must in any case be a common experience, brought on by fear of flying. The test of whether it might be classified as precognitive must be related to the precision of the detail. Suppose you decide to ignore the dream, board the aircraft, and then find you are being ushered to the seat you had in the dream by the air hostess you saw in the dream? You could be forgiven for making an excuse and disembarking. Even then, though, the precognition might only apply to the embarkation. Episodes in dreams of the future are rarely entirely consistent with what eventually happens.

The recurrence of a single detail is often enough to make a deep impression. Kevin Clark had a nightmare in which he 'wandered, "Steppenwolf" fashion, into the underworld twilight zone', where he encountered a journalist, John Feeney, whom he knew only vaguely. He was puzzled by the fact that the dream seemed more 'real' than his waking state, and he wrote down the experience. 'You can imagine my horror when I turned on the early morning news to hear that six journalists had been killed in a plane crash the previous evening in Kent during a Beaujolais Nouveau junket; John Feeney was one of them.'

A retired schoolmaster in the West Country had a vivid dream one night in which he was standing at the door of a house overlooking the sea. Gazing up into the sky, he saw an aircraft break up, hundreds of passengers falling out of it into the water. Although at first he was not unduly disturbed, he had the same dream the next night, and the night after – though on the third night, he saw the crash from a different perspective, as if he were level with the plane when it blew up. As the antibiotics he was taking at the time for an ear infection were making him feel depressed, and he had a fear of flying – he had never travelled by air – he thought his state of health might be responsible; and although he told two friends, who confirm his account, to look out for a report of a catastrophe of the kind he had seen in the dream, he did not intend that they should take him seriously. Between two and three weeks after the dream, at a spot approximately half an hour's flying time out in the Atlantic, but in the direction he was looking in the dream, a bomb blew up an Air India jet on its transatlantic flight, scattering over three hundred bodies into the ocean below.

Not surprisingly, the event was disturbing for him; 'In fact I am haunted by the event to this day. After all, it was an event of global significance.' Chance, he maintains, cannot be the explanation: 'I feel that the dream emanated from beyond myself' – significant in that it appeared to be designed to draw his intention to the impending catastrophe, though in no way directly related to him.

Probability theory might be applied, loosely, to support the case for chance where a single dream episode is involved; but it would be unwise to use it to support chance as the explanation for the precognition involved in, say, the episode reported by 'Diana Finer', from a time when her marriage was breaking up.

I dreamed that I was walking down the platform of Exeter station. (I was in fact taking a train to London the following day and was worried that I might not wake in time to catch it.) As I walked, in my dream, I came face to face with my husband's current mistress. She was standing on the platform with her suitcase on the ground beside her on the left side. I began to turn and run from her, but someone who was invisible to me put his hands on my shoulders and turned me towards her saying that I must speak to her. There was no more to the dream but it disturbed me so much that I told my husband I did not think that I would go to London after all, and told him the reason why. He scoffed at it and said that she could not be on the train as she had not got the day off. This worried me even more because I then thought that they would have planned to meet as I was not going to be at home. However, I did get up and go.

At the station, Mrs Finer looked nervously along the platform to see if the woman, who had been violent towards her, was there, but there was no sign of her. Mrs Finer found an empty carriage and, when the train pulled out, left a newspaper to keep her seat while she went to the restaurant car to have breakfast.

I returned to my seat just before we reached Taunton and saw to my amazement that she was in the seat facing mine. She was equally surprised at my arrival. At that moment the train pulled into Taunton and the carriage was filled with children going to London on a school outing. As I hesitated, meaning to move my place in the carriage, I was reminded of the part of my dream where I had been told to speak to her, and so I sat down. The journey to London took

2½ hours and she spent most of it trying to make me agree to leave my husband so that she could marry him. She told me so many things about their relationship that I did not know that I was both shattered and horribly fascinated. As she spoke I became more and more certain that my marriage was finished. She was flaunting her age before me, and it seemed that she knew a man who I had never met in my own husband.

At Paddington Mrs Finer made her way to the Underground.

As I went I thought about the dream and the fact that I had seen her in the dream, standing on the platform at Exeter, whereas in reality she had been on the train. I walked onto the Underground station and, looking across at the opposite platform, saw her standing facing me with her suitcase on her left just as she had stood in the dream.

Identifying paramnesia

When people in the positivist tradition have a dream of that kind, they may feel compelled to admit that chance really will not do as an explanation. This has led to the invention of some ingenious alternatives, such as the one which Alfred Maury provided following a terrifying nightmare.

I appeared in front of the revolutionary tribunal. I saw Robespierre, Marat, Fouquier-Tinville, all the ugliest faces of that terrible era; I spoke with them; at last, after many events which I remember only vaguely, I was judged, condemned to death, taken by cart to an immense concourse on the site of the Revolution. I mount the scaffold; the executioner binds me to the fatal plank; he makes it see-saw; the blade falls; I feel my head separate from my body; I wake up in a state of intense anguish, and I feel on my head the bedrail which had suddenly detached itself and had fallen on my cervical vertebra, in the manner of a guillotine blade.

Less closed-minded than most of his contemporaries, Maury did not dismiss accounts of apparently supernatural phenomena as inventions, but tried in *La Magie et l'Astrologie* (1860) to offer explanations which could squeeze some of them, at least, into the confines of the laws of nature as they were then laid down. He was not likely to accept that his mind while he slept might be capable not only of seeing the future, but also of constructing an elaborate scenario to coincide with the event foreshadowed – an idea which his fellow positivists would ridicule. As he had had the dream himself, he could not dismiss it as an invention. In *Le Sommeil et les Rêves* (1878) he argued that 'at the moment I was struck, the memory of that redoubtable instrument, whose effect my bedrail reproduced so well, had sparked off all the images of that area symbolised by the guillotine.'

It can be laid down as an axiom that when scientific assumptions harden into a dogma, any explanation which fits the dogma, however far-fetched, may be acceptable. So it was with Maury's; for nearly a century the corollary – that dreams, however protracted they may seem to be, are in reality 'all over in a flash' – was accepted (it still occasionally surfaces, in letters to the Foundation). Not until the 1950s did research into the link between dreaming and 'rapid eye movements' in sleep, conducted by William Dement at the University of Chicago, expose 'all over in a flash' as misleading.

Maury's dream, then, remains unaccounted for except by explanations unacceptable to orthodoxy; as does Rian Hughes' contribution to the Foundation's collection.

I dug out an old alarm clock – it had always been faultless in the past, but had not been in use for some years – to wake me for a morning appointment.

My dreams, early that morning, concerned boxing. Despite my protestations, I was to go several rounds with an enormous bruiser who looked ready to settle the business without bothering about my puny frame. Forced into the ring, I took a deep breath – then the bell went . . .

I woke up. The bell was the alarm clock – ringing *once*, and *once only* (a 'ding'), at exactly the right time in my dream (or my dream had led up to the time the clock went off *exactly*). It had never rung only once before.

Another 'scientific' explanation was put forward by positivists a century ago to explain the '*déjà vu*' experience: 'identifying paramnesia'. The human brain has two hemispheres, which ordinarily run in tandem; but occasionally, the hypothesis was, they may cease momentarily to be synchronous. If one hemisphere has a mind's eye picture of a landscape, or an event, the other, picking up the picture a fraction of a second later, may see it as if it were a memory, leaving the impression 'I have been here before'.

When Dunne studied the accounts of the Martinique disaster (see page 69), he found that his figure of the number of inhabitants at risk, in his dream (4000) and the figure in the *Daily Telegraph* headline (40,000) were both wrong.

So my wonderful 'clairvoyant' vision had been wrong in its most insistent particular. But it was clear that its wrongness was likely to prove a matter just as important as its rightness. For *whence*, in the dream, had I got the idea of 4000? Clearly it must have come into my mind *because of the newspaper paragraph*. This suggested the extremely unpleasant notion that the whole thing was what doctors call 'Identifying Paramnesia'; that I had never really had such a dream at all; but that, on reading the newspaper report, a false idea had sprung up in my mind to the effect that I had previously dreamed a dream containing all the details given in that paragraph.

This was disturbing; but it gave Dunne an idea. The next time he had a dream which made an impression on him, suggesting it might be worth watching out for a linked event, it was of a blaze in which a fire engine was playing a stream of water on a smoke-hidden structure. When a plankway became visible through the smoke, he saw that it was crowded with people 'dropping in heaps'; the air was filled with 'horrible, choking, gasping ejaculations.'

I was taking no chances with 'Identifying Paramnesia' this time. I carefully recalled every detail of the dream after waking, and not till I had done this did I open the morning papers. There was nothing in these. But the evening editions brought the expected news.

There had been a big fire in a factory near Paris. As the ladders were too short to reach a balcony where some of the girl workers had taken refuge, the firemen directed their hoses onto it; but the smoke came rolling out from the building behind them 'in such dense volumes that, although the unfortunate girls were standing actually in the open air, every one of them was suffocated before the new ladders could arrive.'

If Dunne's theory of time, designed to make a belief in dreaming the future acceptable without the need to accept extra-sensory perception, had found favour among scientists, identifying paramnesia could have been ditched; but as few people claimed to be able to understand the theory, and none of those who claimed to understand it agreed with it, the positivist hypothesis has survived.

Occasionally, though, it is challenged. In 1947, Freddie Grisewood, one of the BBC's best-known broadcasters, related in the magazine *Country Life* how as a child, he once had a short succession of dreams in which he appeared to be living on an estate in the seventeenth century. Some years later, staying with friends in Sussex, he was taken to a house he had not seen before, and immediately recognised it as the one he had known in his dreams. When his hostess showed him around, he was able to confirm that it really was the same house. He pointed to a wall in one of the rooms where, he recalled, a tapestry had hung; so it had, she told him, but it had been taken away before he was born. In the bedroom he had used in his dreams, a window had vanished. He tapped the wall; it sounded hollow. The window had been bricked up.

Yet belief in identifying paramnesia has lingered on for lack of an accredited orthodox alternative. On one occasion when 'Mary Farquhar' was ill, and in a comatose condition,

I experienced continuous precognition. The medical explanation was that my brain responses were 'lagging behind' actual events which gave the illusion of precognition, but I find this difficult to believe. How could it account for 'knowing' who would be on the telephone and what they would say?

'For years I was prepared to accept that I was remembering experiences of a fraction of a second before,' Ian Tonothy recalls, 'until in 1967 I had an experience so clearcut that I rejected such explanations.'

I dreamt that I was standing in my kitchen talking to one of my flat-mates who was peeling potatoes, with Wagner playing on the radio in the lounge. The dream was remarkable in being so mundane, unlike the usual twisted, convoluted fantasies. Apart from the fact that I didn't at the time like Wagner, the scene was like a normal waking experience. That's why I remembered it. Three weeks later it happened; like finding myself in the middle of a replayed film.

For several years after this experience Tonothy recorded such dreams; like many of Dunne's in that they were 'distinguished by their mundane nature,' but unlike Dunne's in that there was sometimes a long interval between the dream and the actual event; in one case, five years. Also unlike Dunne's, 'almost all the instances have one thing in common: the period during which the dream "comes true" is always one of significant change for me.'

A recent case where the *déjà vu* experience is backed up by confirmatory evidence has been reported by 'Joan Enders'. In May 1985, she was engaged in visualisation exercises, recording what she saw on tape. In the course of one of them,

> I described a house in very great detail, the exterior, then the interior, the garden, etc. In October 1985 I was invited to go with a group of people to the oldest house in Radnorshire. To my knowledge I had never been in the area at any time in my life. When we reached the house I recognised it immediately as 'my house' on tape. Out of a total of 21 observations, 19 were accurate in every detail.

Mrs Enders played the tape to the woman who had taken her to the house, who confirmed its accuracy. 'I had actually dated the tape, so somehow I had looked into my own future.'

Apparitions

The first of the coincidences which provide Alice Johnson with the main material for her research – 'the apparitions seen at the time of death, or of some crisis in the life of the person represented' – is unlikely, today, to sound a promising line of inquiry, if the aim is to suggest an alternative to chance as the explanation. They would seem to be too rare to pose any threat to probability theory, in its role as chance's companion.

Alice Johnson, however, had good reason to give it pride of place in her list. 'Crisis apparitions' had actually been used to overturn the case for chance, as a result of a suggestion by one of the most eminent of experts on probability theory. If two events, A and B, are both constantly happening, De Morgan had pointed out in his *Budget of Paradoxes* in 1872, it can come as no surprise when occasionally they happen at the same time. But what if A is constantly happening, and that B, however rarely it happens, almost always coincides with A? Take the case of spectres of the dying, appearing to relations or loved ones at what they later find was at, or very close to, the time of death. Such appearances of people who were thought by the percipients to be living (as distinct from ghosts of the known dead), were rarely reported, De Morgan observed, 'without the alleged coincidence of death.'

It remains, then, for all, who speculate at all, to look upon the asserted phenomenon, think what they may of it; the thing which is to be explained, is a *connexion* in time of the death, and the simultaneous appearance. Any person the least used to the theory of probabilities will see that purely casual coincidence, the *wrong spectre* being comparatively so rare that it may be said never to occur, is not within the rational field of possibility.

When, ten years later, Myers and Gurney became Joint Hon. Secretaries of the newly-founded Society for Psychical Research they were able to pursue this line of investigation. First, they assembled a collection of accounts of experiences which could be interpreted as psychic; the title of their book, *Phantasms of the Living*, indicates their debt to De Morgan ('spectre,' they had decided, was too identified with the dead, as was 'ghost'; phantasm was to be used about the living. It did not catch on; later researchers have used 'apparition' where the appearance is of a living, or presumed to be living, person). The report of a 'Census of Hallucinations', which followed, revealed that in probability theory the proportion of well-authenticated apparitions encountered within twelve hours of the time of death was over four hundred times higher, compared to the known statistics for average deaths daily, than chance would account for.

No comparable investigation has been carried out since, but there are plenty of remarkable case histories in recent times, such as Ronald Searle's (see page 79), to suggest that if the resources were available, research might well confirm those findings. In the 1950s, with the help of a questionnaire in *Schweizerischer Beobachter*, Aniela Jaffé collected about 1500 accounts of 'irrational' experiences, including some of 'ghosts who cannot be distinguished from the living', as she described them in her *Apparitions* (1957). One of the accounts she used came from the wife of a confirmed sceptic who had been an adjutant in a regiment; he had been deeply hurt when his colonel, to whom he had been much attached, cut him dead when they met one evening. The colonel had in fact died two days before. In the other two cases, the encounter with the apparition and the death appeared to have been at the same time.

The largest collection of cases in which an apparition has been encountered at the time of death was accumulated by Flammarion. In the three volumes of *Death and its Mystery* (1922) he provided scores of examples of death coincidences of various kinds, ranging from encounters with individuals who appeared to be living but were dead or dying, to the macabre variety of portents in the chapter on 'Deaths announced by noises, by blows struck, by an unexplained uproar, by physical phenomena' – some historical, some contemporary, but most from people of standing in their communities.

In 1768 the great botanist Linnaeus and his wife were woken up by the sound of heavy footsteps in his museum, which he knew nobody could have entered; he recognised the familiar tread of his dearest friend, whom he later found had died 'at precisely the same hour'. Sir Walter Scott and his wife were woken up, half a century later, by an alarming din in one of the rooms which had been newly built for them, as if boards were being dragged along a floor; when it happened again the next night Scott went to investigate, but found nothing. He refused to even consider the possibility of any psychic manifestation; but according to his biographer Lockhart, when he heard that the builder he had employed had died at the time he had first been woken up by the noise, it left a stronger impression on him than he cared to admit.

Sometimes the death warnings were trivial in themselves, but sufficiently unusual to trigger an immediate foreboding, later shown to be justified. The sheer number of such coincidences, Flammarion argued, meant that they should be taken seriously.

We must determine whether the supernormal faculties, the mani-festations we described – presentiments, seeing the future, the will acting without the spoken word, things perceived at distances too great for the eye to reach, the functioning of the soul beyond the physical senses – whether all these could not be attributed, strictly speaking, to unknown properties of our vital organisms.

For Flammarion, the accounts he provided left no doubt that evolution had provided these faculties; 'the facts that are to follow,' he claimed, 'will prove superabundantly the truth of our thesis.' Aniela Jaffé's research and the accounts given by Celia Green and Charles

McCreery in their book – also *Apparitions* (1975) – confirm that such coincidences are still being reported; as does the outcome of a recent research project in Switzerland, a follow-up to Aniela Jaffé's summarised by Andrew MacKenzie in *The Seen and the Unseen* (1989). And our Foundation has its share, including some macabre cases. For example, in 1985 'Joan Wall' was suddenly struck by a horrific impression that the friend with whom she was staying was going to be killed by a blow with a stick on the back of her head. A month later, when the friend rang she cut the call off short because she wanted to watch a television programme; and immediately had the feeling, 'What if that were to be the very last conversation I had with her?' The next day, Mrs Wall suddenly felt more tense than she had ever felt before. Later, she heard that her friend had been murdered that day, by a blow on the back of the head with a wooden implement.

As the Foundation's aim has been to concentrate upon the evidence from spontaneous types of coincidence, the other three varieties which Alice Johnson thought might provide clues to the sources – the findings from research into 'the utterances of at least one trance medium' (it was Mrs Leonora Piper, investigated by William James and Richard Hodgson); from 'the successful experiments in thought-transference'; and from 'the movements of the divining rod over concealed underground water' – lie outside this book's scope. As it happens, over the past sixty years the attention of psychical researchers has been focused mainly on laboratory-type research, in an understandable attempt to convert orthodox scientists to acceptance of the reality of psi. In the 1980s, however, disillusionment grew; the minority who accepted its reality was found to be composed almost exclusively of scientists who had themselves had what they took to be psychic experiences. Hardly anybody admitted to conversion on the strength of the experimental evidence.

It is safe to say that few members of the public have studied that evidence; nevertheless almost four out of five adults in Britain, opinion polls have shown, accept ESP. They accept it apparently largely on the strength of personal experiences of the kind that they feel are more plausibly explained by its existence than by chance. Again, as with dreaming the future, it is often the trivial episodes which make a lasting impression.

Trivial forms of precognition while awake, too, can be curiously striking to those who experience them. Charles Tart, Professor of Psychology at the University of California, Davis, is one of the most experienced of parapsychologists (the term tends to be applied to those psychical researchers who concentrate on laboratory-type research); yet he was clearly greatly impressed by what happened on the morning he found himself saying 'coup d'état' aloud to himself, again and again.

It was rare for him to start saying anything aloud, 'much less over and over'; and as he could not remember ever having said 'coup d'état' aloud before, he was mildly puzzled 'as to why the word had popped into my head and, as it were, on to my tongue'. He occasionally recalled it during the day, but it was soon forgotten. 'The next morning, when I arrived at my office at the university, one of the first envelopes in my mailbox was from a Mrs Coudetat of San Diego' – the first letter he had ever received from anybody of that name.

'Although one can never be certain about just what is and what isn't coincidence in spontaneous cases,' Tart comments,

> I personally regard this 'coup d'état' case as a clear instance of predictive psi. The unusualness of my speaking repeatedly aloud to myself with no discernible motivation to do so at the time, the rarity of the words 'coup d'état' in my life, and the immediate confirmation of their importance the following morning rule out coincidence as a good explanation.

He was using the term predictive psi, he explained, rather than precognition, because it might have been telepathy – picking up what Mrs Coudetat was conveying in her letter.

Psychokinesis
The greater readiness to recognise the importance of such coincidences as of real significance for the study of ESP, however, is not so evident in connection with PK: with the various physical phenomena associated with psi. Alice Johnson did not care to include them in her selection of the main material for psychical researchers in spite of the fact that they had been one of the chief objects of earlier research; and although world-wide interest was aroused in them in the early 1970s by Uri Geller's performances, it has since declined.

In the opening scene of Tom Stoppard's play *Rosencrantz and Guildenstern are Dead*, the two of them are found passing the time by betting on the spin of a coin. Guil's money bag is nearly empty, Ros's nearly full, for a reason which soon becomes apparent: Ros is guessing heads, each time; heads is coming up, each time. When the tally reaches the seventies, Guil despairingly invokes probability theory. 'The law of averages, if I got this right, means that if six monkeys were thrown up in the air for long enough they would land on their tails about as often as they would land on their . . .' At this point, Ros again says, 'Heads'; heads it is.

What could be the explanation? Guil offers a list of possibles: he was willing it; time had stopped; divine intervention; 'un-, sub-, or supernatural forces'. Disturbed, he pauses. 'The scientific approach to the examination of phenomena is a defence against the pure emotion of fear,' he resumes. 'Keep tight hold and continue while there's time' – and he produces a rationalisation to justify his reluctance to accept that such forces could be responsible for the apparent breaking of the probabilities 'law'.

If we postulate, and we just have, that within un-, sub-, or supernatural forces *the probability* is that the law of probability will not operate as a factor, then we must accept that the probability of the *first* part will not operate as a factor, in which case the law of probability will operate as a factor within un-, sub- or supernatural forces. And since it obviously hasn't been doing so, we can take it that we are not held within un-, sub- or supernatural forces at all; in all probability, that is. Which is a great relief to me personally.

Having delivered himself of this notable rationalisation Guil pauses; 'Which is all very well, except that . . .' When he resumes, it is 'With tight hysteria, under control'.

Few people in his position would be able to keep their hysteria under control. Even if the existence of psychokinetic forces is accepted, they are expected to confine their manifestation to poltergeist hauntings and omens at the time of death. Stoppard's play was staged in 1967; ten years later, that opening scene was bizarrely parodied in the course of experiments undertaken with Matthew Manning in California.

Manning was one of the species dubbed 'mini-Gellers' who emerged as psychic in the 1970s, following the publicity given to Uri Geller's performances; and in exhaustive tests in many different countries, Manning ran up a string of positive results until, wearying of the role of guinea-pig, he decided to concentrate his attention on becoming a healer, the career he has followed since. The most remarkable phenomenon, however, was observed not in the course of a test, but in the preliminaries.

What happened was reported by F. W. Lorenz of the Department of Animal Psychology, University of California, Davis. The trials were designed to discover if Manning could influence, among other things, 'galvanic skin response'; he was put in an isolation room, from which he was to try to influence the minds of volunteer subjects in another room. Their reactions (if any) were to be measured on an instrument of the kind best known for its use as a lie detector, by picking up minute changes in the perspiration levels of the palm of the hand. To comply with the accepted protocol for such experiments, the timing of Manning's attempts to stimulate or to inhibit the sweating had to be randomised, so that there could be no question of collusion, in advance, between him and any of the subjects. The outcome was described in Lorenz's report.

Our attempts to specify random sequences had disconcerting results. At first we entered a table of random numbers, using odd numbers for arousal and even numbers for sedation, but each time we obtained abnormally long sequences of odd or even. Then I turned to tossing a coin and obtained nine heads in a row. I refused to use that, and made two further attempts, both of which led to long sequences of the same face before being abandoned.

This was not the only disconcerting evidence of 'un-, sub- or supernatural' forces in the course of the experiments. The 'Pauli Effect' was much in evidence, as it often was when Manning was being tested. Wolfgang Pauli became notorious among his quantum physicist colleagues for the way in which he seemed to be a walking poltergeist. 'Something usually broke in the lab,' George Gamow recalled, 'whenever he merely stepped across the threshold.' On one occasion, according to Gamow, a complicated apparatus for the study of atomic phenomena collapsed in a laboratory in Göttingen; it was later found that Pauli, on his way from Zurich to Copenhagen, had been in a train which had stopped for a few minutes in Göttingen station. 'You may believe this anecdote or not,' Gamow commented in *Thirty Years that Shook Physics* (1966), 'but there are many other observations concerning the Pauli Effect.' Another physicist, Werner Heisenberg agreed; he, too, had encountered it.

There are many other observations concerning Manning's 'Pauli Effect'; recording instruments going haywire, to the researchers' frustration. The investigators of poltergeist hauntings have often had the same experience. In *The Challenge of Chance* Koestler dealt in some detail with the poltergeist which plagued a lawyer's office in the Bavarian town of Rosenheim. The most elaborate of the investigations was staged by two Munich physicists, who introduced an array of gadgetry to detect any human intervention; eventually they had to report that 'although recorded with the facilities available to experimental physics, the events defied explanation in terms of current physical theories.' Not merely had objects been found to move – and were filmed by remote-controlled cameras in the process – but the movements 'gave the impression of being under intelligent control and to have a tendency to evade investigation.'

Coincidences eventually led to the discovery of the source of the trouble. A legal secretary, Annemarie S—, was a victim of the Pauli Effect; among other signs was that if she accompanied her fiancé to the bowling alley, the machine which automatically registered his score would break down. When Professor Hans Bender of the University of Freiburg studied the evidence about the times when the disturbances in the office occurred, he was able to bring the haunting to an end by the simple expedient of persuading her, in her own interest, to leave her job; she had fallen in love with the lawyer, he found, and the maniestations appeared to be linked to her frustration at having him within reach, but being kept at arm's length. On her departure, the office had no more trouble. Nor did she; she married soon afterwards, and the Pauli Effect ceased.

Significantly, no serious attempt has been made to discredit the Rosenheim findings. But if they are accepted, their implications for the study of coincidence are far-reaching. And they can no longer be dismissed on the ground that they would constitute a violation of the laws of nature. Those laws have been repealed; and in the new model which the quantum physicists have been constructing, action at a distance of a kind has had to be incorporated.

6

The Implications of Research

Quantum physics
The discoveries of the quantum physicists have proved to be crucial to the understanding of coincidence – or perhaps it would be safer, at this stage, to call it the removal of certain misunderstandings about coincidence, derived from the materialist principles which emerged in the seventeenth century and hardened into the mechanistic dogma in the nineteenth.

The key features of quantum theory that have challenged traditional mechanism – David Bohm, Professor of Theoretical Physics at Birkbeck College, London, explained in *Wholeness and the Implicate Order* (1980) – are, first, that 'movement is in general discontinuous' (an electron, for example, can go from one state to another, without passing through any states in between); second, that 'entities such as electrons can show different properties, particle-like, wave-like or something in between', and third, 'two entities, such as electrons, which initially combine to form a molecule and then separate, show a peculiar non-local relationship, which can best be described as a non-causal connection of elements that are far apart.' Whereas the mechanistic principle, even when transformed by Einstein, required continuity, strict causality and locality, 'quantum theory requires non-continuity, non-causality and non-locality.'

The significance of 'non-locality' becomes more apparent when the term is translated into colloquial English. 'Physicists have the reputation of coining strange terms, a fact that sometimes irks the philosopher and the historian,' Henry Margenau, Emeritus Professor of Physics at Yale, has jestingly reprimanded his colleagues. They speak of non-locality: 'the good old term "action at a distance" which has had a lively and interesting existence, would do as well.'

The adoption of 'non-locality' was presumably the result of the alarm physicists have long felt at the notion that such action can occur, with no apparent cause. It was this which led Galileo to deride as an occult fancy the notion that the moon acted on the tides; even Newton was to dismiss the idea that one body could act on another through a vacuum, without the mediation of anything else, as 'so great an absurdity that I believe no man who has in philosophical matters a competent faculty for thinking can ever fall for it'. Gravity, however, appeared to obey laws; as did magnetism, in spite of some eccentric quirks. In any case, their effects could readily be demonstrated. They have therefore been classified as causal, though they have remained occult in the sense that no explanation for them can be found. Anomalous forms of action at a distance which cannot be demonstrated – not, at least, in ways acceptable to orthodoxy – have remained outlawed.

Orthodoxy's attitude to non-locality has consequently been ambivalent. The method by which it has been established is not easy to present in colloquial English, but Paul Davies, while he was Professor of Physics at the University of Newcastle (before he was carried away to the United States through the brain drain), has done his best in *God and the New Physics* (1983). The fundamental difference between Einstein's theory and quantum theory, Davies explains, was that Einstein assumed that subnuclear particles, by analogy, behaved much as bullets do when fired from a gun at a target. Niels Bohr maintained that in quantum theory, 'electrons from an electron gun simply turn up at the target.'

> Instead of envisaging the electron at the target as really existing prior to its arrival and being connected to the gun by a precise trajectory, physicists think of the electron leaving the gun as being in a sort of limbo, its presence represented only by cohorts of ghosts.

Each 'ghost' follows its own path, though only one turns up at the target. Not surprisingly, Einstein could not swallow this apparently preposterous notion, and he suggested a way in which it might be possible to show that Bohr was wrong. If a particle split into two fragments, and they were shot off in different directions, each would carry the imprint of its former partner; if one flew off spinning clockwise, the other would continue to spin anti-clockwise. It was not until after his death that the experiment was undertaken; it showed that Bohr had been right. It is as if the fragments, on their journey apart, are represented by two 'ghosts', A and B. 'If a measurement of

A promotes, for instance, the clockwise ghost to reality, B has no choice; it must promote the anti-clockwise ghost.'

As Davies comments,

> It seems baffling, to say the least, how fragment B can possibly *know* for which of its two ghosts fragment A has opted. If the fragments are well separated, it is hard to see how they can communicate. Furthermore, if both fragments are observed simultaneously, there is simply no time for any signal to propagate between the fragments.

Nevertheless the communication happens: 'events without causes, ghost images, reality triggered only by observation – all must apparently be accepted on the experimental evidence.'

Unable any longer to reject the evidence, some physicists have been quick to deny that it lends any support to the findings of psychical research. The fact that subnuclear fragments communicate, they argue, does not prove that messages can pass in the same way from mind to mind. In any case, the brain has no source of power to transmit them. But these arguments reveal a lack of knowledge of the psychical researchers' theories. Before non-locality had been heard of, the physicist Sir William Barrett, one of the founders of the SPR, had asserted that telepathy was not to be thought of as a kind of wireless. The evidence, he insisted in 1924 in a letter to *The Times*, 'all points to the phenomena of telepathy as being due not to any physical transmission across space'; it should be thought of as transfusion, rather than transmission.

Recently Alan Gauld of the University of Nottingham has taken this argument a step further. The term 'extra-sensory perception', he feels, is a complete misnomer, in so far as it conjures up a picture of the perception reaching us in the same way that, say, the sound of a knock on the door reaches us. 'We do not acquire the factual knowledge exhibited in so-called ESP by any quasi-perceptual or transmissive process, though sometimes we may fancy we do, because of the form in which it manifests itself,' he insists. From the point of view of everyday notions about how we acquire factual information, the knowledge obtained is totally anomalous. 'It is not "acquired". The information does not "arrive". The knowledge, so to speak, "happens".'

It 'happens', too, without the need for a source of power within the brain. The evidence, Henry Margenau has commented, suggests that the happenings do not involve 'transfer of energy or any exertion of force'. The energy appears to be latent in the universe – just as the savages (as anthropologists thought of them) assumed, with their belief in *mana*, an occult reservoir of power which could flow through people, and which a few individuals, shamans and sorcerers, could tap to work magic.

Quantum theory implies that what appears to be empty space does in fact lend justification to that belief. Matter turns out to be 'no more than a relatively small wave or disturbance on top of this "ocean" of energy,' David Bohm has pointed out; 'using reasonable assumptions, the energy of one cubic centimetre of space is far greater than would be available from the nuclear disintegration of all the matter in the known universe.'

The mere fact of the energy being available, though, would be of little importance if there were no prospect of tapping it in the way that Emerson suggested in his essay on Fate: 'I believe the mind is the creator of the world, and is ever creating,' he claimed. 'Thoughts rule the world.' Half a century later his mystic's view was surprisingly echoed by two of the early commentators on the impact of the new physics. 'The stuff of the world is mind stuff,' Sir Arthur Eddington wrote in 1927. 'The stream of knowledge is heading towards a non-mechanical reality,' Sir James Jeans confirmed four years later; 'the universe begins to look more like a great thought than a great machine.'

Gradually it began to look even more like a great thought; in 1980 David Bohm described the many analogies which had been established between thought processes and quantum events in *Wholeness and the Implicate Order*. They were still, however, analogies; to obtain an understanding of the actual relationship, he admitted, was proving extremely difficult. In 1988 the Oxford University physicist Roger Penrose took up the challenge. As non-local quantum correlations can occur over widely separated distances,

it seems to me to be a definite possibility that such things could be playing a role in conscious thought modes. Perhaps it is not too fanciful to suggest that quantum correlations could be playing an operative role over large sections of the brain. Might there be any relation between a 'state of awareness' and a highly coherent quantum state in the brain? Is the 'oneness' or 'globality' that seems to be a feature of consciousness connected with this? It is somewhat tempting to believe so.

In *The Quantum Self* (1990) Danah Zohar has surveyed the accumulating evidence, concluding that quantum physics and consciousness can be reconciled without loss of 'face' either to mind, or to individuality. 'Once we have made this connection, once we have seen that the physics of human consciousness emerges from quantum processes within the brain and that in consequence, human consciousness and the whole world of creation share a physics with everything else in this universe,' she feels, 'it becomes impossible to imagine a single aspect of our lives that is not drawn into one coherent whole.'

If this belief turns out to be justified, another of Emerson's contentions will be lent some justification, too. Who, he asked rhetorically in his essay on Power, shall set a limit to the influence of a human being?

> There are men who by their sympathetic attractions carry nations with them and lead the activity of the human race. And if there be such a tie that wherever the mind of man goes, nature will accompany him, perhaps there are men whose magnetisms are of that force to draw material and elemental powers, and, where they appear, immense instrumentalities organise around them.

Biology
'Biologists, who once postulated a privileged role for the human mind in nature's hierarchy, have been moving relentlessly toward the hard-core materialism that characterised nineteenth-century physics,' the psychologist Harold Morowitz has observed. 'At the same time, physicists, faced with compelling experimental evidence, have been moving away from strictly mechanical models of the universe to a view that sees the mind playing an integral role in all physical events. It is as if the two disciplines were on fast-moving trains, going in opposite directions and not noticing what is happening across the tracks.'

One aspect of mind which is of obvious biological significance for coincidence is the presence in nature of, in effect, non-local minds, exercising control of the actions of individual members of certain species such as ants, which do not have individual minds. Its existence is not in question; but the implications for biologists riding on the materialist express have been so disturbing that with few exceptions they have not cared to face the facts.

In a lecture he gave to American biologists in 1910, the eminent zoologist Henry Morton Wheeler urged that the facts ought to be faced. Biological theory, he told his audience, must remain incomplete if the study of 'superorganisms', as he described them, was neglected because of 'our fear of the psychological and the metaphysical'. 'Superorganism' came into use for a while as convenient shorthand for an anthill or a termitary, but Wheeler's plea was ignored. 'It is not just that the idea has been forgotten,' Lewis Thomas commented in *The Lives of a Cell* (1974). 'It is as though it has become unmentionable, an embarrassment.'

It is evidently an embarrassment to Thomas, as well. In his capacity as president of the Memorial Sloan Kettering Center, and subsequently as University Professor of the State University of New York, he has an honoured status in the scientific establishment; but under his other hat, as the most accomplished essayist writing on science today, he has often acted as the establishment's conscience-pricker. And in *Late Night Thoughts* (1984) he has returned to the issue.

To account for the way in which blind termites 'organise in platoons and begin sticking up pellets to precisely the right height, then turning the arches to connect the columns, constructing the cathedral and its chambers in which the colony will live out its life for the decades ahead, air-conditioned and humidity-controlled', as he describes the process, biology has to fall back on 'the chemical blueprint coded in their genes'. This can only mean that the blueprint has made provision for the emergence of a group mind, capable of intelligent advance planning as well as minute-to-minute control. And if this exists at the evolutionary level of the termite, why should it not exist in some form among humans?

I can say, if I like, that social insects behave like the working parts of an immense central nervous system: the termite colony is an enormous brain on millions of legs; the individual termite is a mobile neurone. This would mean that there is such a phenomenon as collective thinking, which goes on whenever sufficient numbers of creatures are sufficiently connected to one another, and it would also mean that we humans could do the same trick if we tried, and perhaps we've already done it . . .

Collective thinking – or, rather, collective behaviour – is in fact familiar in society in the form of mass hysteria. The forms it commonly takes help to explain why it is not more familiar on an everyday level; the evolution of the human race was only possible through a decisive break with the control which operates in termitaries, enabling individuals to make their own decisions, even when they involve overcoming instinct's promptings. Mass hysteria usually represents an unwelcome regression to an earlier evolutionary stage. Yet there are indications that this form of group mind control has itself evolved, and that it may be playing a useful role in people's lives as a prompter. This was Jung's assumption; to understand synchronicity, he believed, the idea of the psyche being connected simply with the brain would have to be abandoned and replaced by the model of 'the "meaningful" or "intelligent" behaviour of the lower organisms, which are without a brain.'

This ties in well with Rupert Sheldrake's theory of formative causation, expounded in *A New Science of Life* (1981) and *The Presence of the Past* (1988). Orthodoxy has tried to explain evolution in terms of genes; Sheldrake has put the case for the supplementary role of morphogenetic fields – non-material regions of influence like gravity and magnetism. They operate through resonance, as in 'the sympathetic vibration of stretched strings', but without involving any transfer of energy; and they influence behaviour as well as physical development.

Jung assumed that the contents of the collective unconscious had never been in consciousness, owing their existence 'exclusively to heredity'; but he was unable to explain how such inheritance could occur. It could not occur through straightforward genetic transmission; yet it 'makes very good sense in the light of the hypothesis of formative causation,' Sheldrake argues. 'By morphic resonance, structures of thought and experience that were common to many people in the past contribute to morphic fields.' Should his hypothesis be confirmed as co-existing with genetic influence, synchronicity will become both more plausible and simpler to understand.

Hostile though orthodoxy's reaction has been to Sheldrake's ideas – *Nature*'s editorial described *A New Science of Life* as 'the best candidate for burning there has been for many years' – even so dedicated a geneticist as Richard Dawkins has lent them a measure of support by agreeing that 'we must begin by throwing out the gene as the sole basis of our ideas on evolution'. Human culture, he admitted in *The Selfish*

Gene (1967), needs its equivalent, for which he coined the term 'meme'. He held meme responsible for, among other things, fashions in clothes or in music; 'just as genes propagate themselves in the gene pool by leaping from body to body via sperms or eggs, so memes propagate themselves in the meme pool by leaping from brain to brain via a process which, in the broad sense, can be called imitation.'

Dawkins was employing 'imitation' in the sense of conscious or unconscious copying. Formative causation opens the doors further, Sheldrake surmises.

> If we are influenced by morphic resonance from particular individuals to whom we are in some way linked or connected, then it is conceivable that we might pick up images, thoughts, impressions, or feelings from them, either during waking life or while dreaming, in a way that would go beyond the means of communication recognized by contemporary science. Such resonant connections would be possible even if the people involved were thousands of miles apart. Is there any evidence that such a process actually happens? Perhaps there is, for such a process may be similar to, if not identical with, the mysterious phenomenon of telepathy.

Psychology
Although academic psychologists have shown little interest in the phenomenon of coincidence itself, a few have explored a region which is of obvious significance: the remarkable concurrences in the lives of identical twins who have been separated after birth, and who in some cases have not even been aware of each other's existence.

Dorothy Lowe and Bridget Harrison were separated in 1945, and did not meet until 1979, when they were flown over from Britain for an investigation by Dr Tom Bouchard, a psychologist at the University of Minnesota. They found when they met that they were both wearing seven rings on their hands, two bracelets on one wrist, a watch and a bracelet on the other.

Various possibilities were canvassed. Although they had grown up in families of different social class, they had well-off husbands; their genes had endowed them with long, slender hands which naturally they would wish to show off; and chance could account for the coincidental distribution of the jewellery. Before the investigation concluded, however, the coincidences – as Peter Watson, describing what happened in his book *Twins*, commented – were 'much more difficult to explain away'.

Among them: they had worn identical wedding dresses and carried the same flowers. Dorothy had named her son Richard Andrew, and her daughter, Catherine Louise; Bridget had named her son Andrew Richard, and her daughter Karen Louise (she had wanted to call her Catherine). Both had a cat called Tiger. Dorothy loved the historical novels of Catherine Cookson; Bridget loved the historical novels of Caroline Merchant (Catherine Cookson's other pen name). They had a string of similar mannerisms when nervous . . . and so on.

Dorothy and Bridget 'share the single most perplexing coincidence in this entire book', Watson comments; but there are others almost as striking. Can they *really* have been the outcome of their common genetic inheritance? The problem here is that the issue has been confused by the existence of the fierce running battle between the backers of nature and of nurture; between those psychologists who believe that individual development is in the main innate, genetically ordered, and those who put more emphasis on environmental influences. Tom Bouchard's remarkable findings have inevitably been a gift to the 'nature' school. The evidence from this and other investigations actually prompted a speaker at the 1989 meeting of the American Association for the Advancement of Science to claim that family resemblance for personality 'appears to be entirely genetic in origin'.

Bouchard himself was rather more cautious. He told the meeting that he had been startled by the findings which psychological tests with separated twins had provided. 'I would have placed money on some traits having no genetic influence, and others strong genetic influence,' he claimed; but in fact, they had averaged out. He was particularly astonished, he admitted, by the fact that religious views showed genetic links. But they can be interpreted as showing genetic links only if it is assumed that there is no alternative except the environmental one, ruled out by the separation. If morphic resonance and psi were to be accepted, they would provide a manifestly more plausible explanation for the weird resemblances between the lives of Dorothy and Bridget; and sometimes, to judge by some of the Foundation's contributors, of non-twin siblings.

A common source of amusement among siblings is the tendency to choose the same present for each other. Some years ago Mrs R. Graham noticed that she and one of her sisters had chosen the same wrapping paper for each other's husband's Christmas presents, which were of the same size and shape.

I remarked confidently that they could not be the same presents, as I had bought mine in advance, the previous summer in Madrid. She had bought hers in Dublin in December. They *were* the same – a double pack of playing cards with prints of Persian miniatures on the front.

The day before sending this account to Godfrey Smith at the *Sunday Times*, Mrs Graham and her sister had a similar experience. Mrs Graham had bought a polar bear toy for one of her nieces in a tiny village in Portugal; it turned out that the year before her sister had bought the same toy for the same niece at a shop in York.

May there be a link, here, with 'couvade'? According to the Shorter Oxford English Dictionary, 'couvade' was 'Tylor's name for the "man-childbed" attributed to some uncivilized races, and the custom according to which, on the birth of a child, the man is put to bed, and treated as if he were physically afflicted by the birth.' This is a travesty of Edward Tylor's attitude. The founder of anthropology as an academic discipline in Britain, he was himself singularly free from academic inhibitions. Couvade, he explained, was widespread, in different forms.

It shows a number of distinct and different tribes holding the opinion that the connection between father and child is not only, as we think, a mere relation of parentage, affection, duty, but that their very bodies are joined by a physical bond so that what is done to the one acts directly upon the other

Tylor linked couvade with sorcery and divination as examples of the mental condition of tribal communities; but this did not entail mocking it. Unlike Sir James Frazer, whose *The Golden Bough* was to become anthropology's bible in spite of its glaring imperfections, Tylor was open-minded enough to assume that there must often be something genuine lying behind the spurious façade of tribal magic.

Couvade crops up in Britain only in flippant reports of husbands sharing their wives' labour pains; but to judge from some of the coincidences sent in to the Foundation, cases where, say, parents suddenly suffer from severe symptoms which they later find are related to actual pains from which their children have suffered, it deserves serious study.

Neurophysiology
Until quite recently, neurophysiology had little to offer for the study
of coincidence. Its practitioners were chiefly concerned to explain
what goes on in the mind by what goes on in the brain. One of the
most eminent of them, Wilder Penfield, had established his reputation
by linking human memories to specific areas of the brain so that they
could be 'tickled' into remembrance by the prick of a needle. But in his
Second Thoughts (1970), while agreeing that there had been a steady
advance in the understanding of the workings of the brain, he insisted
that this had not led to the mind being explained.

> It seems to be a phenomenon of another order. Somehow it is
> capable of reason, discretion, intuition, creative thought, con-
> sidered judgment. Somehow, too, the mind can exert control over
> attention. Those things that are ignored leave no trace in the brain.

No mechanism has been found to compel the brain to think, Penfield
pointed out.

> The mind continues free. This is a statement I have long considered.
> I have made every effort to disprove it. The mind, I must conclude,
> is something more than a mechanism. It is, in a certain sense, above
> and beyond the brain, although it seems to depend on brain action
> for its very existence.
>   Yet it is free.

If Penfield was right, the materialist case against communication
between mind and mind collapses. And his view is shared by the
Nobel Prizewinner Sir John Eccles. 'The more we discover about the
brain, the more clearly do we distinguish between the brain events and
mental phenomena,' he maintains, 'and the more wonderful do both
the brain events and the mental phenomena become.'

Parapsychology
Many people who experience very striking coincidences in their lives,
Robert Morris, holder of the Koestler Chair at Edinburgh, has
observed, attribute considerable meaning to them.

> The study of such coincidences is important for depth psychology,
> as it may have profound implications for our understanding of the

psyche and its relationship with the universe, as well as for the usage of such material in therapy. Parapsychology is interested, because by definition it deals at least with a subclass of coincidences, those involving unexpected correspondences between events in an organism and events in the environment.

Parapsychologists have made a number of attempts to present hypotheses about the way in which psi works to promote coincidences. A consensus has been developing derived from the assumption that psi is an early evolutionary development – the 'sixth sense' being effectively the first, later supplemented by the five, and eventually being swamped by them because, Henri Bergson suggested, the human brain evolved as a necessary filter, selecting what is immediately necessary for survival from the mass of inchoate information pouring in through the senses. The sixth sense, however, has never been entirely lost. It gets its messages across, the psychiatrist Jan Ehrenwald has surmised, partly through leakage – the brain's filter allowing information through when consciousness is dulled, as in sleep or trance conditions; partly through need – the brain concedes the urgency of the message. And psi 'happens' by the same process as non-locality – and, presumably, as termites 'get the message'; ESP and PK appear to be bound together.

If non-local information transference is accepted, it follows that many coincidences can be atttributed to it; a prospect which has recently been attracting parapsychologists' attention. Visiting some friends in New York, Rex Stanford got off the subway by mistake one station too soon, which ordinarily would have entailed a longer walk. As it happened, while he was on it he encountered his friends; doubly lucky, as they would not have been at home if he had reached it after getting off at the right station. This and similar coincidences have led Stanford to present his hypothesis of 'psi-mediated instrumental response', a clumsy title usually compressed into PMIR.

Up to a point, PMIR can be equated with intuition. But intuition is normally regarded as a form of subliminal prompting which reaches consciousness, urging a course of action, whereas PMIR may remain subliminal – Stanford did not *intend* to get off at the 'wrong' station. It comes closer to serendipity, as it is usually applied to the process by which people appear to be guided to something which fulfils a conscious need. It is as if the mind has undergone an evolutionary development adapting the rigorous control of a termitary to more flexible human requirements. Whereas the individual person in mass hysteria outbreaks is under a form of group dictation, PMIR appears to operate through and on behalf of the individual.

'On behalf of' may suggest that the process is beneficial; perhaps it should be emphasised that some people from time to time appear to be victims of a PMIR version of 'Murphy's Law', by which their slice of toast, whenever it falls on the floor, inevitably lands butter-side down. One of Myers' correspondents wrote to tell him of an occasion when he suddenly felt the conviction that if he went by his usual route he would meet a friend whom he particularly did not wish to meet; 'I therefore, without hesitation, took another road, and having arrived at one of the street corners, whom should I meet but my friend.' His premonition, he insisted, had not been just conjecture: it had seemed to him as if it had been 'an instantaneous intimation to my soul'. Many of the coincidences in the 'joker' category which are being reported today leave the victims with the feeling that their PMIR has operated to mock or even to punish them.

The 'Murphy's Law' aspect of coincidence has been explored by Jule Eisenbud. Parapsychologists are often mocked with the question why, if certain individuals really have psychic powers, do they not use them to make their fortunes on the horses, or on the Stock Exchange? The stock answer is that psi operates at the unconscious level; if it were under voluntary control, things would be different. Would they be so different, though? Eisenbud suggests that not merely is psi beyond voluntary control; the goals it serves 'may often be at variance with those which are consciously espoused, and which we all too un-thinkingly imagine to be the "natural" or "normal" goals of the individual.' The goals which it serves, he argues, are those which arise out of *un*conscious needs.

As a Freudian psychoanalyst, Eisenbud has often been able to observe the process at work in a patient's life. Psi, he has found,

> may be presumed to operate not just in dreams and other events that we classify as 'mental', but also to have a part in determining where he goes, who he meets, what he does, and so forth. It has been possible to show the strong presumption of psi factors at work in leading a person to be unconsciously guided out of his accustomed orbit and, as if in fulfilment of a strong sense of guilt (which could be independently demonstrated at the time), orientated toward potentially 'punishing' events.

Eisenbud has been more concerned as an analyst with the people who are that way orientated than with those whose lives direct them to potentially fulfilling events; but the same principle presumably applies. The force which propelled Myers' friend towards an encounter he was seeking to avoid may facilitate the promotion to Field Marshal of a man under 'Mars rising' by nudging him into the right place at the right time.

It may do the same for lovers, by the process Proust described in *Cities of the Plain*. Marcel, the narrator, happens to be the witness of the first meeting between the Baron de Charlus and Jupien, at a time and place where the Baron would normally never have been; only the indisposition of Mme de Villeparisis could have made him pay a call, 'perhaps for the first time in his life, at that hour of the day.' The Baron was one of those men whose sexual satisfaction 'depends upon the coincidence of too many conditions, and of conditions too difficult to ensure.'

> The feud of the Capulets and Montagues was as nothing compared with the obstacles of every sort which must have been surmounted, the special eliminations which nature has had to submit to, the hazards, already far from common, which result in love, before a retired tailor, who was intending to set off soberly for his office, can stand quivering in ecstasy before a stoutish man of fifty; this Romeo and Juliet may believe with good reason that their love is not the caprice of a moment, but a true predestination, prepared by the harmonies of their own temperaments, and not only by their own personal temperaments but by those of their ancestors, by their most distant strains of heredity, so much so that the fellow creature who is conjoined with them has belonged to them from before their birth.

Eisenbud believes that psi represents an early evolutionary process designed not just to facilitate propagation, but also to serve a more wide-ranging ecological purpose. Why does a tarantula spider allow a digger wasp to crawl over it to find the precise spot to insert its paralysing sting, though the tarantula is perfectly capable of escaping from or killing a wasp of another species? As this is only one of numerous examples of similar predator–prey relationships there must, he argues, be some ecological balancing act in operation; 'the thing that would most efficiently fill this bill would be some kind of universal unconscious psi linkage.'

7

Kammerer Revisited

To what extent have developments since the publication of *The Law of the Series* and *Synchronicity* lent credence to the theories? In Kammerer's case, it has to be said, very little, or his book would surely have appeared in an English translation. Nevertheless a case for seriality was presented in *Nature* in 1953. This is at first surprising, in view of *Nature*'s notorious mistrust of such unconventional notions. Evidently neither the writer nor the editor had any idea that this was how it could be construed.

The aim of the writer – the mathematician George Spencer Brown of Trinity College, Cambridge – was to present an ingenious theory to explain away the evidence from laboratory research into ESP, in particular the card-guessing trials at Duke University and elsewhere. As the normally sceptical Professor Hans Eysenck felt compelled to admit in *Sense and Nonsense in Psychology* (1957), unless there was a gigantic conspiracy involving hundreds of respectable scientists all over the world 'the only conclusion the unbiased observer can come to must be that there does exist a small number of people who obtain knowledge either existing in other people's minds, or in the outer world, by means as yet unknown to science'. Spencer Brown had agreed – up to a point: the trials, he thought, had been 'well designed and rigorously controlled'. But the strength of the evidence from them lay mainly in the fact that the positive results obtained by a few of the people tested were significantly above chance, statistically speaking. They were not, however, *spectacularly* above chance; and even the most proficient guessers tended to succumb to 'decline effect', their scores eventually dropping to chance level. This, he argued, meant that they need not be interpreted as providing evidence for ESP. On the contrary, they provided a good reason for 'beginning to doubt the universal applicability of classical frequency probability.' Randomness, in other words, may not be random; it may throw up patterns which give the impression of being caused by ESP.

Irritating though this might be to parapsychologists, by rendering some of the evidence for ESP suspect, it was even less welcome to orthodox scientists, if their faith in probability theory was put at risk of being undermined. Spencer Brown's idea was hard to prove, or to disprove; it was allowed to fade away. Pointing out that it could not in any case account for some of the results obtained in ESP trials, Sir Alister Hardy nevertheless gave it a cautious welcome on the grounds that if it were eventually to be accepted, it would introduce an important new principle to science. Koestler went further, emphasising its importance for research into coincidence. Spencer Brown's contention that there is something anomalous in the concept of randomness, he pointed out, bears a remarkable resemblance to Kammerer's theory, which is in fact 'the reciprocal of the concept of randomness'.

Otherwise, Kammerer's theory has not attracted support. Perhaps the closest that anybody has come to providing it has been an article 'What are Coincidences?' (1978) by Ivor Grattan-Guinness.

I appear to be 'coincidence-prone', whatever that means. There is a saying that things happen in threes, but mine are usually twos; a constant succession of pairs involving all aspects of daily life, mostly mundane and unworthy of further discussion. In addition, in many cases elementary calculation of probabilities shows that the chances of their occurrence are much *better* than one might imagine. But some coincidences are 'long shots' by any probabilistic standards.

After listing examples, and emphasising the problems they raised, Grattan-Guinness commented that he thought of them 'as a kind of *converse telepathy*'; instead of two people sharing the event, the events are sharing a person – which is why studying them is so difficult: 'the effect does not reside in the person in the same way as it does in many other psychic phenomena.' Grattan-Guinness went on, however, to warn that 'it is particularly dangerous to seek for any overall or holistic explanation'. He was suspicious of synchronicity, too, on the grounds that as a theory it is not falsifiable; 'I prefer the synchronists to the sceptics, but their intellectual record so far does not seem to me to be impressive.' Most of his own cases could be fitted into the hypothesis of psi as the causal agent, along the lines Eisenbud had suggested; but there were problems with that, too.

Jung, though critical of Kammerer's theory, believed that up to a point it could be fused in with synchronicity. In a letter to Rhine in 1945 he provided an example of 'synchronistic seriality'; he had noticed on one occasion that the number of his streetcar ticket was the same as the number of the ticket for the concert to which he went the same evening, and it had then cropped up in a telephone conversation. Quite why this qualified as synchronistic he did not make clear; but it was to provide Vaughan with the more impressive example which he recalled in his *Patterns of Prophecy*.

Vaughan had come across Jung's letter to Rhine on the morning of 19 April 1968, as his diary entry for that day confirmed.

Having read an account of Jung's finding a synchronistic relationship between his streetcar ticket number, his theatre ticket number, and a phone number, I studied my streetcar ticket number. It was 096960. Then I realised I was looking at it upside down. But it was the same: 096960. The number of the streetcar could also be read upside down: 111. But instead of finding a third number, like Jung, I nearly tripped over an ashcan with the name JUNG written on it.

Kammerer and his theory may not have attracted attention, but 'clustering' evidently still arouses interest, sometimes amusement, occasionally uneasiness. A cluster is not as a rule thought of as having a particular relevance to the individuals experiencing it, unless it happens to have some significance – say, a succession of their 'lucky' numbers; but it can prompt speculation on whether some unexplained force is at work.

8

Jung Revisited

In a lecture given in 1977 John Beloff recalled that although when he read Jung's *Synchronicity* he had been intrigued, regarding it as 'one of the more extravagant products of Jung's fertile imagination', he had not expected it to catch on. Events had proved him wrong; 'fourteen years later, although it could not be said to occupy a paramount place in contemporary parapsychological speculation, it has become a firm fixture.'

Thirteen years later still, it has spread out to establish itself among what used to be described as the intelligentsia, a species which today lacks an identification, but for convenience can be described as the readers of the 'quality' newspapers and magazines. Synchronicity can no longer be closely identified, however, with Jung's concept; partly because Jung himself did not claim to present it as a fully-fledged theory. In the foreword to his essay on the subject, he explained that he was making good a promise which for many years he had lacked the courage to fulfil; 'the difficulties of the problem and its presentation seemed to me too great; too great the intellectual responsibility without which a subject cannot be tackled; too inadequate, in the long run, my scientific training'. His research into symbols, however, had brought the problem closer; and as he had been alluding to synchronicity for twenty years he felt it was time to explain what he had in mind by it – though this would entail, he feared, 'uncommon demands on the open-mindedness and goodwill of the reader.'

It still does, not least because Jung was not good at elucidating obscurities in his ideas. His 'scarab' illustration of synchronicity (see page 5) gives a clearer picture than his attempts to describe it as a theory: the unconscious minds of therapist and patient, brought into collaboration by the need of the patient to find a way out of her problems and the need of the therapist to help her, are assisted by synchronicity in the form of a contribution from the collective unconscious – an archetype, the scarabeid beetle, arriving at the opportune moment in the session.

How, though, was this done? Jung turned to Pauli to explain that the new physics left the door open for the acceptance of acausal forces; and to Rhine, for the evidence which his research at Duke University had provided for the reality of psi phenomena, showing how the intercommunication between individuals – and, presumably, between individuals and the collective unconscious – could be accounted for. But this pushed Jung into accepting that the phenomena should be considered acausal: a source of confusion.

It was Jung's harping on acausality which chiefly irritated Koestler when he came to examine the theory of synchronicity. Starting from the acausality premise, he complained, Jung had nevertheless ended up with the notion that the archetypes had somehow engineered the scarab's appearance at the window. The confusion had arisen, John Beloff has explained, because of Jung's arbitrary decision to restrict the meaning of causality to the way in which it is understood in physics. Jung had taken for granted that because trials had shown that telepathic communication appeared to be instantaneous, regardless of the distances involved, it must be acausal, as this was how quantum physics classified acausality. But 'what this argument overlooks is that the concept of cause was not invented by physicists'. It was surely nonsensical to claim that the findings from card-guessing trials for telepathy, if they were positive, were not causally related. Whether Uri Geller bends keys by normal or paranormal means, 'the one thing we can be sure about is that he *causes* them to bend.'

'Meaningful' has also raised problems. When Jung recalled that his interest in synchronicity had been roused by coincidences which were connected 'so meaningfully that their "chance" concurrence would represent a degree of improbability that would have to be expressed by an astronomical figure', he was using the term in a special sense. It is usually employed – as, for that matter, is 'synchronicity' – to describe a coincidence which has a meaning for the person or people it has involved, in the sense of giving the impression that it may have been designed for them, for good or ill. An improbable coincidence excites curiosity, but the improbability does not make it meaningful in this second sense; whereas a coincidence which ordinarily would be readily attributed to chance can become meaningful if it leaves those concerned wondering if it has implications for them, personally.

Synchronicity may be the best known theory to account for meaningful coincidences, Grattan-Guinness has observed, but it is 'probably the most feeble' – he is one of many parapsychologists who share Koestler's irritation with it. As an alternative Grattan–Guinness offers 'propensity', a hypothesis covering a group of theories which have in common the assumption that 'nature', including the person involved and his environment, 'has a propensity to fall into certain states of affairs which are favourable (or unfavourable) to psi events' – a notion related to Sir Karl Popper's theory of probabilities, set out in his *Logic of Scientific Discovery*. The most convincing criticism of Jung's theory, however, is Eisenbud's. Jung had the idea of synchronicity, and then contrived to fuse psi into it. But if psi is accepted on Eisenbud's or Sheldrake's model, there is less need for synchronicity. Most meaningful coincidences can be accounted for without it.

As things stand, therefore, it would be unwise to try to resuscitate synchronicity in its original form. Nevertheless the basic idea of an acausal connecting principle, as Beloff concedes, 'is not devoid of meaning'. The concept of acausality may have to be dispensed with, 'but the type of cause that we are left with is very different from the type of cause we associated with mechanical forces'. The essential point, David Peat claims in *Synchronicity* (1987), is that Jung presented a hypothesis which spanned the apparently unbridgeable gap 'between the objective and subjective approaches to the question of the universe and our role within it.'

> Synchronicity provides us with a starting point, for it represents a tiny flaw in the fabric of all that we have hitherto taken for a reality. Synchronicities give us a glimpse beyond our conventional notions of time and causality into the immense patterns of nature, the underlying dance which connects all things and the mirror which is suspended between inner and outer universes. With synchronicity as our starting point it becomes possible to begin the construction of a bridge that spans the worlds of mind and matter, physics and psyche.

9

Where, From Here?

Approved of or not, 'synchronicity' seems likely to continue in colloquial circulation, along with 'meaningful'. The fact that they are so loosely defined may even be an advantage, in view of the number and variety of alternative explanations for those coincidences which suggest unexplained forces at work. From the accounts submitted to the Foundation it is evident that the existence of such forces is taken for granted by many people who are neither superstitious nor gullible, simply on the evidence of personal experience. They are not prepared to accept that orthodox science has all the answers.

The first stage in the construction of an improved model of synchronicity, based on such evidence, is to examine the accounts as far as possible without doctrinaire preconceptions – as was indeed urged in a paper, 'Coincidence', read at a meeting of the Royal Society of Literature in 1896 by Friedrich Max-Müller, Professor of Comparative Philology at Oxford and an internationally renowned expert on early languages and religions. Muller was mainly concerned with the remarkable coincidences he had found while comparing the early Buddhist writings and the Bible. He had come across the tale familiar as 'the judgment of Solomon', for example, in a Buddhist tract, in a slightly different and, he felt, a 'more clever, more true psychologically' version. After a man had died, two of his widows claimed the custody of a child. The wise Visakha, asked to arbitrate, told them to see which of them could pull the child from the other by main force. 'This was done, but as soon as the child began to cry, one of the women let go; Visakha declared at once that she was the real mother and gave the child to her.'

Such parallels were of great philological and historical interest, Muller contended. They had been noticed and commented upon, 'unfortunately not in a purely historical spirit, but in the impassioned tone of theological controversy.' Christians felt threatened when told that, for example, the New Testament miracles – the star seen over the

stable where Jesus was born, the walking on water, the feeding of the
five thousand with loaves and fishes, and many more – could be found
in Buddhist texts centuries before Jesus's birth. Theologians had at
first rejected such evidence; later, when it became incontrovertible,
they had simply averted their eyes from it, as too embarrassing to
contemplate. Some of the coincidences, Muller was sure, could be
accounted for by the same process which leads to similar myths arising
in countries far apart; some, by chance. 'But in a few, the parallelism is
too clear to be denied.' In such cases, it was surely the duty of scholars
to try to find out whether, and if so, how, they were carried from India
to Palestine; if not, how else could they be explained.

Synchronicity arouses much the same reaction today, dismissed as
it is as 'unscientific' in orthodox circles. 'Scientists tend not to ask
themselves questions until they can see the rudiments of an answer in
their minds,' Sir Peter Medawar acknowledged in *The Future of Man*,
excusing this attitude as an understandable fault of temperament.
'Embarrassing questions tend to remain unasked or, if asked, to be
answered rudely.' Medawar might find it understandable, but some of
the most eminent of scientists have denounced such intolerance. In
1956 Michael Polyani, widely regarded as the premier scientist-
philosopher of recent times, wrote an article for *Science* begging that a
ten-year ban should be imposed on the use of the term 'scientific' for
the harm it had been doing, 'applied in a way which is absolutely
destructive'. Sir John Eccles agrees; 'We have to learn to live with
problems beyond our present understanding,' he has urged his fellow
scientists, 'and not impulsively to deny either the existence or the
reality of such problems.'

As it happens, however, with the emphasis so heavily on controlled
laboratory-type experiments, coincidences are not an attractive
subject for scientific research. It can only be conducted by members of
the public. They too, need to recall Müller's plea: 'Whatever value we
may attach to our most cherished convictions, there is something
more precious than all of them, and that is a perfect trust in truth, once
we have seen it.'

An investigation of coincidences should be primarily designed to
get at the truth, or at least make progress towards it. But as Koestler
pointed out, it should also have another aim: to clear away the murk
that has collected around them. The moment that chance ceases to be a
convincing explanation, uneasiness sets in – as has been shown by the
number of people who have asked the Foundation to maintain their

confidentiality. Often, of course, this is for readily acceptable reasons; but in some cases the mere fact of having an interest in coincidence must not be disclosed because of 'what people might think'. 'Peter Savage' for one, tells us he believes many people have had similar experiences to him 'but are embarrassed to speak out in case they are thought of as cranks'. His experiences appear to have been commonplace enough – the occasional precognitive dream; spontaneous perceptions; *déjà vu*; thinking of somebody a moment before he rings up – yet he insists on preserving his anonymity.

Other contributors express relief that the subject has at last been brought out into the open. After the publication of *The Unknown Guest* letters came into us at the Foundation expressing heartfelt gratitude for the revelation that certain experiences which had caused alarm were not merely commonly encountered, but were nothing to be alarmed about. A typical example was sent in by Mrs A. As a young child, she had a vision of a boy in a sailor suit, standing on a roof and holding a plant in his hand. He had smiled at her; 'I smiled back, and a friendship began'. He always appeared when she went to bed; but when her mother died, and she was put into an orphanage, he came no more. After the war Mrs A obtained a job as a receptionist to an optician, and in 1950 they married. In 1965, after both his parents had died, he brought home with him an album of photographs, some taken of him as a child in the 1920s. At the sight of one of them, 'My heart stopped, and I felt physically ill,' she recalls. 'There in front of me was the little boy from my childhood.' The photo showed him in a sailor suit standing on the roof of a block of flats; although he was not actually holding a plant, a tomato plant was at his side.

'For so long I have felt alone with my story, not daring to discuss it fully with anyone for fear of being thought a crank,' she has told us. 'I have never told my husband.' But she had read some accounts of such happenings, collected by the Foundation; 'Now I know that other, far greater minds than mine, have had the inexplicable happen to them.' Again and again, she has been asking herself whether chance, coincidence 'or some great mathematical order of things', could have been responsible. Asked whether she would permit us to use her account here, she told us she still did not want to be identified, but 'I can't tell you of the relief I felt at getting the story out in the open at last'.

Her coincidence, admittedly, was 'spooky'. But a surprising number of people who clearly regard themselves as free from irrational fears are ready to admit that even mundane coincidences can be disturbing, as Bernard Dixon, a former editor of the *New Scientist*, has confirmed. One day while he was European editor of the science magazine *Omni*, on his way to visit his office in New York, he bought a ticket at the Heathrow parking lot, and got back into his car.

But it wasn't my car. It was precisely the same model and colour as mine and it had been parked right next to mine. Just as I was doing a double-take, its owner appeared from the office. We grinned at each other and drove off to our allotted places in the maze of auto-mobiles. As we locked our vehicles – again alongside each other – I noticed the man's suitcase was virtually identical to mine. We boarded the minibus and commented on this extraordinary coinci-dence. There was more to come. When the driver inquired which terminal we wanted, our replies were identical. We were booked on the same flight.

It was not a particularly striking succession of coincidences, and Dixon had 'long been sceptical about the "meaning" of such events'. Yet he was bothered, 'not because I saw any deep meaning in the happening. It was simply the realisation of how profoundly baffled and disturbed it had left me.' He could just accommodate it intellectually; but his imagination conjured possible sequences of the same kind which would have been harder for him to take.

If Dixon could have been so disturbed by what was hardly, after all, of any great moment – it was not as if, say, he had found that the man was eventually going to get him a new job, or in some other way influence his life – it is not surprising that more significantly meaningful coincidences can be still more worrying.

Research
Of the thousand or so people who filled in Jane Henry's Christmas Eve questionnaire in the *Observer*, two-thirds sent in stamped addressed envelopes asking to be involved in a follow-up study. The final form this will take has yet to be decided upon; but is open to anybody to begin research on the Foundation's behalf. The most important step is to write accounts of coincidences as soon as possible after they occur, and if practicable to have them witnessed. The questionaire will be found on page 209. It will be useful, too, to have not just the events themselves, but also your reactions. One contributor, for

example, emphasises that what has been significant for him is the number of times coincidences have been brought about by a change of plan, causing him to break a habit – as when on impulse he happened to pick up an *Observer*, a paper he did not normally buy, and found himself confronted with the questionnaire on coincidence, a subject which fascinated him.

Where coincidences come in series, as when mothers and children, siblings or lovers appear to enjoy telepathic links, or to experience community of sensation, it is useful to know not just if the linkage is frequent, but also whether it is consistently reliable. Parents with children can also keep an eye out for spontaneous perceptions of the kind Keith Kissack has contributed. Serving with the Green Howards in Italy in 1944, he was leaving battalion HQ after a briefing (which had included synchronising watches) at about 2 pm, when he was knocked unconscious by shell splinters.

Back in Monmouth that day my wife was washing up after lunch. My daughter, aged 2½, to whom I was only a name as she was born after I joined up, was playing with some bricks on the kitchen floor. She suddenly got to her feet, went over to my wife, said, 'Daddy's hurt', and went back to her bricks.

Pets are another potential source of coincidences; stories of dogs and cats who seem on occasion to 'know' what is happening to their owners are legion.

One of the simplest devices coincidence-watchers can employ is the one recommended by J. W. Dunne: a pad and a pencil at the bedside, coupled with the resolution to write down everything remembered about dreams immediately on waking. When J. B. Priestley was preparing a television programme on Time, viewers were asked in advance if they would submit experiences which appeared to contradict conventional notions of the past, present and future; he was inundated with letters (after the first thousand, he admitted, he stopped counting), most of which were about dreams of the future, and many of the best-attested cases came from men and women who had followed Dunne's recommendation. Without it, Priestley surmised, at least a third of those cases would not have come his way.

'Dunne dreams' were not mentioned in my *Observer* article as one of the types of coincidence we were looking out for; but from the replies, they clearly have continued to intrigue those who experience them, and they offer an unusual opportunity for individual research – as A.E. noted. 'It is rarely that profound ideas present themselves to the common people in a form which attracts them, so that they can begin to apply them to life, to experiment with them for themselves and make a really exciting game out of their experiments,' he observed. The founders of great religions might have had this ability, but not the philosophers.

It is quite possible that a man of our time, who is neither a great writer nor a great philosopher but who has only a very acute intelligence, may have found a way of exciting the common people to make explorations in that Everliving. Dunne's book may possibly be the pivot around which great numbers of people may turn to the practical consideration of that transcendental conception of an Everliving in which past and future glow in an eternal present. Any who dream can, if they read *An Experiment with Time*, become fishermen in that Great Deep.

Techniques of meditation and visualisation also offer a useful opportunity for individual research. A trawl through the accounts of coincidences shows how often they are linked to subliminal processes, and are less likely to occur, or are missed, when the conscious mind is active. Everybody knows that when a forgotten name is on the tip of the tongue, the best way to recapture it is not to try, but to think of something else or, better, stop thinking of anything particular; the subliminal will soon present it. What is less known is that the method can be adapted to release intuition, and allow it to pick up information which would otherwise not reach consciousness.

Groups practising meditation can experiment along these lines, as Mrs M. E. Mitchell and some friends did between 1984 and 1986. The method they used was to form mental images and try and project them; at their next meeting, they would compare what they had projected with what, if anything, had been received. They did not have particularly striking results, and often there would be 'displacement effect' – a message intended for one would be picked up by another. But they were impressed by 'the great mass of small coincidences' which they began to experience, leaving them in no doubt that some form of thought-transference was operating. 'It almost certainly happens to everyone all the time,' they decided, '*but* . . . it is not recognised. In the very nature of things it cannot be noticed unless one does some sort of study such as ours.' It is responsible, they feel, 'for the great majority of what we call "coincidences".'

One of the experiments which drew Jung towards the theory of synchronicity, he recalled in *Memories, Dreams, Reflections*, was with the *I Ching*, the 'Chinese Book of Wisdom' dating back to the fourth millenium BC. He cut himself a bunch of reeds, and would sit for hours casting them on the ground in front of him; according to the way they fell, he would look up the appropriate hexagrams in the book, and assess how appropriate the answers were to each question. Time and again, he encountered 'amazing coincidences which seemed to suggest the idea of an acausal parallelism.' Some of our contributors recommend following his example, as a research preliminary, using coins as more convenient than stalks. 'Meaningful coincidences between throwing the coins and the answer are the rule, not the exception,' one enthusiast claims; an answer which will carry particular conviction comes if you impatiently ask a question that has just been answered, and you get the hexagram Four – 'the first time he asks, I answer; but if he asks again and again, it is annoyance. No answer.'

Contributors who have been keeping a record of coincidences in their lives often emphasise that they have not been recording them simply out of curiosity, but because they are useful. 'I have come to think of them as hints, or cues, from my intuition,' Michael Swain comments, listing examples; they appear to be saying, 'sit up and take notice because there is something happening, or about to happen, that is important.' David Kettley, artist and designer, finds coincidences prompt him in his work; 'to be aware of synchronicity, to be "in tune" with it, has led me to lead a much less stressful life.' Dearbhla Molloy has come to feel she can rely on synchronicity to back her intuition; and she cites the occasion when she had to make the kind of crucial, often painful, decision which working in the theatre can impose. In 1986 she had reached what she realised was a crossroads in her career, and had begun training as a psychotherapist. Deciding, after all, to return to the stage, she was offered a job in a fringe theatre. Should she take it, or hold out for something better?

On an impulse I drove to Ellen Terry's cottage. Upstairs, I stopped outside a glass case, mesmerised by an extraordinary dress on a stand. It was metallic green, made from beetles' wings; the attendant told me she had worn it as Lady Macbeth. I went out into the garden and sat beneath a tree. I closed my eyes and inside my head I said, 'Ms Terry, I don't know if I'm a solo singer any more, or a member of the chorus, so to speak. Help me recognise the signs that tell me which I am?' I drove home, feeling very peaceful. When I got in, my agent had called. About the time I was sitting under the tree, the Bristol Old Vic had telephoned to offer me Lady Macbeth.

Dearbhla Molloy had had no interview with the director, whom she had never met; nor had she ever worked in Bristol before.

Bibliography

I have included only those books and articles which deal directly with coincidence, or which have struck me as being valuable for a better understanding of the subject. Translated works are in their English titles.

A list of source references has been deposited with the Koestler Foundation at 484 King's Road, London SW10 0LF. Anybody wishing to consult it should write for a copy, enclosing s.a.e.

A.E. (George Russell), *The Living Torch*, London, 1937.

Beloff, John (Review of *The Challenge of Chance*) *SPR Journal*, March 1974.
Beloff, John, 'Psi Phenomena: Causal versus Acausal Interpretation', *SPR Journal*, September 1977.
Bender, H., 'Meaningful coincidences in the light of the Jung-Pauli theory'. In Shapin and Coly (eds) *The Philosophy of Parapsychology*, New York, 1977.
Bohm, David, *Wholeness and the Implicate Order*, London, 1980.
Bohm, David and F. David Peat, *Science, Order and Creativity*, London, 1989.
Bolen, Jean Shinoda, *The Tao of Psychology*, San Francisco, 1979.
Brown, George Spencer, 'Statistical Significance in Psychical Research', *Nature*, 25 July 1953.
Brown, George Spencer, *Probability and Scientific Inference*, London, 1957.

Close, Frank, 'Chance Encounters', *New Scientist*, 19 May 1988.
Comfort, Alex, *Reality and Empathy*, New York, 1984.

Davies, Paul, *God and the New Physics*, New York, 1983.
Davies, Paul and J. R. Brown, *The Ghost in the Atom*, Cambridge, 1986.
De Morgan, Augustus, *Essay on Probabilities*, London, 1838.
De Morgan, Augustus, *A Budget of Paradoxes*, London, 1872.
Diaconis, Persi, and Frederick Mosteller (On Probability) *Journal of the American Statistical Association*, December, 1989.
Dunne, J.W., *An Experiment with Time*, London, 1927.

Eisenbud, Jule, *Parapsychology and the Unconscious*, Berkeley, 1984.
Emerson, R. W., Essays on Fate and on Power, *Works*, vi, London, 1883.
Evans, Christopher and Peter Evans, *Landscapes of the Night*, London 1983.

Flammarion, Camille, *The Unknown*, London, 1900.
Flammarion, Camille, *Death and its Mystery* (3 vols), London, 1922.
Flew, A. G. N., 'Coincidence and Synchronicity', *SPR Journal*, November 1953.
Freud, Sigmund, *New Introductory Lectures*, London 1933.

Gauld, Alan, 'ESP and attempts to explain it'. In Thakur, *Philosophy and Psychical Research*, London, 1976.
Gauld, Alan, *Mediumship and Survival*, London, 1982.
Gauquelin, Michel, *The Truth about Astrology*, Oxford, 1983.
Godley, John, *Tell Me the Next One*, London, 1950.
Grattan-Guinness, Ivor, 'What are coincidences?', *SPR Journal*, December 1978.
Grattan-Guinness, Ivor, 'Coincidences as spontaneous psychical phenomena', *SPR Journal*, February 1983.
Greenwood, Frederick, *Imagination in Dreams*, London, 1894.
Gurney, Edmund, *Phantasms of the Living*, London, 1886.

Hardy, Sir Alister, *The Spiritual Nature of Man*, Oxford, 1979.
Hardy, Sir Alister, Robert Harvie and Arthur Koestler, *The Challenge of Chance*, London, 1973.
Heywood, Rosalind, *The Sixth Sense*, London, 1959.
Heywood, Rosalind, *The Infinite Hive*, London, 1964.

Inglis, Brian, with Ruth West and the Koestler Foundation, *The Unknown Guest*, London, 1987.

Jevons, William Stanley, *The Principles of Science* (2 vols), London, 1874.
Johnson, Alice, 'Coincidences', *SPR Proceedings*, 1898–9, xiv.
Jung, Carl, 'Synchronicity: an Acausal Connecting Principle', in *Collected Works*, viii.
Jung, Carl, *Memories, Dreams, Reflections*, London, 1962.
Jung, Carl and Wolfgang Pauli, *The Interpretation of Nature and The Psyche*, New York, 1955.

Koestler, Arthur, *The Case of the Midwife Toad*, London, 1971.
Koestler, Arthur, *The Roots of Coincidence*, London, 1972.
Koestler, Arthur, (with Hardy and Harvie), *The Challenge of Chance*, London, 1973.
Koestler, Arthur, *Janus*, London, 1978.
Kolata, Gina, 'One-in-a-trillion coincidence', *New York Times*, 27 February 1990.

Laplace, Pierre Simon, Marquis de, *A Philosophical Essay on Probabilities*, Paris, 1812.
Laver, James, *Nostradamus*, London, 1942.

MacKenzie, Andrew, *The Seen and the Unseen*, London, 1989.
McNish, Robert, *The Philosophy of Sleep*, Glasgow, 1830.
Margenau, Henry, *The Miracle of Existence*, Boston, 1984.
Maury, Alfred, *La Magie et l'Astrologie*, Paris, 1860.
Max-Muller, F., 'Coincidence', *Fortnightly Review*, July 1896.
Medawar, Sir Peter, *The Limits of Science*, London, 1985.
Mill, John Stuart, *A System of Logic* (2 vols), London, 1843.
Morris, Robert, 'Spontaneous synchronous events as seen through a simple communication model' (unpublished paper).

Noakes, Ben (ed.), *I Saw a Ghost*, London, 1986.

Paulos, John Allen, *Innumeracy*, New York, 1988.
Peat, F. David, *Synchronicity*, New York, 1987.
Penfield, Wilder, *Second Thoughts*, London, 1970.
Penfield, Wilder, *The Mystery of the Mind*, Princeton, 1975.

Penrose, Roger, *The Emperor's New Mind*, Oxford, 1989.
Popper, Karl and John C. Eccles, *The Self and its Brain*, New York, 1977.

Randles, Jenny, *Beyond Explanation*, London, 1985.
Roberts, Peter, *The Message of Astrology*, Wellingborough (Northants), 1990.

Sheldrake, Rupert, *A New Science of Life*, London, 1981.
Sheldrake, Rupert, *The Presence of the Past*, London 1988.
Stanford, R. G., 'Towards re-interpreting psi events', *Journal of the American Society for Psychical Research,* July 1978.
Stokes, Douglas M., 'Billiard Balls & Brahms', *Parapsychology Review*, September 1985.

Tanous, Alex, *Beyond Coincidence*, New York, 1976.
Thomas, Lewis, *The Lives of a Cell*, New York, 1974.
Thomas, Lewis, *Late Night Thoughts*, New York, 1984.

Vaughan, Alan, *Patterns of Prophecy*, New York, 1973.
Vaughan, Alan, *Incredible Coincidences*, New York, 1979.
Venn, John, *The Logic of Chance*, London, 1866.

Watson, Peter, *Twins*, London, 1981.
Weaver, Warren, *Lady Luck*, New York, 1963.

Zohar, Danah, *The Quantum Self,* London, 1990.
Zohar, Danah, *Through the Time Barrier*, London, 1982.

Appendix

Coincidence Questionnaire

We would like to have a better picture of the coincidences people experience. You can help by filling in this questionnaire and sending accounts of coincidences you have experienced, particularly those which you feel have been 'meaningful'.

1–5

Please ring the appropriate number.
1. Have you ever experienced coincidences which you feel were in some way meaningful?

Yes	1
Not sure	2
No	3 Go to Q5.

6

If yes
2. Please describe *on a separate sheet* a meaningful coincidence that you have experienced. Please note what happened and why you think it is meaningful.

3. Were any of the coincidences you experienced in one or more of the following categories? If yes, how often have you experienced them?

		Never	Once	Occasionally	Often	
i.	Clusters, or sequences, of related names, numbers or events.	1	2	3	4	*7*
ii.	Spontaneous association (e.g. when a name comes to mind, and you hear it on the radio or meet the person.)	1	2	3	4	*8*
iii.	Spontaneous perception (e.g. when you perceive or sense something happening at a distance)					
	a. in space	1	2	3	4	*9*
	b. in time	1	2	3	4	*10*
iv.	'Small-world' (encounters with people in improbable circumstances)	1	2	3	4	*11*
v.	'Hidden hand'					
	a. problem solving	1	2	3	4	*12*
	b. prayer answering	1	2	3	4	*13*
	c. guardian angel	1	2	3	4	*14*
	d. library angel	1	2	3	4	*15*
	e. other	1	2	3	4	*16*
vi.	'Mind over matter' (e.g. clocks stop, pictures fall, as if influenced by some event)	1	2	3	4	*17*
vii.	Recovery of lost property	1	2	3	4	*18*
viii.	Other (write in)	1	2	3	4	*19*

4. Has your experience of coincidences left you with the impression that they are ever:

		Usually	Sometimes	Never	Don't know	
i.	Significant	1	2	3	4	*20*
ii.	Useful	1	2	3	4	*21*
iii.	Personally meaningful	1	2	3	4	*22*
iv.	Other (write in)	1	2	3	4	*23*

5. Do you believe that meaningful coincidences can be accounted for, or influenced by any of the following?

		Yes	No	Don't know	
i.	Pure chance	1	2	3	*24*
ii.	Destiny/Fate/Karma	1	2	3	*25*
iii.	Planetary positions at birth	1	2	3	*26*
iv.	Divine or diabolic intervention	1	2	3	*27*
v.	Seriality (Kammerer's theory)	1	2	3	*28*
vi.	Synchronicity (Jung's theory)	1	2	3	*29*
vii.	Psi (ESP,PK)	1	2	3	*30*
viii.	Intuition, hunch	1	2	3	*31*
ix.	Serendipity	1	2	3	*32*
x.	Other (write in)	1	2	3	*33*

6. Are you?

Male	1	*34*
Female	2	

7. How old are you?

17 or less	1	*35*
18–34	2	
35–49	3	
50–64	4	
65 or over	5	

8. What is your occupation? *36,37*

Thank you for your help.

Please return questionnaire to: **Coincidence**
The Koestler Foundation
484 Kings Rd
London SW10 0LF

If you would like to be involved in a follow-up study please enclose s.a.e. Replies will be analysed by Jane Henry, of the Open University, and Ruth West, Director of The Koestler Foundation. Please state if you wish your reply to be treated as confidential.

Index

A., Mrs, 200
acausality, 196–7, 204
action at a distance, 178–9
A.E. (George Russell), 22, 126–7, 131, 203
Alister Hardy Research Centre, Manchester College
    (formerly Religious Experience Research Unit), 8, 150
Alkemade, Flight Sergeant Nicholas, 157–8
Alpbach symposium, 30
alternatives: principle of, 12
American Rose Society, 27
Amoore, Susannah, 120
Amory, Derick Heathcoat (later 1st Viscount), 37
Ansell, F.E., 15
Antigonus, 100
ants, 182
apparitions, 170–4
Arc, Joan of, 84
Ashe, Geoffrey: Miracles, 153
astrology, 141–7
Atkins, J.B., 138
Aubrey, John: Brief Lives, 26
Ayers Rock (Australia), 80–1

Bacon, Francis, 149
Badman, May, 121–2
Ball, Sir Robert: Story of the Heavens, 28
Barnes, Tracy, 83–4
Baroda, Gaekwar of, 161
Barrett, Sir William, 180
Bates, H.E., 132; The Blossoming World, 30
Bell, Thomas, 112
Beloff, John, 1, 146, 195–7
Bender, Hans, 177
Bennett, Arnold: The Old Wives' Tale, 33
'Bentley, Jack', 62
Bergson, Henri, 189
Bernhard, Prince of the Netherlands, 74
Bingham, Revd Charles, 20
biology, 182–5
Birdwood, Mark William Ogilvie, 3rd Baron, 54–5
Birkenhead, F.E. Smith, 1st Earl of, 139
Bland, John, 55–6
Blunt, Anthony, 30
Blyth, Kate, 48–9
Boggle (game), 39–40
Bohm, David, 181; Wholeness and the Implicate Order, 178,
    181
Bohr, Niels, 179
Bok, Bart J., 142
Bolen, Jean Shinoda: The Tao of Synchronicity, 60
Boswell, James, 66
Bouchard, Tom, 185–6
Boussac, Marcel, 156
Brice, Barbara, 20–1, 75
Britt, Edgar, 161
Brookes, Edward, 38
Brougham, Henry Peter, Baron Brougham and Vaux, 77–8
Brown, George Spencer, 158, 192–3

Bryson, George D., 22
Buber, Martin, 133
Buddhism, 198–9
Burgess, Anthony, 73
Burke, John: The Florian Signet, 36–7
Burrswood Healing Centre, 42
Burton, Revd Dr, 109
Butterworth, Arthur, 19

Caesar, Julius, 2
Callil, Carmen, 51
'Cameron, Laura', 88
'Carr, John', 152
Cavendish, Richard, 147
Cayley, Sir George, 49
chance, 1–3, 8, 35, 97, 99–106
Chatsworth (Derbyshire), 23
Churchill, Sir Winston, 138–40
Cicero: De Divinatione, 100
clairvoyance, 127
'Clapton, Bernard', 95
Clark, Kevin, 164
Clarke, D.H. 'Nobby', 157–8
Clemens, Samuel (Mark Twain), 35, 108–9, 158–9
Clinton, Charles Henry Rolle Trefusis, 20th Baron, 89
clustering, 8–9, 22–5, 107, 194
coincidence: defined, 97; statistical analysis of, 98–9; and
    chance, 99–106
collective thinking/behaviour, 183–4
Colvin-Snell, Sonia, 80–1
Committee for Scientific Investigation of Claims of the
    Paranormal, 99, 144
community of sensation, 87–8
concurrence, 111–12
consciousness, 181–2
Cooke, Alistair, 50
Cooper, Lady Diana, 118
copycat experience, 20–2
Corder, William, 66–7
couvade, 187
Cromer, Evelyn Baring, 1st Earl of, 138
Cronin, Anthony: Dead as Doornails, 156
Crosland, Anthony, 79
crossed lines, 57–59
crosswords, 106–7
Crowley, Jeananne, 99
Cumberland, Stuart (and 'Cumberlandism'), 113–14

'D., Mr and S., Mrs', 61
Daily Telegraph: crosswords, 107
Danson, Trevor, 152–3
Dare, Monty, 24
Darwin, Charles, 112
Davies, Paul: God and the New Physics, 157, 179–80
Dawe, Leonard Sidney, 107–8
Dawkins, Richard, 184–5
Dean, Clifford, 44

Dean, Glenys, 92–3
death *see* apparitions
déjà vu, 167–70
Dement, William, 167
De Morgan, Augustus, 33–5, 48; *Budget of Paradoxes*, 34, 170–1
Deschamps, Emile, 1
destiny, 129–41
'*Deus ex Machina*', 8
Diaconis, Persi, 97–9, 106, 111, 126, 143, 160
Dickens, Charles, 67–8; *Great Expectations*, 132
Dictionary of Psychology (Penguin), 114, 126
Dimitrov, Georgi, 43
displacement effect, 203
Dixon, Bernard, 201
Dixon, Jeane, 110–11
Don, Monica, 136
Donald, Tan, 16
Donoghue, Joyce, 85
Doyle, Sir Arthur Conan, 53
dreams, 65–79; and precognition, 160–1; duration, 167
Drem airfield, 82
Du Bois, Cora, 46
Duke University (North Carolina): experiments, 7, 192, 196
Dumas, Alexandre, the elder, 91
du Maurier, Dame Daphne, 51
Dunne, J.W.: *An Experiment with Time*, 68–70, 73, 81, 162–3, 168, 170, 202–3
Duthie, Alan, 121

Earl, Sebastian, 70
Eccles, Sir John, 188, 199
Eddington, Sir Arthur, 181
Edinburgh University: Chair of Parapsychology, 10
Einstein, Albert, 6, 178–9
Eisenbud, Jule, 190–1, 193, 197
Elliot, Liam, 135
Elliott, Alan, 46
Ellis, Paul G., 25
Elstob, Peter, 18–19
embroidery and exaggeration, 108–11
Emerson, Ralph Waldo, 133, 158, 181–2
'Enders, Joan', 170
energy, 181
ESP (extra sensory preception), 9, 11, 158–60, 173, 189, 192–3
European Review, 34
Evans, Christopher: *Landscapes of the Night*, 162–4
Eveleigh, Laurence and Diana, 62
evolution, theory of, 112
Eysenck, Hans, 161; *Sense and Nonsense in Psychology*, 192

fallibility, human, 106–8
'Farquhar, Mary', 117, 169
Farrell, J.G., 154–5
fate, 131–3; *see also* destiny
Fatima (Portugal), 128
Fawcett, Lt.-Colonel Percy Harrison, 32
Fearnhead, Peter, 21–2
Feeney, John, 164
Feifer, George, 52
fiction into fact, 28–30, 37
'Finer, Diana', 165–6
Fitzgerald, Charles, 27
Flammarion, Camille, 1–3, 59, 90, 96, 100, 102; *Death and Its Mystery*, 172; *L'Inconnu*, 1, 3
Fleming, Peter: *One's Company*, 31–2
Fontgibu, M. de, 1
Ford, Ford Madox: *The Good Soldier*, 133
Forster, E.M.: *A Room with a View*, 132
Forster, John, 67–8
Forster, Margaret, 51
Forsyth, Dr David, 23

Forsyth, Frederick, 94
Fourier, Jean Baptiste, 50
Francis, St, de Sales, Bishop of Geneva, 90
Franz Ferdinand, Archduke of Austria, 73
Frazer, Sir James: *The Golden Bough*, 187
French, Ronald, 107–8
Fresnel, Augustin Jean, 34
Freud, Sigmund, 94–5; *New Introductory Lectures on Psychoanalysis*, 23
Freund, Dr Anton, 23
Froshaug, Judy, 125–6
Fuller, John G.: *The Airmen who Would Not Die*, 78
Fyall, Andrew, 52

Galileo Galilei, 178
Galton, Francis: *Inquiry into the Human Faculty*, 76
Gamow, George, 176
Garner, Tony, 129
Gauld, Alan, 180
Gauquelin, Michel and Françoise, 142–7
Geller, Uri, 174–5, 196
genes, 184–5
Gerhardie, William, 155–6
ghost in the machine, the, 88–96
Gibbs-Smith, Charles, 49–50
Girtin, Tom, 25–6, 136
Gissing, George: *The Crown of Life*, 132
Glenavy, Charles Henry Gordon Campbell, 2nd Baron, 140
Gobbi, Tito and Bruno, 84–5
Goddard, Air Marshal Sir Victor: *Flight Towards Reality*, 82
Godley, John *see* Kilbracken, 3rd Baron
Goering, Hermann, 43
Goethe, J.W. von, 147; *Conversations with Eckermann*, 14
Goldwater, Barry, 28
golf: holes in one, 98
Graham, Mrs R., 186–7
Grattan-Guinness, Ivor, 50, 145, 196–7; 'What are Coincidences?', 193
Graves, Robert, 25–6
gravity, 178–9
Green, Celia and McCreery, Charles: *Apparitions*, 172–3
Green, Charla, Daniel and Joshua, 92
Greene, Graham, 59–60
Greenwood, E.M., 44
Greenwood, Frederick, 68
Grisewood, Freddie, 169
guardian angels, 41–8, 153
Gurney, Edmund, 76, 171

habit breaking, 56–7
Haines, Bill, 50
Hall, John Henry, 104–5
hallucinations, 76–81
Hannah, J.W.: *The Futility God*, 29
Hannibal, 100
Hardy, Sir Alister, 8, 112, 150, 158, 193
'Harper, Joan', 116
Harrison, Bridget, 185–6
Harris, Harold, 10
Harrison, Michael, 86
Harvie, Robert, 8
'Harold', 7
Hawkins, Hildi, 150
Hawthorne, Nathaniel, 34
Heads, Barrie, 17
Heiseler, Joy, 14
Heisenberg, Werner, 176
Henry, Jane, 201
Heywood, Rosalind, 2, 'orders', 115–16; *The Infinite Hive*, 115
Henderson, G.L.P., 78
Higgs, Mary, 117
Highley, John, 136–7

Hill, Peter, 98
Hill, Susan: *People*, 154–5
Hinchliffe, Captain Raymond, 78
Hitler, Adolf, 43
Hodgson, Richard, 89–90, 173
Hollis, Christopher, 163
Holmes, Oliver Wendell, 13–14, 25
Holroyd, Michael, 155–6
Hooper, Bari, 72
Hopkins, Anthony, 52
horoscopes *see* astrology; stars
horse-racing: in dreams, 69–70, 156, 161
Howard, Jack, 124
'Howe, David', 16–17
Hudson, Andrew, 27
Hudson, W.H.: *A Hind in Richmond Park*, 81
Hughes, Rian, 167
Hunter, Ian, 71
Hurt, John, 32

I Ching ('Chinese Book of Wisdom'), 204
indentifying paramnesia, 166–70
Inglis, Brian: *The Unknown Guest*, 10, 123, 200
intuition, 114–26, 204
Ireland, John A., 23
Ivory, Mrs B., 55

Jaffé, Aniela: *Apparitions*, 171–3
James, William, 173: *Principles of Psychology*, 76
Janson, Hank, 36
Jardin, Ian, 27
Jardine, Douglas, 80
Jaynes, Julian, 76
Jeans, Sir James, 181
Jenkins of Hillhead, Roy, Baron, 78–9
Jevons, William Stanley, 102; *Principles of Science*, 148
Johnson, Alice: enquires, 2–3, 12, 111; classification of
    coincidences, 8, 13; seeks attestation, 10; and recurrence,
    14; and library angels, 48–9; and physical phenomena, 89;
    and telepathy, 90; on Hall and *Rocket*, 105; on
    numerology, 148; on investigation into ESP, 160; and
    apparitions, 170, 173; and PK, 174
Johnson, Samuel, 66
Johnston, Howard, 83
Jones, Ernest, 23
Jones, Raymond E., 92
Joseph (Bibical figure), 2, 66
Joyce, James, 59; *Ulysses*, 22, 156
Joyce, Nora (*née* Barnacle), 59
Jung, Carl Gustav: on synchronicity, 4–7, 30–1, 195–7, 204;
    property restoring, 53–4; van der Post dreams of death
    of, 79–80; and Freud's materialism, 94–5; and
    numerology, 149; and group mind, 184; and Kammerer's
    theory, 194; and acausal forces, 196–7, 204; *Memories,
    Dreams, Reflections*, 87, 204

Kammerer, Lacerta, 31
Kammerer, Paul; suicide, 6, 31; and seriality, 13–15, 30,
    134, 192–4; and clusters, 107; and numerology, 149;
    Koestler's life of, 155; *Das Gesetz der Serie (The law of the
    Series)*, 3–4, 6, 8, 11, 192
Kavanagh, Patrick, 156
Kearey, Ilona, 44
Kendall, Ena, 141
'Kelly, Peter', 40–1
Kennedy, John F., 27–8
Kesey, Ken: *One Flew Over the Cuckoo's Nest*, 71
Kettley, David, 204
Kilbracken, John Godley, 3rd Baron: *Tell Me the Next One*,
    69–70, 103
Kipling, Rudyard, 52, 162–3
Kirkpatrick, Ivone, 14
Kissack, Keith, 202
Kitchener, Horatio Herbert, 1st Earl, 138

Kloepfer, Maria, 91
Koestler, Arthur: and seriality and synchronicity, 6–8, 13,
    134, 196; classification of coincidences, 8–11; and
    Kammerer, 30–1; attempted suicide, 43; and Maria
    Kloepfer, 91; and crosswords, 106–7; and Rosalind
    Heywood, 116; and Malraux, 131; life of Kammerer,
    155; and Thomas Mann, 159–60; and ESP, 193; and
    Jung's causality, 196–7; and investigation, 199; *The Act of
    Creation*, 10; *Arrow in the Blue*, 133; *Beyond Reductionism*,
    30; *The Case of the Midwife Toad*, 4; *The Challenge of
    Chance*, 8–9, 14, 30, 42, 57, 106, 158, 160, 177; *The Ghost
    in the Machine*, 89; *The Roots of Coincidence*, 5, 7, 105
Koestler, Cynthia, 10
Kormis, Fred, 74
'Kuoppa, Mrs Raili', 57

Laithwaite, Eric, 85
Lane, Jennifer, 88
Lang, Andrew, 161
Lanyi, Monsignor de, Bishop of Grosswardin, 73
Laplace, Pierre Simon, Marquis de, 100, 103
Laver, James, 129–30
Laversuch, Robert, 151
Law, Arthur, 29
Leaf, Walter, 14
Lee, John, 89
Lennon, John, 65
Leventhal, Con, 156
Levin, Bernard, 51
Lewis, Elaine, 119
Lewis, Julian ('Jules'), 60
library angels, 8, 14, 48–53, 135
Lincoln, Abraham, 27–8
Linnaeus, Carl, 172
Livingstone, Ian, 62
Llewellyn, Harriet, 135
Lockhart, John Gibson, 172
Loewenstein, Tirzah, 92
London, David, 24
London Transport, 7–8
Lord, Graham, 59–60
Lorenz, F.W., 176
Louis XVI (Capet), King of France, 129
Lovell, Sir Bernard, 42
lovers' allies, 59–64
Lowe, Dorothy, 185–6
luck, 157–8
Lyell, Sir Charles, 112

McEwan, Ian: *The Innocent*, 73
McGlashan, Dr Alan, 20
McHarg, James, 59, 87
Mackay, Elsie, 78
MacKenzie, Andrew: *The Seen and the Unseen*, 173
McNish, Robert: *The Philosophy of Sleep*, 67, 161
McVicar, Kate, 87–8
Maddox, Brenda, 59
Maistre, Joseph De: *L'ange distributeur des pensées?*, 14
Malraux, André, 131
Mann, Thomas: *Buddenbrooks*, 159
Manning, Matthew, 175–7
Manning, Olivia, 155
Manvell, Roger and Fraenkel, Heinrich: *The July Plot*, 43
Margenau, Henry, 178, 181
'Marjorie', 116–17
'Marsh, Jane', 151–2
Marten, Maria, 66–7
Martin, Mrs J., 123
Martineau, Harriet, 41–2
Martinique, 69, 168
Maupassant, Guy de: *L'Auberge*, 53
Maury, Alfred, 166–7
Max-Müller, Friedrich, 198, 199
Medawar, Sir Peter: *The Future of Man*, 199

meme, 185
Mendel, Gregor Johann, 111–2
mental telegraphy, 159
Meyer, Michael, 56
Mill, John Stuart: *A System of Logic*, 101–2, 109–10
Millay, Edna St Vincent, 113–14
Milsted, Veronica, 84
mind reading, 70–1
Mitchell, Clio, 118–19
Mitchell, Mrs M.E., 203
Mitford, Jessica, 39
Molloy, Dearbhla, 204–5
monkey on a typewriter, 102–3, 106
Montgomery, Ruth: *A Gift of Prophecy*, 110
morphic resonance, 184–6
Morris, Robert, 188
Morris, William, 124
Morowitz, Harold, 182
Moscardi, Peter, 57
Mosteller, Frederick, 97–9, 106, 111
Muffett, Thomas, 26
Murchison, Dee, 17
Murphy's Law, 190
Myers, Frederic, 76, 78, 171, 190–1; *Human Personality*, 121; (with Edmund Gurney): *Phantasms of the Living*, 171

Nature (magazine), 192
neurophysiology, 188
Newcastle upon Tyne Journal, 150–1
New Scientist (magazine), 8
Newton, Sir Isaac, 179
New York Times, 97
Nicholson, Michael, 140
Noakes, Ben: *I Saw A Ghost*, 79–80, 118
Nostradamus: *Centuries*, 129–30
numbers (numerology), 12, 147–50

Observer (newspaper), 201–2
odours, 86–7,
Oedipus, 2, 131
Oldmeadow, Rivers, 78
Ono, Yoko, 65
O'Nolan, Brian (Flann O'Brian; Myles na gCopaleen), 156
O'Rourke, Hanne, 18
O'Sullivan, Seumas, 126–7
Oxford Companion to the Mind, 114, 126

Paine, Albert Bigelow, 35, 108
Parade (magazine), 110
paramnesia, identifying *see* identifying paramnesia
parapsychology, 188–91
Parker, Richard, 29
Parsons, D.J. and John, 121
Pascal, Blaise, 100
Paul, Philip: *Some Unseen Power*, 85
Pauli, Wolfgang, 6, 176–7, 196
'Peace' rose, 27
Penfield, Wilder, 188
Penrose, Roger, 181
Perceval, Spencer, 66, 76
Perelman, Laura and Sid, 79
Philip of Macedon, 100
Phillips, Grenville Tudor, 25
pictures, falling, 91–2
Pilaar, Dr Marinus, 38
Piper, Leonora, 173
Playfair, Guy Lyon, 128
Plutarch, 100
PMIR (psi-mediated instrumental response), 189–90
Pocock, Tom, 37–8
Poe, Edgar Allan: *The Murders in the Rue Morgue*, 101; 'The Narrative of A. Gordon Pym', 29
Pokhara Bookshop, Nepal, 15
Polyani, Michael, 199

poltergeists, 89
Popper, Sir Karl: *Logic of Scientific Discovery*, 197
positivism, 33
Postgate, Raymond: *The Ledger is Kept*, 30
'practical joker', 8, 39, 62
prayer, 150–6
precognition *see* prevision
Prescott, Heather, 26
Press, Valerie, 137
prevision (precognition), 67–70, 160–6, 169, 173
Priestley, J.B., 46, 202
Pritchard, Colonel D., 80
probability theory, 10, 97–100, 103, 105, 165
propensity hypothesis, 197
property restoring, 53–6
Proust, Marcel: *Cities of the Plain*, 191
providence, 33–41
psi, 7, 11, 158–60, 173–4, 186, 189–91, 197
psychokinesis (PK), 174–7, 189
psychology, 185–7
Purvis, Ian, 20

quantum physics, 178–82

Ralph, Anthony, 108
'Randall, Jean', 58
Randles, Jenny: *Beyond Explanation*, 83
recurrence, 4, 14
Redgrave, Major-General Sir Roy and Lady, 58
Religious Experience Research Unit *see* Alister Hardy Research Centre
Relph, Michael, 63
resonance, 30–2
Rhine, Louisa, 194; *The Invisible Picture*, 76, 196
Richardson, Peter, 127
Roberts, Ann Victoria: *Louisa Elliot*, 135
Roberts, Peter: *The Message of Astrology*, 38–9, 146–7
Robertson, Morgan: *Futility*, 29–30
Rocket (journal), 104–5
Rose, Harold, 74
Ross, Jim, 150–1
Rotha, Paul, 36
Roszak, Theodore, 65
Rumble, Dorothy, 45
Runnowitsch, Jay, 58
Russell, George *see* A.E.
Russell, Mary, 61
Ryle, Gilbert: *The Concept of Mind*, 88

Saint-Saëns, Camille, 59
Salam, Ardus, 140
Sales, Louis de, 90
Salisbury, Robert Arthur Talbot Gascoyne-Cecil, 3rd Marquess of, 138
Satterthwaite, Dr Stephen, 27
'Savage, Peter', 200
Scholz, Wilhelm von, 53–4
Schopenhauer, Arthur, 77, 130; 'On Death', 159
Schreiber, Mark, 120
Scott, Sir Walter, 172
Scull, Philip, 146
Searle, Ronald, 79, 171
second sight, 66–8
Selkirk, Malcolm, 123
Senarmont, Henri Hureau de, 34
'Senex' (i.e., Armine Wodehouse), 41
serendipity, 126–9
seriality, 4, 7, 11–12, 192
Sertorius, 100
Shakespeare, William, 149
Sheldrake, Rupert, 184, 197
Sidgwick, Eleanor and Henry, 2
Simmerson, Geoffrey and Margaret, 71–2
Simmons, Jeffrey, 36

Simner, Peter, 98
sixth sense, 189
Skidelsky, Robert, 155
small-world experiences, 15–20, 32
Smith, Lord Justice A.L., 105
Smith, Godfrey, 108, 187
Smith, Logan Pearsall: *All Trivia*, 105
Smyth, Frank, 124
Society for Psychical Research, 2, 159, 171; *Proceedings*, 2
Socrates, 84, 116
Somerskjold, Mrs Grete (*née*Wiesenthal), 31
Somerville, E.O. and Ross, Martin: *The Real Charlotte*, 99
Somerville, John, 120
Somerville, Stuart Scott, 120
Spencer, Herbert, 5, 161, 163
Stanbury, Elizabeth, 42
Stanbury, Commander R.N., 42
Stanford, Harriet, 137
Stanford, Rex, 189
stars and horoscopes, 141–7
Stauffenberg, Colonel Claus Philipp Schenk, Count, 43
Stedham, Patrick, 125
Steere, Douglas: *Dimensions of Prayer*, 150
Stent, John, 154
Stoppard, Tom: *Rosencrantz and Guildenstern are Dead*, 174–5
Stuart, Douglas, 27
Stuart, Francis, 140
subliminal component, 12
Sunday Times, The, 9–10, 20
superorganisms, 183
Swain, Michael, 204
Swift, Jonathan: *Gulliver's Travels*, 28
synchronicity, 4, 9, 11–12, 193, 195–9, 204

'talk of the devil', 13–15
Tart, Charles, 173–4
Taversham Hall, Norfolk, 19–20
Taylor, Louise, 56
Taylor, Mary, 64
telepathy, 113, 159, 180
telephone numbers, 57–9
Temple, William, Archbishop of Canterbury, 150
Tenhaeff, W.H.C., 73–4
termites, 183, 189
Terry, Ellen, 204–5
Thackeray, William Makepeace, 29
Thomas, Lewis: *The Lives of a Cell*, 183
'Thorneycroft, Mrs', 122
Thornton, Abraham, 13–14

Tickell, Tom, 8
time warps, 25–8
Titanic (ship), 29
Tonothy, Ian, 169
Toure, Ali Farke, 17
Townley, Claire, 58
trance, 65–6
Treuhaft, Bob, 39–40
Tuckett, Ivor: *Evidence for the Supernatural*, 29
Twain, Mark *see* Clemens, Samuel
twins, 87, 185–6
Tylor, Edward, 187

van der Post, Sir Laurens, 60, 79–80
Vaughan, Alan: *Patterns of Prophecy*, 110, 118, 194
Venn, John: *The Logic of Chance*, 101–2
Villenave, Matthieu Guillaume, 91
visions, 81–4
voices, 84–6
Voltaire, François Arouet de: *Philosophical Dictionary*, 129
Vonnegut, Kurt, 118

Wade, John, 74–5
'Wall, Joan', 173
Wall, Mary, 95–6
Wallace, Alfred Russel, 112
Watkins, Roy, 39
Watson, Peter: *Twins*, 185–6
Weaver, Warren, 105; *Lady Luck*, 22
Weiss, Paul, 30–1
Wells, H.G.: 'The Purple Pileus', 133
West, Dame Rebecca, 48
Wheeler, Henry Morton, 183
Wiesenthal, Grete *see* Somerskjold, Mrs Grete
Wilde, Oscar, 133
Williams, Elma, 87
Williams, John, 66, 76
Williams, Richard, 35
'Wilson, Mrs', 119
Wilson, Edmund, 113–14
Wilson, James, 161
Wodehouse, Armine *see* 'Senex'
Wolpert, Lewis, 140
Woo, Dorothy, 54
Wright, Steve, 141

Yeats, W.B.: *A Vision*, 131
Young, Michael, Baron, 93

Zohar, Danah, 182